Additional praise for

𝕷𝖎𝖛𝖎𝖓𝖌 𝕷𝖔𝖆𝖉𝖊𝖉

"This tome hits you like a shot of Jägermeister on an empty stomach. Here is a man living life the way it ought to be lived."

—Mark Steines, host of *Entertainment Tonight*

"Often funny, sometimes sad, and always entertaining, this honestly refreshing guide to living the good life should be read by everyone who's ever picked up a drink and enjoyed it."

—Taylor Plimpton, author of *Notes from the Night*

"Dan Dunn's time studying at the feet of the master and mentor Hunter S. Thompson could best be described as 'one cheek on the bar stool and one foot on the floor.' His latest handbook, *Living Loaded*, celebrates his booze-scribe lifestyle in liquoricious detail. I love it!"

—John Oates, of the rock and soul duo Hall & Oates

"Dan Dunn lives a life most people fantasize about. True degeneracy with panache. This book is an essential primer for the joys of the drinking life."

—Jonathan Goldsmith, actor,
aka The Most Interesting Man in the World

"Profoundly profane, profanely profound, *Living Loaded* will win your heart, seize your liver, and probably steal your wallet. But you'll forgive it, because Dan Dunn is the best—and almost certainly the worst—drinking companion you'll ever have: charming, hilarious, and always, it seems, on the brink of a bar fight."

—Steve Rushin, author of *The Pint Man*

Living Loaded

DAN DUNN

Living Loaded

TALES OF SEX, SALVATION,
AND THE PURSUIT OF THE NEVER-ENDING
HAPPY HOUR

THREE RIVERS PRESS
NEW YORK

Published in the United States by Three Rivers Press, an imprint of the Crown Publishing Group, a division of Random House, Inc., New York.

www.crownpublishing.com

Three Rivers Press and the tugboat design are trademarks of Random House, Inc.

Library of Congress Cataloging-in-Publication Data

Dunn, Dan, 1968–
    Living loaded : tales of sex, salvation, and the pursuit of the never-ending happy hour / Dan Dunn.—1st ed.
        p. cm.
    1. Drinking of alcoholic beverages—Humor.   I. Title.
    PN6231.D7D86 2010
    818'.607—dc22   2010012353

ISBN 978-0-307-71847-1
eISBN 978-0-307-71848-8

Printed in the United States of America

BOOK DESIGN BY ELINA D. NUDELMAN
COVER DESIGN BY DAN REMBERT
COVER PHOTOGRAPH © STUDIO 504/GETTY IMAGES

10 9 8 7 6 5 4 3 2 1

First Edition

This book is dedicated to Scott Alexander,
for his tireless efforts on my behalf

And to Scott's wife, Anne, for not divorcing him
over his tireless efforts on my behalf

And to my brother, Brian, who I miss more than anything

And to Radiohead, for "Creep"

CONTENTS

CONTENTS

AUTHOR'S NOTE
ON COCKTAIL PAIRINGS

At the beginning of each chapter of *Living Loaded* you will find cocktail recipes designed to be "paired" with the corresponding chapter. These delicious drinks were created exclusively for this tome by sixteen of the world's finest mixologists, all of whom I am honored to call friends. And while I am eternally grateful to each and every one of these great barmen and barwomen for their invaluable contributions, what I'm most excited about is the prospect of people who might otherwise have dismissed this book as the incoherent ramblings of a besotted fool buying it anyway just for the recipes. *Cha-ching!*

Right, then. Let's get this party started right with the world premiere of an aperitif designed by the Italian Stallion himself, Vincenzo Marianella....

"THE DUNNer"

2 oz. Oxley gin

1/2 oz. Amaro Nonino

1/2 oz. Aperol

1 dash Jerry Thomas Bitter Truth

Grapefruit peels

Add all ingredients to a mixing glass over ice and stir until cold. Strain into a chilled rocks glass over two ice cubes. Release the essential oil of two grapefruit peels on top of the glass.

"Immerse yourself in a hot tub with this book and relax, because there is nothing better after a day spent riding your motorcycle than a hot tub, a cool cocktail, and a great read ... unless you can substitute a woman for any of the above. Once you finish the first drink, be sure to have a second one ... then stay off the motorcycle for the rest of the evening and let Dan's book take you on a wild ride instead."

—**VINCENZO MARIANELLA** digs motorcycles. In 2006 he was named Best Bar Chef by StarChefs.com and L.A.'s Best Bartender by esteemed critic Anthony Dias Blue. He hasn't done jack-squat since. (Kidding!) In addition to owning and operating a beverage consulting business, MyMixology.com, Vincenzo runs Copa d'Oro in Santa Monica, one of California's finest drinking establishments.

Living Loaded

"Lowballing"

CREATED BY DALE DEGROFF

1 oz. *Alize Red Passion*

1 oz. *cognac*

1 oz. *fresh pineapple juice or Dole unsweetened pineapple juice*

1 *dash Angostura bitters*

Shake all ingredients well with ice and strain into a rocks or lowball glass. A nice foam will result from a well-shaken drink, and that is garnish enough.

"First off, let me say that it's a real pleasure to offer up a special drink that Dan Dunn and the readers of this deliciously twisted tome can call their own.

"I've always thought Dan was a smart kid . . . could've been a bank president or chairman of a big insurance company if he were so inclined. But I think he made the right choice with drinking his way around the world, doing as much highballing and lowballing as he can along the way. Hell, it's a lot more fun than finance anyway, *and* Dan has somehow managed to stay out of jail so far . . . which is more than I can say for a lot of guys on Wall Street.

"So mix yourself a drink, find a cozy place to hunker down, and enjoy *Living Loaded. Salud!*"

—**DALE DEGROFF,** aka King Cocktail, is a James Beard Award–winning bartender (that's a first, folks), founder of the Museum of the American Cocktail, and the author of *The Craft of the Cocktail* and *The Essential Cocktail.*

ONE

Fuck Your Fucking Job

𝕴t was the last day of Summer.

"Fuck your fucking job," is what she told me. Summer, that is. The woman I was living with.

"Who the fuck has a fucking job like yours anyway, you fuck?"

I'm pretty sure it was a rhetorical question, but at that point it didn't matter much. She was gone. Walked out the door for good after two tumultuous, if not completely sex-lacking, months. The delicious irony that it happened around Labor Day was the only bit of pleasure I could wring from this otherwise wholly unpalatable set of circumstances.

Granted, I'd signed on for this crazy experiment in monogamous cohabitation despite the preponderance of evidence that such an arrangement simply cannot work. At least, not for me. I know this. I've always known this. Yet, inexplicably, I ignored that little voice in my head reminding me of that inescapable fact. Again. Because I thought Summer and I would be *different*. Turns out every couple believes they'll be *different* when it comes to bucking the overwhelming odds stacked against lasting romantic bliss. It's the enduring delusion that such a thing exists that lines the pockets of everyone from wedding planners to couples' counselors to hitmen—further proof that nothing in this world generates more wealth than pure stupidity. (Just ask Goldman Sachs.) As it turns out, nine couples out of ten are *no different* at all. That's right, just 10 percent of couples have the good fortune to die together in a fiery car crash or double suicide before they ever get around to realizing how much they can't stand the fucking sight of each other anymore.

It may have been the drinking that finally sent Summer over the edge. Or my relentless travel schedule to exotic women–filled ports of call the world over (to be clear, the point is that the women—not necessarily the locations—are beautiful and exotic). She was within her rights to take issue with the womanizing, I guess. But what was I supposed to do about it? Seriously. I mean, when you have a job like mine—nightlife columnist for *Playboy*—flying, drinking, and screwing come with the territory. Hell, it's right there in the job description. Literally.

Crapulous, she called me. A goddamn crapulous jerk.

I looked it up after she left. It means "given to or characterized by gross excess in drinking."

I'll give her points for honesty. Along with an A+ in vocabulary.

Look, I get paid to crisscross the globe covering the adult beverage beat for what is arguably the world's most notorious and iconic magazine. And for that, I make no apologies to anyone. I'll admit I go overboard with the partying from time to time, but for chrissakes, that's not a crime in these United

States. At least, not yet. Besides, I have a hard time justifying moderation when there are so many children going to sleep sober every night in Africa. The poor little bastards.

Still, a high-profile job predicated on excessive alcohol consumption does not come without its perils. Here's an example of how such an existence can yield nightmarish results.

Once, while touring Ireland with a small group of spirits journalists, I was very nearly beaten to death in a pub just outside of Dublin.

One of the members of our group was a fresh-out-of-the-frat douche-nozzle from New York on assignment for some atrocious laddie magazine that doesn't even exist anymore. Guy looked like Billy Zabka, the dude who played Johnny the smirking bad guy in the first *Karate Kid* movie. He acted like him too. Indeed, on more than one occasion during the course of that trip I wanted to rear up on one leg like a crane and kick him in the teeth. A maneuver, I might add, that if executed properly is unstoppable.

So we're in this pub and I go up to the bar to get a drink. Place is packed, there's a soccer game on TV—St. Patrick's Athletic versus Galway United. Premier division. Lots at stake. The score is tied 2–2 late in the second half, and everyone in the pub—St. Patrick's fans, all—is totally blotto. Wait, sorry, I didn't mean to be redundant; I already established that they were Irish and in a pub. Anyhow, just as I grok all this, Billy Zabka sidles up next to me. Him and that fucking smirk of his.

He points at the TV. "Soccer game, eh?" he says.

Observant kid. Without looking over at him, I nod.

"You like soccer?" he continues.

"They call it football over here," I reply flatly.

He snorts. "Yeah, I know. So fucking stupid!"

I let that one go and wave to the bartender. I need strong drink. Badly.

"I'll get this one," he says.

"Um, OK," I say warily. "I'll have a Redbreast Irish Whiskey. Neat."

He looks at me and smiles. A stupid Billy Zabka smile.

"No, no, no, bro-ha." He clucks. "I got a better idea."

It wasn't. A better idea, that is. In fact, it was a breathtakingly stupid idea. The kind of shit-brained stratagem that makes you feel not so much angry as sorry for the guy. But also very angry.

"Two Irish Car Bombs!" he shouts.

Now, for those of you unfamiliar with this particular concoction and the reasons why ordering it in a pub in Ireland is such a sterling example of poor judgment, here is some background: To make an Irish Car Bomb, you combine half a shot of Jameson with half a shot of Bailey's in a shotglass, then drop the shotglass into a pint of Guinness and chug it. This little abomination was invented by a man named Charles Burke Cronin Oat at Wilson's Saloon in Norwich, Connecticut, in 1979. Norwich, Connecticut, being, of course, in America. So, to recap, an American bartender invented a drink that appropriates three of Ireland's most beloved adult beverages as ingredients and named it after an act of terrorism that has caused catastrophic social and political upheaval—not to mention countless deaths—for generations of Irish citizens.

To fully appreciate the import of this, imagine that in the wake of 9/11, a cheeky Irish pub owner dreamed up a drink that combined America's native spirit, bourbon, with sweet vermouth (a Manhattan) in a shot dropped into its most popular beer, Budweiser, and called it a Manhattan Ground Zero because, as he explained, drinking it "left a big fat hole in your gut." Now imagine you're sitting in a pub down around Wall Street in what was once the shadow of those fallen towers, and a group of Irishmen on holiday storm in and order a round of Manhattan Ground Zeros. Now just imagine all those Irishmen were rowdy and obnoxious (sorry, there I go, being redundant again) and looked just like Billy Zabka.

So Zabka shouts "Two Irish Car Bombs!" in this very packed pub, and all activity comes to a record needle–screeching halt. Everyone—and I mean every single person—stares daggers at us. It's the silent death stare—the worst kind. Then, in what ranks in the top five bad-to-worse moments of my life, Galway scores the go-ahead goal in the final minute of play. Game over. Match Galway.

The first thought that crosses my mind is *I'm going to die in Ireland and I didn't even get to meet the Blarney Stone or kiss Bono.* I'm expecting my life to flash before my eyes, like people say happens when you reach the pearly gates (OK, so I'm an optimist; sue me), but instead something Martin Luther King Jr. once said pops into my head: "A man who won't die for something is not fit to live."

There are myriad things I'd like to think I'd be man enough to die for—my family, dear friends, a roll in the hay with Rachel McAdams—but defending some Neanderthal I'd quite frankly like to pummel myself from a mob of angry Irish soccer hooligans is not even worth being eighty-sixed from the pub, let alone beaten to death. (And for the record, yes, I did just invoke Martin Luther King Jr. to illustrate a barroom tale. I have no defense. My brain is my brain.)

With no time to waste I spring into action, going "crane" on Zabka before anyone has a chance to realize I'm with him. Of course, I don't actually have the space, coordination, training, or discipline to properly execute the crane move, so I do the next best thing: deliver a wicked elbow to Zabka's jaw while bellowing "What the feck is wrong with you, you dumb fecking yank!" I'm suddenly feeling emboldened, fierce. Like I'm going to pull this off. Yet despite being in possession of what

I'd *thought* was a solid Irish brogue, a face that I thought made me appear quite the Irishman, and a common Irish surname, it's immediately discerned by each and every local in that pub that I am, in fact, a dumb fecking yank as well.

The reason dawns on me immediately: I'd recently had my teeth whitened. A dead giveaway in that part of the world. Curses.

But just as the mob begins to close in on us we catch a break. Turns out the pub owner, a burly ex-cop who commands the respect of all who enter his joint, had been tipped off by the publicist who'd arranged our junket that we were journalists, wielders of the almighty pen. There's no question this guy would have liked nothing more than to see that angry mob scatter our teeth all over the pub floor, yet he recognized the potential fallout of letting two American booze scribes get brutally assaulted and left for dead in his establishment.

So instead of suffering deep, perhaps permanent, bodily harm, all that happened was we got thrown out of that pub with a wholly unnecessary warning never to return again. Still, close call.

Zabka never did broach the subject of me elbowing him in the kisser, by the way. I expected as much. In my experience, brawny blowhards who wear prep school sweatshirts and strut around acting like they own the joint invariably fold like a French prizefighter once you show them you're capable of real street violence. That's one of the many valuable lessons I learned from my grandma back in our hardscrabble area of Philadelphia. She also taught me a few other things, like never trust rich people, empty cardboard refrigerator boxes are the greatest toys ever invented, and a penny saved is still just a fucking penny.

But, so listen, my job is alternately wonderful, brutal, glamorous, reprehensible, dangerous, hangoverific, toxic, deadly, a gift from the lipid solvent gods, and the best excuse for pretty much any horrible behavior you can think of. The pages that follow are littered with examples of all of these. But you should know going in that most of the book is also about consequences, good and bad. It's an unsparing look at the complexities and contradictions, the shortcomings and strengths of men like me, and the many ways alcohol—to paraphrase Homer Simpson—really is the cause of and solution to all of life's problems. As a professional booze scribe who's seen countless drunks from all walks of life at the highest of highs and lowest of lows (a particular bar in Gary, Indiana, comes to mind), I'm all too familiar with this. And who knows? Maybe, just maybe, along the way I'll stumble upon—perhaps even literally—some wisdom about why men like me drink so copiously, and find us some other outlet for coping with our deficiencies.

Of course we'll be closely examining my own personal failings as a human being, and the very real possibility that many of them might be related to my boozing. We'll take an unflinchingly honest look at whether the things Summer repeatedly pointed out in the waning days of our doomed dalliance might actually not have all been complete bullshit. And while I certainly don't agree with most of what she had to say, I will admit in these pages that I am not the great man Young Me once imagined I'd turn out to be.

I'd be lying if I claimed there isn't some small part of me that occasionally wonders if Summer might have had a point. It's this little lingering thought that I've gotten really good at ignoring but haven't quite been able to shake for good—kind of like a pebble stuck in the sole of my cross-trainers. At forty years old, can I justifiably explain away all manner of what polite society calls "bad behavior" as merely a professional obligation, or is it time to start entertaining the notion that I could just be a developmentally arrested lush?

From one perspective—let's say, the grown-up female one—my lifestyle choices might be construed as reckless, even pitiable; a desperate cry for help from my wounded inner brat. Peter Pan Syndrome writ large. Or, well, OK, writ medium-sized. But I digress.

The wife of one of my oldest friends subscribes to this point of view. We'll call him Bob—and her, Andi. Bob and Andi got married at twenty-four after a four-year courtship, and then promptly squeezed out three seemingly well-adjusted children together. Perfect family and all that. For years Andi chided me for carousing and bedding young women, insisting such behavior was merely my way of avoiding meeting life's adult challenges head-on. I'd defend myself by saying I was simply having a good time, at which time she'd point to the fact that I'm unmarried and childless and have business cards with bunny ears on them that list my title as "Public Menace" as proof that in actuality I'm dreadfully unhappy and destined to die alone of herpes or liver failure or some hideous combination of the two.

Bob, on the other hand, swears I'm his hero.

Is it worth mentioning that Andi left Bob last year for another man? Now, that's what I call meeting life's adult challenges head-on! Hell, none other than Mötley Crüe drummer Tommy Lee himself—who got hitched to Pamela Anderson when she was in her PRIME, mind you—once told me that unless you're dead set on having children, there's absolutely no reason to ever live with or marry anyone. He also told me that because his dick is so big, it hurts to jog. He's got a poet's heart, that Tommy Lee.

And here's the weird part: In a lot of ways I envied Bob and Andi. Because my job/lifestyle combo is like a supermodel serial killer—it might look great and be a whole lot of fun, but it will cut your throat if you take your eye off it for a second.

As the poet said, writing about music is like dancing about architecture. If that's true, then what I do is like smoking crack about crack. I am a professional risk-taker. I am the king's taster: the medieval peasant who got to live the good life, eating a steady diet of foie gras until his luck ran out and one of the one-in-a-thousand morsels with arsenic in it landed on his plate. There's a saying among commercial deep-sea divers that "there are old divers and there are bold divers, but there are no old, bold divers." This profession isn't all that different. In a heartbeat that breezy walk in the park can turn into a sprint through the fields away from a tornado.

That said, it is the best job for picking up chicks. Too bad it's also the worst for keeping them. In fact, writing this book is only serving to underscore the central conflict of my existence: On one hand, I want nothing more than for *Living Loaded* to become a huge bestseller, because I've found that stunningly beautiful women are prone to sleeping with famous authors. On the other hand, if I do a truly great job of writing an unsparingly honest exposé of my working life, any self-respecting woman who reads it will likely prefer to date Tom Sizemore or Charlie Sheen or Eliot Spitzer over me. (Note: This reminds of me of something else Tommy Lee once told me—that the true definition of fame is being able to pick up the *Sports Illustrated* swimsuit edition, find a model you like, and have your manager set up a date with her. "And you bang her the first night too, dude," he added. Again, a poet's heart, that Tommy Lee.)

But let's return for a moment to the time before I'd ever even heard of alcohol—also before I became a screw-up. Coincidence? It's circa 1976, I'm seven years old and just as cute as can be (but so was Son of Sam at age seven). I was a little short on comic book money, but since I've always been the sort who thinks outside the box, I didn't do lemonade stands like other kids. Instead, I decided to hawk homework help for a dime from a stand that *looked* like a lemonade stand, which I set up in front of my childhood home.

"What are you dooooing, you reeetard?" jeers a pretty little blond girl about my age but easily a head taller. She is clearly the alpha blonde of a pack of equally pretty little tow-heads, whose body language betrays them as being beyond merely unimpressed with my wares. Their eye-rolling actually looks like some madly perfect modern-dance expression of scorn.

The other girls chime in on cue, teasing me cruelly and relentlessly until tears begin streaming down my dusty little-boy cheeks. My eyes burn and I hide my face in shame. When my mother emerges from the house to see what all the commotion is about, the little girls quickly scamper away.

"How's business today, sweetie?" she asks, beaming with the maternal glow of a 1970s-style Donna Reed. Which is strange because she was the furthest thing from it.

"The girls think I'm dumb 'cause I don't have a lemonade stand like everyone else," I say, sniffling and wiping a tiny trembling hand over my tear-streaked face.

My mother comforts her enterprising little man with a tender kiss on the forehead.

"That's what they think, huh?" she says. Her eyes, suddenly ablaze, trail my tormentors as they beat a hasty retreat. "Well, someday, when you're running a successful Fortune 500 company, and those budding little bimbos are all on drugs and flunking out of junior college, we'll see who's dumb."

Then she pats me on the head, drops a dime in my money can, and goes back inside the house. And Young Me smiles, my fabulous future unfolding in my young mind's eye . . . girls on drugs . . . junior college dropouts. Something about bimbos budding . . .

And look at me now. I'm a forty-year-old, childless single dude who drinks for a living. Young Me would be deeply ashamed. Certainly he'd be shocked and embarrassed to learn that my two-month stint living under the same roof as Summer is as close as I can recall to being a real commitment with a woman. It sounds odd even saying it now, but long before I became the hard-living "Playboy Imbiber," as I've come to be known, I wanted to be a family man—to live a non-ironic *Leave It to Beaver* lifestyle. Where I grew up there didn't seem to be any other alternative. Getting married young and having kids is what normal people *did* in northeast Philadelphia. And from a very young age I desired nothing more than to be perceived as normal. At least, in the way that is felt by people who first suspect, then know, that they will never truly feel that way.

Instead of actually feeling "normal," we ask ourselves "What would a normal person feel, say, think, or do in this situation?" And then we try to do, think, say, and, we hope, feel exactly that way. And that (plus the boozing) is a recipe for my problems with women—the cause of what I have come to think of as my first "net loss" in that department . . . er, "Annette" loss is more like it. But we'll deal with that in chapter 4.

At any rate, to fully understand what I hope to deliver here, right now it's time for the first of many informative (and crowd-pleasing) how-to lists you'll encounter throughout this book.

How to Write a Book About Your Life As a Professional Drunk

My friend and spiritual advisor, the late Dr. Hunter S. Thompson, once opined that writing is like sex in that it's only fun for amateurs. Indeed, there is nothing quite so dreary as sitting alone day after day in a windowless home office, hungover, staring at a computer monitor and praying—most often futilely—for inspiration to strike, your millstone and your only respite being the gigantic pile of free booze in the cabinet that you have received, gratis, from liquor-company reps.

Ah, but it takes more than strong drink, discipline, and a near limitless capacity for self-flagellation to crank out a winning seventy-thousand-word tome about drinking and carousing—especially when all you'd really like is to be doing something much more enjoyable with your time. Like drinking or carousing with amateurs.

This being my second go-round with a boozy memoir, I've learned a thing or four about the process.

1) Embarrassing revelations about your past are good.

Whether it's for reasons of schadenfreude, sympathetic connection, or just to feel better about themselves, people get off reading confessions about how magnificently fucked-up other people are ... particularly if those scribes are practicing or recovering drunks, junkies, or sex freaks. For proof, look no further than enormously popular memoirists such as James Frey and Elizabeth Wurtzel. Throw in a life lesson or two gleaned from the experience and you're golden.

For instance, I remember the time Young Me was ogling a *Penthouse* magazine with pages still sporting the little circle indentations from the box spring where, until a few moments earlier, it had resided under the pressure of my parents' mattress. My eyes were wide, my heart delighted. It was my first close encounter with real naked-lady pictures. I had no idea what was happening to me as my organ swelled inside my Toughskins; all I knew was that life was suddenly richer and deeper than before. It was like discovering a room in my home that I never knew existed. And in that room were pictures.

Lots of pictures. Pictures of girls thoroughly unlike the ones at school, or even at the public swimming pool. Then, just as suddenly as a whole new world of prurient delights had revealed itself to me, an adult hand swooped in and Young Me found myself over a lap, being spanked.

I learned two lessons that day: (a) Sex is the best and worst thing in life, and (b) When people are mad at you, it's kind of hot.

See? Don't you feel good about yourself now?

2) Admit you are powerless over your addiction.

In my case, I'm powerless over my addiction to dropping the names of famous people with whom I've crossed paths. We're but one chapter in, and already you're aware that I'm friendly with Mötley Crüe's drummer and knew the literary giant who gave the world gonzo journalism. See what I did there? By copping to my celebrity compulsion I set myself up as a sympathetic (there's that word again) rather than merely pathetic figure. So later on, when I follow the tale of the time I got trashed with Seann William Scott in Scotland with details of the time I got wacked with Bill Murray in Santa Monica, instead of thinking me a shameless blood-sucking sycophant, perhaps you'll be impressed with the bravery I've exhibited in openly sharing my addiction. Hey, where's my "Thank you, Dan"?

3) When in doubt about how to wrap up the first chapter of your drinking book, include a cocktail recipe that'll make everyone happy. Plus, if there's one thing I've learned, it's that nothing takes people's mind off your massive shortcomings more than getting them drunk.

Fish House Punch

1 1/2 cups superfine sugar

64 oz. water

32 oz. lemon juice

64 oz. amber rum

32 oz. brandy

4 oz. peach brandy

In a large punch bowl, use just enough water to dissolve the sugar. Add lemon juice, liquor, and the remaining water. Refrigerate for an hour. Add large block of ice. Serve. No garnish necessary.

4) Honesty is the best policy.

It is not, however, the most entertaining policy. So I'll cop to something else: A few of the events recounted in these pages are what overzealous litterateurs and The Smoking Gun website might call "subject to debate" or "remembered clearly, but may have been a dream." I drink for a living, folks, and as a result my memory is foggier than a San Francisco morning after a Grateful Dead show (in the early days, before the cops caught on). Plus, having grown up in a highly dysfunctional environment, as a coping mechanism I developed a vivid imagination, which I now have a hell of a time keeping in check. For instance, I'm not entirely sure that I have, as reported in chapter 5, made time with golf legend Greg Norman's daughter. Then again, I'm not sure I *haven't*. The truth depends largely on the tenacity of her legal representation.

Same goes for Danny DeVito and Seann William Scott. In fact, the same goes for anyone in this book, including those in the acknowledgments. *Especially* those people, because I always fear I'll end up drunk and homeless, babbling to imaginary friends. The sad part is, the people will actually exist, I'll just imagine they're my friends.

"The ManBag"
CREATED BY GAZ REGAN

2 1/2 oz. straight rye whiskey

2 dashes sweet vermouth

2 dashes Luxardo Maraschino liqueur

2 dashes Green Chartreuse

3 dashes Angostura bitters

Stir all ingredients over ice and strain into a chilled cocktail glass. Add the garnish. On second thought, scratch that last part. There ain't no goddamned garnish! Garnish is for sissy boys.

"This drink is loosely based on the Police Gazette Cocktail, as detailed in the 1912 book *The Hoffman House Bartender's Guide*. It highlights the style of drink preferred by sporting gents around the turn of the twentieth century, when the pugilistic art was greatly admired by anyone with balls. The name prevents wimps from ordering this drink. You gotta be a man to order a ManBag."

—**GAZ REGAN,** from ArdentSpirits.com, is the author of *the bartender's GIN compendium, The Joy of Mixology,* and numerous other works of cocktailian splendor.

TWO

Drink Like a Fucking Man, Man

$\mathfrak{I}$ used to be a regular at P&J's Tavern, a hole-in-the-wall in a down-and-out section of northeast Philly known as Summerdale. P&J's was the first drinking establishment I ever went to, and over the course of a long summer many years ago it's where I became a pinball wizard and honed my now considerable pool, darts, and shuffleboard skills. It's also where I received a crash course in drunkenness, sex, obscene drunkenness, fisticuffs, and all manner of other types of unseemly behavior. Not that I engaged in any of it firsthand. At least, not that summer. After all, I was only seven.

It was a different time, one people seem to now think less enlightened. But I would argue that life was infinitely more interesting for kids in the seventies than it is now. I usually went to P&J's with my dad. Back then, a heavy drinker taking a first-grader to a bar every day was no more frowned upon than that same guy driving the wee lad home after tying one on, then letting him play with lawn darts or listen to the Carpenters unsupervised. Dangerous, sure. Also really goddamn fun. I think it's the toys of the era that I miss the most. Like those Click Clack Clackers with the two heavy acrylic balls on a string that when "clacked" together with enough force had a tendency to shatter, sending eye-piercing shards everywhere. Come to think of it, I should have picked some up for Timmy McFadden (more on that guy later).

But irresponsible as it might seem now, spending damn near every day with my pops at P&J's in the summer of 1976 is one of two truly meaningful father-son bonding experiences I can recall from my childhood. The other happened when I was five and he kidnapped me and fled to Maryland. No shit. I'm going to leave that story be for now, though, except to say that I honestly believe the guy had my best interests at heart. Plus, I've got to set aside some material for my follow-up to this book, a weepy tell-all companion tentatively titled *A Heartbreaking Work of Running with a Million Little Pieces of Scissors*. Oprah, I hope you're ready.

But back to P&J's. P&J's was my indoctrination, that watershed moment that changes everything. No matter who you are or where your own personal relationship with alcohol has taken you, your first encounter with booze is a singular event from which there is no turning back. In that moment you are set upon a journey toward becoming one of four different types of people: (1) a person who drinks; (2) a person who doesn't drink; (3) a person who wishes he could handle drinking yet cannot; or (4) a person who is dead.

And while I'm sure there are a few teetotalers reading this in the interest of getting a peek behind the curtain, I think it's a good bet that most of the folks reading this book are, like me, firmly entrenched in the first category. It would be naïve to rule out, however, that any one of us might become a three or four down the line somewhere. We're all fours eventually, after all. And as far as number three goes, my extensive field research has revealed a cruel irony: A given person's unwillingness to acknowledge their category-three potential vastly increases the possibility of it happening. Because alcohol does funny things to your brain. Sometimes it's the ha-ha kind, and sometimes it's the peculiar kind. And sometimes it's the "I take my first-grader to the bar then drive him home drunk" kind. Hilarious, right?

Better Gin Than a Gun

My parents divorced when I was three. It wasn't amicable. Not by a long shot. Still isn't, even here on the other side of the millennium. My father, as you might have suspected based on the above, is an alcoholic, and my mother is crazier than a paisley snowflake in Jamaica. Check that—my dad is a *recovering* alcoholic. And while the one-day-at-a-timers at AA would no doubt strenuously object to my saying so, I'd even venture to say he's *recovered*, since he's not so much as touched a drop in more than twenty-five years. Mom, however, is definitely not a recovering crazy person. Turns out manic-depressive disorder with psychotic episodes is a bitch of a hard habit to break.

Now, I'm not here to wallow in self-pity or whine about how my parents fucked me up so badly it drove me to drink. That's what therapy is for. And while there's no doubt that my parents' various issues have contributed to my love of the bottle, I'm not going to get all Freud on you. Instead, I'd like to address their impact on the *type* of drinker I've become. I remember reading a few years ago that England's Department of Health came up with a list of the various types of problem drinkers. In my interpretation, they go a little something like this:

1) Pity-Party Drinkers: These are the poor bastards who drink because their lives suck. Whether they're bereaved, divorced, dumped, in financial ruin, or just plain old sad sacks, alcohol is a comfort to these guys, a form of self-medication used to help them cope with their miserable existences in a godforsaken world. On the bright side, they make other people feel much better about themselves.

2) Five P.M. Sharp Drinkers: These folks have high-pressure jobs and stressful home lives that send them running to the nearest bar the second the clock strikes happy hour. In other words, 90 percent of the adult population. They use booze to help them relax, unwind, and ease the transition between their equally hellish work and personal lives.

3) Bachelor Party Drinkers: These are the guys with such busy social calendars they can find the time to get together only on special occasions (generally ones that involve strippers). But when they *do* manage to get together, they know how to make up for the lost time—and then some. The memories from their frat house days may have faded, but the bond of drunken sex with strangers lasts forever. Note: These are the people you want to go to Vegas with.

4) Barstool-Glued-to-Their-Ass Drinkers: These people believe that going to the pub every night is "what men do." The bar is their second home, and it should be, since their tabs are about on par with their mortgages. We all know these people. They're the cast of *Cheers*.

5) Desperate Housewives Drinkers: These are those for whom alcohol is company, making up for an absence of, you know, real people. Think Eva Longoria unwinding with a glass (or three) of vino after a long day of cleaning, cooking, and scheming. For these women (as the name implies, they are mostly women), drinking often marks the end of the day, when they've finished working around the house and are getting ready to work at pretending they can stand their husbands.

6) "Punch Me As Hard As You Can" Drinkers: These are the macho dudes who have cultivated an alpha-male persona revolving around their drinking prowess to compensate for their lack of brain, brawn, and overall appeal to women. These dudes feel a constant need to prove their masculinity—i.e., their ability to pound shots of Jäger—to themselves and others. Also known as "drunk assholes."

And, last but not least, the old classic:

7) Binge Drinkers: Everyone over the age of fourteen has friends like these. Drinking excessively is their way of having fun, and as far as they're concerned, the more drinks, the more fun. Which would lead one to believe that their idea of the ultimate good time is a five-hour blackout and a night with their head in the toilet. These are basically hedonists who use alcohol to release inhibitions. Hey, I didn't say I was knocking it.

I know what you're thinking. I was as shocked as you to find that they did not include a category for Professional Drinkers. However, after pausing for a moment of self-examination, I have since determined that, as a consummate professional,

I am actually a combination of all of these types. This is either a gut-wrenching tragedy or the all-time most towering achievement in the history of adult-beverage consumption. And I honestly have no idea which.

No doubt some of these tendencies came from my mentally unstable mother, while I can thank my dear old formerly besotted dad for others. I'd like to think I brought some of these jiggers to the mix all on my own, though. After all, it would be humiliating to admit I didn't learn *something* worthwhile during those six long years spent in college.

The psychological community appears to be in agreement that children who hail from bipolar and/or alcoholic households grow up believing emotional chaos is normal. And they say this like it's a bad thing. Look, I recognize that long-term exposure to a delusional mother and a dad fighting a losing battle with Jack Daniel's has, on occasion, left me feeling as unstable as weapons-grade plutonium. Still, I'd take the high-octane cocktail of contradictions that is my drunk self over being "normal" any day of the week. What the hell does "normal" mean, anyway? Show me a "normal" person and I'll show you someone who has never once snorted lines in Metallica's tour bus or had mind-blowing unprotected sex with a total stranger in the stairwell at a Lake Tahoe casino. And where's the fun in that?

So, on second thought, I *am* going to give my 'rents some credit for steering me toward the career path I've been wobbly navigating for the past decade or so. Consider this a heartfelt thank-you, Mom and Dad, for screwing me up enough to be "abnormal," yet not so much that I wound up in an insane asylum, homeless, or, worse, on a reality-TV show. Sure, I raise a bottle to my lips most days. Better gin than a gun, I say. Had it not been for my batshit-crazy mom and fall-down-drunk pops, I might be barely making ends meet at a data-entry job in a drab office building in Boringtown, USA, instead of getting paid a pretty penny (well, a penny anyway) to be a globe-trotting boozehound for *Playboy*. Score one for abnormality.

Man Shall Consume No 'Tini

Now, it wouldn't be right to dole out gratitude to those who played a seminal role in my development as a world-renowned dipsomaniac without mentioning a guy I once knew from South Philly named Denny Capriotti. He was a former Golden Gloves boxing champ turned, ahem, "collection agent." Everybody called him Knuckles. There were two certainties whenever you hit the town with Knuckles and his crew: (1) You were gonna get drunk, and (2) you were gonna get into a brawl. Sometimes we were the ones savagely beaten, but most of the time—due in large part to Knuckles's proficiency in the sweet science—the other guys got the worst of it.

I lost touch with Knuckles in my early twenties, which was (coincidentally?) around the time I realized my future lay in rearranging words, not faces. To this day, though, I still credit him with teaching me some extremely valuable lessons about life. His pearls of wisdom included "Never take a swing at someone when you're wearing a nice watch" (he'd had too many bands break on him) and "Never go bowling in shorts" (this one I can't explain, but I know instinctively that it's true). But the one piece of advice that stuck with me the most has become one of the fundamental cornerstones of my close personal relationship with alcohol. It is, to wit: "Drink like a fucking man, man!"

As it turns out, though, this seemingly simple rule is not always so simple to follow. In today's world of nebulous and ever-shifting gender roles, how is a guy to know what a man drinks like? Where exactly do we draw the line between drinking like a man and drinking like a metrosexual? Or between drinking like a metrosexual and drinking like Steven Cojocaru at a Gaultier show after-party during Fashion Week? (And believe me when I say that if you're the sort who might actually be at a Gaultier after-party during Fashion Week, you don't need me to tell you how to drink.)

Sometimes it's simple. There are drinks that are impossible to sissify. Scotch rocks. Bourbon rocks. A Manhattan. Draft beer. Tequila shots. But then there are those calls that fall right in the gray zone. For instance, from time to time I enjoy a premium vodka with soda water on the rocks with a squeeze of lime. It's refreshing, it gets you drunk, and, let's face it, chicks don't dig the beer belly. Plus, I'd argue vodka is quintessential hard-guy hooch; after all, it is the spirit of choice among Russian mobsters and burly professional hockey players with names like Vladimir and Uwe. However, others will tell you the high-priced vodka-soda-lime combo is better left to neutered yuppies and supermodels. I do not subscribe to this view, although if Knuckles were around, I'd switch to Jameson in a hot minute.

There are some basic rules for "drinking like a man" that everyone can agree on, such as the fact that it's never acceptable to order a cocktail the color of a Smurf (or any other Saturday-morning cartoon character, for that matter). But even for that we need an exception. Namely, the frozen rum drink, which is acceptable if and only if you're on a beach or poolside in an exotic locale with a hot chick and she orders one too. (Note that this applies to daiquiris only. Piña coladas are the banana hammocks of tropical adult beverages. Just don't go there.)

Another easy one is this: Man shall consume no "'tini"; that is, save a *real* martini, if and only if made the way God—and the Rat Pack—intended. And that means gin, bub. The vodka martini is the gibbering bastard child of Jay McInerney and the guy from *American Psycho*. The only thing less manly than drinking a vodka martini is drinking it at a bar with interior designers on call.

You see how complicated it all becomes?

Then there's the delicate conundrum of how to handle a situation where a known badass—someone who could easily mop the floor with anyone in the room—orders off the swishy side of the drinks menu. Is it OK for the rest of us to follow suit, or does the Male Code of Conduct call for us to keep our scotches neat and our mouths shut? And who is this peculiar and rare breed whose manliness is so unassailable he can order an amaretto sour if he wants to without fear of repercussion? I'll tell you.

A few years back I found myself hunkered down with Sugar Ray Leonard in a private booth at a Las Vegas nightclub on a Saturday night. Though the legendary boxer had not fought professionally in quite some time, he appeared to be in tip-top shape—or at least in good enough shape to beat the pants off a mouthy booze writer who hadn't seen the inside of a gym in months. So it was with a fair amount of trepidation that I called him out on what I observed to be some surprisingly lightweight drinking habits.

"No mas!" I shouted, harking back to Ray's most memorable bout with Roberto Durán. However, I was referring not to boxing but to the Cape Codders he kept ordering (for the record, it's the cranberry juice, not the vodka, that makes it girly).

"What's wrong with Cape Codders? I really enjoy them," Ray replied, instantly topping my list of Top 10 Things I Never Thought I'd Hear a Guy Who Kicked Marvin Hagler's Ass Say.

"You're one of the toughest fighters of all time, man. You should be drinking something harder than Cape Codders! A

Rusty Nail, at the very least!" I instinctively looked at his watch and was relieved to find he was wearing a top-of-the-line Movado. Still, I feared it was only a matter of time before the words "I'll have a Shirley Temple, please" escaped the lips of the guy who once TKO'd Tommy "The Hitman" Hearns. Who knew what would happen after that?

"Well," Sugar Ray said thoughtfully as our waitress sized me up for my casket, "I like cabernet, too. Two glasses?"

Relief washed over me as I recalled something else Knuckles once told me, back in Philly. "Real men do drink wine ... but only red, and only on Sundays." I peered over at Ray's Movado. Half-past midnight—in the clear. We ordered a bottle and polished it off like champs. Good thing for him, too. I've got a killer right hook I like to follow with my signature cower-in-the-corner-and-beg-for-mercy move.

So all you hard-living, "I'd rather be caught singing 'Total Eclipse of the Heart' at karaoke than uttering the words 'with a splash of lime'" manly men out there may take comfort in the fact that wine is not off-limits, as long as it's consumed within the parameters I've just described. For the rest of you wine lovers who are less inclined to taking drinking tips from my old buddy Knuckles, however, there exists a whole other set of complicated (if just as arbitrary) guidelines. In honor of the fermented nectar of the goddesses and its peacemaking abilities, I'd like to dedicate this next bit of oenological wisdom to the greatest pound-for-pound wine-sipping pugilist of all time.

How to Kill at Wine Tastings

As you can probably guess, as an adult-beverage columnist, I end up at a lot of wine tastings. This means I routinely encounter pompous schmucks who believe they possess God's own palate, and that they deserve the adulation of everyone around them for swirling some cabernet around their mouths and pronouncing it "troubling, yet brilliant." The technical term is "wine snob," and I'll admit that I can't legitimately hang with a lot of them, knowledge-wise. But however adept they may be at sniffing out hints of ambrosia or narrowing the origins of a grape down to a five-mile radius, I also think many of them are missing the point. Knowing, for them, has become more important than enjoying. Trust me, there's no better way to bring a good time to a screeching halt than having to listen to someone (even if it's you) running their mouth about how variances in soil types and altitude affect the pH levels of '05 Alexander Valley cabs.

Besides the fact that these people are annoying, why should you care? Because even though you didn't come to a tasting to compete, they did. And the more pernicious of this breed will use any opportunity to make you look an unsophisticated lout so they can mack on the waitress in the little black dress in your stead. This injustice must not stand. So to avoid becoming a glass-swishing, ambrosia-sniffing douchebag without losing your shot at the hottie waitress, the key is to exhibit a happy medium of wine knowledge: to know enough so you're perceived as an urbane sophisticate, but not so much that you become an insufferable bore who spends all his time reading oenology journals (or, worse, pretends to). Lucky for you, I've isolated six rules to help you achieve this delicate balance. Master them, and you'll ace wine tastings without looking like you just matriculated at Asshole University.

1) Know your go-to modifiers.

Look, wine tasting is subjective. I don't care what anyone says—figuring out what's happening flavor-wise in any given vintage is a crapshoot for all but the most refined palates. Luckily, even when you're at a loss to pinpoint precisely what it is you think you're tasting, if you know these five simple words—which can be used indiscriminately and interchangeably—no wine snob will ever look at you sideways. They are as follows: "complex," "balanced," "layered," "intense," and "well-rounded." A wine taster who uses these words to describe a wine is like a psychic who tells a rube they sense concern over affairs of the heart, money, or health. In other words, it's bulletproof, never-fail bullshit. Use one or more of these terms, and you can rarely go wrong no matter what you say next. Trust me; you could follow up by proclaiming you detect hints of yak wool or banana oil in a Pinot Gris, and everyone else around would start nodding knowingly. Bonus tip: When it comes to a wine's "nose," the bolder the better. Who cares what it means if it will help you score (with the snobs *and* with the waitress)?

2) Ditto for your aphorisms.

You would think that original ideas would be embraced by a roomful of intelligent, curious people of the ilk that attend a wine tasting. And you would be wrong. Dare to utter something like "What the hell does Robert Parker know, anyway?" and they very well may stone you to death. Instead, stick with safe, unoriginal bromides such as "Wine is made in the vineyard, not the winery," or "The scoring system employed by the mainstream wine media is bogus," or, better yet, "Oak should not go into Chardonnay." That last one's got the added advantage of being true.

3) Memorize the triple crown of vintages.

The mere mention of the following three years and regions at a wine tasting is like shouting, "Hey, look, it's Michael Jordan!" in a room full of Chicago Bulls fans; it's guaranteed to stop everyone in their tracks. The winning trifecta is: 1982 Bordeaux, 1996 Champagne, and 1970 Northern California. Once you've won everyone's undying awe and respect by citing said vintages, use the opening as a springboard into subject matter you're more familiar with. As in, "Oh, yeah, that 1970 Mayacamas is a real killer. Did you know that Black Sabbath released their debut album on Friday the thirteenth that same year?"

4) Be obnoxiously deep in one—but only one!—area.

Be careful here; this skirts close to wine snobbery. Still, it can actually be very helpful to have just one area of serious knowledge, if only to brush back a know-it-all when he tries to hijack the conversation and mess with your game. For me, it's corks. Yep, I know all about straight corks, diamond corks, and nova corks, and I have an almost autistic level of knowledge about the chemical scourge of vintners everywhere: 2,4,6-Trichloroanisole (TCA for short), the naturally occurring fungus that makes good wines go bad. I'm also well versed in the relative merits of cork alternatives—screw caps, agglomerates, Vino-Seal, etc. Carefully deployed, this knowledge can make you look like a badass without pushing you over the line into blowhard territory. The key is to drop some obscure nuggets of wisdom—say, "Hmm, these look like high-tech, cork-based closures made up of cork granules that have undergone CO_2 saturation"—that the snob has to sheepishly ask you to explain. Be brief and nonchalant about it, and it's an instant panty-remover.

5) Embrace the value play.

If you overdo number four a little, not to worry; there is an antidote. Nothing gets the snob-stink off you faster than talking smack about the expensive stuff. Learn a few excellent bottles in the $10–20 range so you can drop statements like "I'd put a seventeen-dollar Hahn Estates Central Coast

Meritage up against a seventy-five dollar Stag's Leap any day of the week." Good candidates for this include Shoofly Buzz Cut ($11), Tiziano Chianti ($11), and Daniel Gehrs Un-Oaked Chardonnay ($15). When the snobs tut-tut and fuss, just say, "No, really, with the money I save I can afford bleacher tickets for the Cubs." If you want to get an even bigger rise out of them, follow that up with "I like to smuggle in a Peachy Canyon Zinfandel for the seventh-inning stretch." Then leave them there, scratching their heads over whether you're being ironic or just a classless idiot (either one will probably get you laid).

6) Don't slurp, don't spit, don't use the phrase "nice legs."

I think these speak for themselves. It's a wine tasting, not a construction site.

OK, so now that you've got these weapons in your arsenal, you should be able to emerge from any wine tasting unscarred by the worst the world's snobs can dish out. But just to be sure you're *really* ready to feign enough sophistication to handle yourself ably in the company of arrogant jerks who believe they're God's ass-pounding gift to oenological exploration, I'm going to let you in on a little trade secret: When wineries send out samples of their wares to media types like me, they include detailed product information sheets—cheat sheets, if you will—including everything from the harvest dates to recommended food pairings to the winemaker's tasting notes. We, in turn, use much of this information when writing up reviews and features (and by "use" I mean "copy verbatim") to make ourselves seem smarter than we are. The beauty is that any lazy ass with an Internet connection can easily access those very same product information sheets. So let's say you happen to be attending an event showcasing wines from the esteemed Trefethen Family Vineyards of Napa Valley. All it takes is a few clicks of the mouse, and suddenly you're able to offhandedly mention that the '07 Estate Pinot Noir is deliciously spicy, but with a velvety texture, and has a subtle yet complex nose of anise, cloves, dried cherries, ripe plums, and liquid smoke that blooms into a soft and elegant palate. Beats the hell out of trying to work all that out on the spot when you're buzzed, doesn't it?

I Hope You Don't End Up Fifty and Still Leading This Lifestyle

Truth be told, I was a pity-party drinker the night I started writing this chapter. After drinking one or seven glasses of Macallan 18 neat, I wound up flat on my back on the cold tile floor of my unfinished home office, arms outstretched Christ-on-cross style, staring absently for God knows how long as drops of water ran along an exposed pipe, reached a precarious angle, dangled momentarily, and plummeted through the air before—PLOINK!—splashing on my forehead.

I'd drifted into one of those self-reflective altered states I've been prone to of late, thinking about something Summer put in an e-mail not long after she'd decided to move out but before her mood turned truly foul. She wrote, "I hope you don't end up fifty and still leading this lifestyle. I worry about your health and happiness is why I say that. You deserve to be happy, Dan."

PLOINK! Another droplet struck my brow, and I didn't even blink. My hair was sopping wet, and my head was now resting in a rapidly expanding puddle of water. Each drop that landed on my forehead seemed to be an indictment of my failings as a man. I was a defeated lover—PLOINK! I was a haunted artist—PLOINK! I liked to drink vodka sodas with a splash of lime—PLOINK!

It was difficult to wrap my booze-addled mind around the notion that I *deserved* happiness. Do I? And what reason could Summer, to whom I'd, to put it bluntly, been sort of a dick, possibly have for wanting this for me? Harder still was imagining myself at fifty. I was already exceedingly worried about scrotal sag and the fact that I simply didn't care about keeping up with the latest music anymore. Christ, what horrors awaited me at fifty? Would I become a Republican?

The phone jolted me out of my drunken soul-searching. I let the machine pick up. (Yes, I still own an actual answering machine, replete with little cassette tapes and a blinking red message alert light. "I'm not in, say whatever you want—" *BEEP!*)

"Dan, it's your mother. If you're there, please pick up the phone." I didn't budge. I was the emotionally distant progeny— PLOINK!

"I need to talk to you about these people who keep crawling around inside the attic," my mother's voice said. "They're stealing things, and then putting them back. They're trying to make me crazy. I tried to get your cousin Dennis to come over here with his gun, but he said to call you. Hello?"

I closed my eyes tightly. I am the man who pawns the responsibility for his mentally unstable mother off on his cousins—PLOINK!

"Dan, are you there?" my mother asked. "Where are you? DAN?"

I was exhausted. The people in the attic would undoubtedly still be there the next morning; I would call her then. Plus, it's all her fault I was passed out drunk on the floor anyway, right? My mother's voice faded as I succumbed to sleep.

"The Professional"

CREATED BY JON SANTER

1/2 oz. Smith and Cross Jamaican rum

2 oz. The Balvenie Single Barrel 15 (cask strength)

1/4 oz. 3/1 honey syrup

1 dash Regan's bitters

Orange peel for garnish

Coat the inside of a rocks glass with the Smith and Cross. Add a large chunk of ice and build the rest of the drink on top of the chunk. Stir 8 times. Express the orange peel over the top and rim, toss in, or discard. Not for amateurs!

"I met Dan at Beretta in San Francisco at about ten p.m. on a Sunday night, after Ryan Fitzgerald texted me from behind the bar, 'Your friend is here and he's a bit ... um, lifted.' I left my apartment, walked across the street, and sat down at Dan's table with his friends to introduce myself. Dan, who had gotten my name from a mutual friend who told him to seek me out, was in the gloaming of a twelve-hour drinking day. We had a Nuestra Paloma and a couple of laughs and then I excused myself the way people do when they conclude that there's just no catching up to the others on that long hazy path of the all-day session. The next day Dan wrote me a thank-you note. I tell you this story because of the thank-you note, not because Dan was blotto.

"Those of us who make drinks for a living, or talk about making drinks for living, or both, understand the inevitability of the accidental marathon Saturday/Sunday (occasionally Tuesday) session. It happens. You start out with perfectly pedestrian plans for brunch with friends, oysters and Champagne or a Bloody Mary or two. Then the manager sends you out a couple of drinks off the new menu she wants you to try (because you used to work together ten years ago at . . .). Those go dry, then another bottle of wine magically appears on the table and thirteen hours later you find yourself across town wondering where the fuck your sunglasses are (you're wearing them) and feeling 'a bit . . . um, lifted.' It takes a certain kind of constitution to keep this up for years on end, as well as the rare composure to have companies consistently pay you to do it on their behalf.

"The Professional is my liquid thank-you note back to Dan. Unless you were nodding your head and wincing during the preceding paragraph, please don't try this at home."

—**JON SANTER** served as president of the San Francisco chapter of the United States Bartenders' Guild from 2007 to 2009. He has been a part of the opening teams at Bourbon & Branch, Beretta, and Heaven's Dog. He's been featured in publications including *GQ, Playboy, The San Francisco Chronicle, Sante',* foodnetwork.com, and *The Wall Street Journal.* In 2008 he was chosen by Bev Media as one of the Top 10 Trendsetting Mixologists in the United States. He currently serves as director of the Beverage Academy at Bourbon & Branch, and ambassador for Hendrick's Gin.

THREE

Never Forget the Tire Iron

$\mathcal{I}$ should point out that, contrary to popular belief, I'm not always completely to blame for my drunken shenanigans. And while I do make my best effort to be a professional at all times, sometimes my best just isn't good enough. Alcohol is a slippery mistress. One day she brings out the charismatic charmer; the next, the irate hothead. All of which is to say that occasionally on booze junkets like the one I'm about to describe, I get wasted (my hosts' fault entirely for overserving me, you understand) and wind up behaving in a manner polite society deems inappropriate or—as a former editor of mine at the Tribune Company observed moments before firing me—"completely and utterly assholish."

For instance, when the cultured, respectable folks who organize the Pebble Beach Food & Wine Festival invited me to attend their second annual event back in 2009, it probably never occurred to them that things—and by things, I mean me—could spin so badly out of control. In their defense, they were not the first to make that mistake.

In *my* defense (though my attorney suggested I try a different approach if we wound up in court), I was out of my element. Pebble Beach is a long, long way from where I live—not only geographically but spiritually. Plus, I showed up battling a touch of the flu. Turns out NyQuil doesn't pair all that well with fine wine.

In a preweekend informational e-mail, the Pebble Beach event organizers described the land to which I was about to journey as "where verdant valleys meet a pristine coastline, where there is often a chilly fog bank that can unexpectedly move in." Then they suggested that a lightweight cashmere sweater wrapped around one's neck is "a perfect accessory for most daytime events."

Which perfectly sums up what I mean about being out of my element: In the places where I normally hang out, the only reasons you would have a cashmere sweater wrapped around your neck is if you were stealing it or being strangled.

But no matter. I graciously accepted their invitation and showed up at the appropriate time and place, showered and shaved and—as presentable as my Irish genes and ripped jeans would allow—pressed onward, for I am a professional. And as a professional, I make a point of carrying two things with me at all times: a notebook and a voice recorder. What happened that weekend is why I carry them. The following transcript reflects my best attempt at a true, real-time account.

WEDNESDAY, 12:30 P.M.—While I'm driving in on Highway 68 near Spreckels in Monterey County, my iPod shuffles from Winger's "Seventeen" to Mozart's "Symphony No. 40," which is the road-trip soundtrack equivalent of a groin pull. Also, Spreckels? What the hell is that? I'd say it's a pet's name at best.

But a farming community where hardworking folks live, pay taxes, and drive pickup trucks? These people should be allowed to live somewhere that doesn't sound like a skin condition.

WEDNESDAY, 1:07 P.M.—After a five-hour drive north up the Grapevine, I check into the Monterey Hyatt under the name Arthur Bach. If you have to ask who that is and why I use that pseudonym, take a drink. If you don't have to ask, take two. I certainly did, as I promptly kicked the weekend off with two snifters of single-malt Scotch. It just feels right in this highfalutin setting. (I actually remember this part!)

WEDNESDAY, 2 P.M.—The wonderful people from Pebble Beach Resorts have comped me a round of golf at the magnificent Links at Spanish Bay. As I stand on the tee box at the first hole and gaze out toward the white-capped Pacific Ocean, I can't help but reflect upon how pissed God must still be at me for that time I made out with my eighth-grade girlfriend in the confessional at St. Albert's. I mean, really, how else do you explain 65 mph winds blowing in my face no matter which direction I turn? I reach into my golf bag, dig out one of the airplane mini-bottles of booze I keep stashed inside (in this case, rum), and gulp it down in an attempt to compensate.

WEDNESDAY, 2:01 P.M.—I just hit a perfect drive. The ball went 17 yards. Gonna be a long day.

WEDNESDAY, 3:18 P.M.—The wind just loosened several of my teeth. Seven holes? I'm going to go ahead and call that eighteen. I bet Phil Mickelson never shot a 45 at Spanish Bay.

WEDNESDAY, 7:45 P.M.—I'm having dinner with my buddy Larry Olmsted, who wrote a wonderful book titled *Getting*

Into Guinness. After pounding a rather stiff drink (my memory of what, exactly, is a bit fuzzy), I tell him I've got a feeling I may shatter some sort of world record myself this weekend. (There is actual, honest-to-God thunder at this point on the recording.)

WEDNESDAY, 10:45 P.M.—Why am I hugging Larry Olmsted?

THURSDAY, 8:22 A.M.—We're about ten minutes away from the shotgun start of the celebrity chef/winemaker golf tourney, and I'm already on my third drink. Unless you count the Cristal. And the Stella. Does beer even count? I think I've found the problem with my methodology here. The problem is counting. In any case, the way I see it, if you play golf sober you are officially part of the problem.

THURSDAY, 8:32 A.M.—We're starting on hole thirteen. And I'm rapidly approaching drink number thirteen. This is not a good sign.

THURSDAY, 9:14 A.M.—One of my randomly assigned playing partners, a nice if somewhat skittish man from San Francisco who I'll call Marlon, pulls me aside and says, "Hey, man, remember—Pebble Beach is hallowed ground." Not sure if this is meant to inspire or discourage me from dropping trou on the sixteenth tee box. I drink a vodka-lemonade instead.

THURSDAY, 9:30 A.M.—Five holes in and I'm starting to hit my stride. Unfortunately for the rest of the team, my stride looks a lot like Mel Gibson during a roadside sobriety test.

THURSDAY, 10:26 A.M.—Just bumped into famed chef Thomas Keller. I told him I was a professional scribe for an esteemed publication and that I'll be visiting New York City soon and wouldn't mind dropping by his acclaimed restaurant Per Se to see if it lives up to the hype. On the house, of course, I added with a wry grin. Keller sort of smiled too, but was clearly uncertain as to whether I was kidding or just a raging asshole. Not at all sure myself at this point, actually.

THURSDAY, 12 P.M.—I may need to change my pants. I just thwacked a golf ball to within two feet of the pin on the par-3 seventh here. If there's a more beautiful hole in golf, I'd like to make love to it.

THURSDAY, 12:01 P.M.—Marlon just slapped me on the ass and shouted, "You can be my wingman anytime!" Not that there's anything wrong with that, mind you. Some of my best friends quote Tom Cruise movies.

THURSDAY, 2 P.M.—Too God-many-fucking-ass drinks to the wind, and we're at an awards ceremony at Club XIX, which overlooks the stunning eighteenth green. How'd we do? Well, we didn't come in first, but we didn't disgrace ourselves either. Regardless, I am choosing to pretend I've won. So this is what it feels like to be Jack Nicklaus. Hordes of attendees are now falling over one another to get at ... OK, at Thomas Keller, who's looking cool as a cucumber in his wraparound shades. The guy's like Bono with a skillet. I'm convinced it's only a matter of time before dry cleaners, like chefs, get their due on reality TV and become international superstars. Hopefully, booze writers are right behind those Martinizing bastards in line.

THURSDAY, 4:30 P.M.—Back at my hotel room. Officially lost count of how much alcohol I've consumed. I wonder if Jack Nicklaus ever gets bedspins?

THURSDAY, 7:35 P.M.—The opening-night gala at the Inn at Spanish Bay is a saturnalia of gustatory delights. Among the many well-known chefs strutting their stuff are Tom Colicchio, Michelle Bernstein, Alex Stratta, Roy Yamaguchi, and Nancy Silverton—which is to say, the cream of America's culinary crop. The wines on hand also represent the best of what our great nation has to offer: Big Basin Rattlesnake Rock syrah, a medium-bodied gem from the Santa Cruz Mountains; Symmetry, a delightfully spicy fruit bomb from Rodney Strong; and Oliver's Blend from Skipstone, the boutique Alexander Valley winery. Its symphony of plums, berries, and currants is so profoundly delicious, it damn near moved me to tears. Cab-merlot blends with intense mid-palates get me every time.

THURSDAY, 8:43 P.M.—The highlight of my evening just happened. I met Morgan Leigh Norman, daughter of golfer/wine mogul Greg Norman and gorgeous enough to render me speechless. As you've gathered by now, it takes a lot to render me speechless.

THURSDAY, 11:22 P.M.—Back in the hotel room, everything's become awfully fuzzy. And squishy. No problem. I'm a professional. And professionals make notes before they pass out. I hereby note that for my money Pierre Seillan of Vérité in Sonoma County is making the finest wines in the U.S. right now, but we all know how I'm a sucker for that Bordeaux-style business. Oh, and I also note what good fun it was running into Ted Allen, of *Queer Eye for the Straight Guy* fame. I think he told me he's got a new show on the Food Network. Good fun. Must set TiVo. Why am I suddenly using phrases like "Good fun"? At this point my speech becomes a bit garbled. Must have been a problem with the voice recorder. What's that? The Au Bon Climat paired well with the risotto? Or was that pudding? No, it was pillows. Pillows filled with fromage blanc and herbs made by Chris Kostow of Meadowood in Napa. Pillows. Fromage. Viognier. Oh, yeah, the Skipstone Viognier was nice too. Ooh, *Top Gun* is on cable. I'm gonna watch me the shit out of some *Top Gun*. I should use "saturnalia" somewhere in here—that's a good foodie word. And "gustatory." People say "gustatory" all the time here. Dammit, where's Morgan Leigh Norman's business card?

FRIDAY—My voice recorder has not a single entry from Friday, though I do have this written in my notebook: "Never forget the tire iron." If you know what that means, please get in touch.

SATURDAY, 10:17 A.M.—Fuck fuck fuck fuck fuck. I lost my wallet. This fucking sucks.

SATURDAY, 12:30 P.M.—Some guy just passed me at the Lexus Grand Tasting and said, "Nice work last night. Did you get her number?" Then he winked. I don't recall ever meeting this joker in my life. And whose number? Was it Morgan Leigh Norman? For the love of all that's good and holy let it be her, and let the answer be yes. Must check BlackBerry.

SATURDAY, 12:31 P.M.—The only Norman saved in my phone is Norman Mailer. And that's a dude from my kickboxing class, not the brilliant dead demigod. That guy never picks up anyway.

SATURDAY, 1:04 P.M.—I have a new favorite chef! David Pasternack of the seafood joint Esca in Manhattan, winner of the 2004 James Beard Foundation Award for Best New York Chef, but what's more appealing than his cooking is his attitude. No bullshit, just pure New York vitality. And a sense of humor to boot! I tell him I'm a professional scribe for an esteemed publication and that I'll be visiting New York City soon and that I wouldn't mind dropping by his acclaimed restaurant to see if it lives up to the hype. "On the house, of course," said with a wry grin (I use this line a lot, as you may have gathered). He comes back with "Hell yeah, brotha!" It's good to be back in my element.

SATURDAY, 4:26 P.M.—A woman from the front desk just called up to my room. Turns out my wallet was right where I left it: in the room of someone named Kris. "They left it at the front desk for you," she says. Out comes the BlackBerry again. There it is—a Kris who wasn't there before. No last name, though. A 310 area code. I hope she's hot.

SATURDAY, 4:28 P.M.—I have not reached the desk yet, but a thought has occurred to me. "Kris" could very easily be "Chris." As in Christopher. As in a dude. Was I that drunk on Friday? In all likelihood. Not that there's anything wrong with that, mind you. Some of my best friends are occasionally drunkenly gay. Now I'm trying to recall the front desk woman's exact words. Did she say "she" left it? Probably, right?

SATURDAY, 4:29 P.M.—The front desk woman says the wallet was there when she came on duty and she has no idea of the gender of the person in question. But there's a note inside. "You dropped this, hot stuff. Great time last night. Had to head back to L.A. See you there, neighbor!" The handwriting is neat, but not too neat. And what does she (I hope) mean, "neighbor"? Is that a figure of speech, like when somebody calls you "cowboy" even though you're from Philly or "homey" even though you're white?

Living Loaded

(Editor's note: The remaining entries from Saturday have been omitted by request of the Crown Publishing Group's legal department.)

My memory picks up again Sunday morning, what with the long drive ahead of me. Checkout time. What an amazing weekend. At least, I think. Oh, look, it's that guy from the Grand Tasting, the one who asked me about the phone number. Greg? Gary? Yes, Gary! He's more distinguished than I remember, at least judging from the cashmere sweater wrapped around his neck.

"Hi, Gary. What's up, man? Hey, this is kind of a weird question, but I was just wondering who it was you were talking about when you asked if I got *her* phone number."

He squints at me quizzically through the dark circles under his eyes.

"I'm really sorry, but I don't recall meeting you," he croaks. "It was a loooong weekend, you know."

"Indeed it was," I say, smiling and feeling whole again as Gary wraps an arm around his trophy wife and walks gingerly toward a courtesy Lexus, which will presumably take him to the airport.

Me? I jump in my 4Runner and gun it back toward L.A. Somehow, several days have passed and the deadline for my weekly Playboy.com column went whooshing by. Not a good thing, but not disastrous, either. At least I can use the weekend's events as my next topic. If only I could remember them.

In the end, even though I didn't technically bring back any memories from my little jaunt to Pebble Beach, I did emerge with one thing—a big fucking hangover. And the blinding rays of—ouch—sunshine streaming through my windshield and piercing straight into my pounding skull as I zoom down the Pacific Coast Highway aren't helping, either. Luckily, as a professional, there's no hangover I can't cure. And now, I impart this invaluable wisdom to you.

Hangovers and How to Beat Them

I have always lived violently, drunk hugely, eaten too much or not at all, slept around the clock or missed two nights of sleeping, worked too hard and too long in glory, or slobbed for a time in utter laziness. I've lifted, pulled, chopped, climbed, made love with joy and taken my hangovers as a consequence, not as a punishment.

Those words by John Steinbeck are one of the most honest assessments I've seen of the perils and pleasures of what I call The Life Gigantic. And that last bit—about hangovers being a consequence rather than a punishment—has helped sustain me through many a morning curled up next to the toilet on a cold bathroom floor, shaking, sweating, and swearing to all that is good and holy that I would Never. Ever. Drink. Again.

Yeah, right.

After many years of making a living by indulging in mass quantities of adult beverages, I've come to understand that while one is suffering the ill aftereffects of overconsumption, the urge to promise yourself you'll never drink again can be overwhelming. But for incorrigible louts and inveterate pleasure-seekers like me, "I'm done with booze" is to drinking as "just the tip" is to one-night stands—a bald-faced lie, and one that should be dispensed with, provided everyone in the room is prepared to act like an adult. Which is to say, admit that they like to drink and fuck far too much to stop anytime soon.

So to those who *are* ready to grow up and admit that morning-after vows of sobriety are bullshit, yet who still wish to avoid future pain on the magnitude of that which I suffered following my Pebble Beach bender, never fear. There is an antidote.

Now, in scientific terms, when you're trying to cure a hangover what you're doing is trying to counteract the unpleasant physiological effects of acetaldehyde, the misery-inducing substance that alcohol turns into after holding court in your liver for a while. Since we're living in the real world here, we're going to ignore the fact that the best way to prevent a hangover is to avoid it in the first place by taking commonsense steps such as avoiding excessive amounts of brown liquors and sweet, sugary concoctions (let alone sweet, sugary concoctions made with brown booze), downing a glass of water after every other alcoholic beverage, eating lots of carbs prior to drinking (to slow down the rate of alcohol absorption), and—yawn—moderation.

For the sake of reality we're also going to acknowledge that when strong drink is involved, the chances of a practicing imbiber remembering to use said hangover-prevention measures are on par with the chances of him remembering he's married. So let's get our heads out of our asses and forget about this prevention crap. The hangover is going to happen, so here are my hard-earned, lab-tested solutions for what to do about it.

1. Don't Panic

First of all, realize there's more to surviving a wicked hangover than making false promises and memorizing passages from lesser-known Steinbeck novels (the quote above is from *Travels with Charley,* by the way). For instance, anyone who regularly awakens with five angry midgets playing grabass

behind their eyeballs is familiar with the following checklist:
wallet, cell phone, car keys, hat, pants, outgoing cell-phone call
log. But once you've secured the basics and satisfied yourself
that the previous evening didn't end in complete and utter
disaster, it's time to do something about the midgets—sorry,
little people—and their horrible, horrible games.

When in the throes of a particularly acute hangover—say,
one precipitated by excessive consumption of Southern
Comfort—it's possible that some parts of your body may claim
temporary independence. The key here is to remain calm. You
can ride this out. Remind yourself that your right eye has its
reasons for not opening, and that your left hand will almost
certainly be able to grasp things again tomorrow. In rare instances your bowels may go rogue. Hey, I'm not here to judge,
but if that happens, you're beyond my help. All you can do is
pray to God you're in a hotel room with enough cash in your
wallet for a Hail Mary tip and chalk it up as fodder for your
memoirs.

2. Smoke 'Em If You Got 'Em (And Have Nothing Else to Do That Day)

If legendary stoner Jeff Spicoli taught us anything in that
memorable scene from *Fast Times at Ridgemont High* where
he gleefully whacks himself in the skull with a checkered Vans
sneaker, it's that getting baked makes you virtually invulnera-
ble to head trauma. I mean, seriously, if cancer patients use the
sticky icky to mitigate the ill effects of chemotherapy, what
chance does a hangover have?

3. Retox

There are many theories regarding the origin of the phrase
"hair of the dog," but they all amount to the same thing. To
avoid the aftereffects of a night of binge drinking (or what

sticklers and losers might call alcohol withdrawl), you're going to have to start drinking again the next morning. Wonderful long-term strategy; see you at Betty Ford. But the dirty secret of this method is that it works. Just bear in mind that the trick is to drink enough to cure the hangover but not get hangover-worthy again. You're aiming for a nap-worthy buzz here. Get really, really drunk and you will experience the Double Hangover. And friends, I have met the Double Hangover. I *know* the Double Hangover. You do *not* want the Double Hangover.

Now, most seasoned drinkers have their preferred hair-of-the-dog remedy (I once knew someone who swore by the dubious method of chasing three PBRs with a shot of Jäger), but my advice to those with an uncommonly well-stocked bar is to go with an amazingly curative shot of the digestif Fernet-Branca. It's a bitter, aromatic spirit made with lots of soothing herbs. Best tool for the job by a mile.

For those who prefer the classics, of course, there's always the mother of all morning-after drinks, the Bloody Mary. This delightful libation (which has the added benefit of containing at least two of your daily required servings of vegetables— practically salad in a glass) was invented at the King Cole Bar in New York City's St. Regis Hotel, and the good folks there were kind enough to provide us with their original recipe for the "Red Snapper," which they still serve. To wit:

1 oz. vodka

2 oz. tomato juice

1 dash lemon juice

2 dashes salt

2 dashes black pepper

2 dashes cayenne pepper

3 dashes Worcestershire sauce

Lemon wedge, for garnish

Combine ingredients in a cocktail shaker. Shake vigorously. Strain over ice cubes. Garnish with a lemon wedge.

Now, the proportions here are dainty (so double 'em), and I prefer a celery stalk (and wouldn't discourage you from adding celery salt and Tabasco, if you're asking). That said, I completely understand if you're too hungover to make it out to brunch and all you have in your fridge is Cheez Whiz and mustard. Basically, if it's booze and you can keep it down, drink it. If that means three parts vodka and one part prayer, shaken over ice, I'm not going to call the cocktail police on you.

4. Hydrate

You've heard it before, but water really will flush the bad stuff out of your bloodstream—it helps you pee out the poison, if you will. So drink tons of liquids, and maybe pop a few analgesic tablets for good measure. Then, posthaste, you should . . .

5. Have Sex

Ideally with someone besides yourself. It won't be the best lay of your life (and may be only barely tolerable for your generous and understanding—or equally hungover—partner), but it'll get the blood pumping. Really. Sex will actually kill pain by increasing the amount of oxygen in the body. In lieu of a willing partner, you can always take matters into your own hand. Now, wash up and follow that with a heaping plate of . . .

6. Bacon, Eggs, and Toast

First off, yum. Second off, bacon and eggs are full of protein, which breaks down into amino acids. You need those. Third off, bacon has grease. Your body wants a little greasy love right now. Fourth off, toast is starch, and that horrible mess in your stomach wants something to soak its horribleness into. And if you're having all that, you should probably toss in a little ...

7. Coffee

The magical caffeine in coffee will constrict the blood vessels in your brain, making them hurt less. I don't know why this works, but it does. Which is why I'd also recommend a ...

8. Cold Shower

Cold water also constricts your blood vessels, but without dehydrating you or throwing a wrench into your naptime plans. Added bonus: If you suddenly feel like you're about to vomit up the huge, greasy meal I just implored you to consume, you'll be in the right room.

If you've had coffee, pot, booze, water, sex, bacon, and a cold shower and are still hungover, then I put it to you that you do not actually exist. Either that or you're Charles Bukowski. That dude's been dead sixteen years and he's *still* hungover.

"Freudian Flip"

CREATED BY JONATHAN POGASH

1 oz. Bols Genever

3/4 oz. Rothman & Winter Orchard Apricot Liqueur (from Austria)

1 whole egg

1/2 oz. demerara syrup*

Rinse of Zirbenz stone pine liqueur (also from Austria)

Nutmeg, for garnish

In a cocktail shaker, dry hump . . . I mean shake all ingredients (that means shaking without ice) except for the Zirbenz, for as long as your arms can handle it. Then add ice, and switch arms if you need to, and then shake again with all the vigor you can possibly drum up. Your palms should stick to the shaker tin at this point. When this occurs, strain ingredients out into a fancy cocktail glass that has been rinsed with the Zirbenz. Garnish with freshly grated nutmeg.

"This drink is reminiscent of the flips, nogs, and other fancy drinks served during the heyday of the cocktail: the nineteenth century. It's a creamy, frothy, milky, refreshing kind of drink that sits nicely on the palate and goes down smoothly. Um . . . that sounds weird now that I'm reading it back to myself. Scratch

---

*Demerara syrup is equal parts demerara sugar dissolved in water.

that. Let's try this again. The egg, when combined with the strong force of the Genever, enters the body, slowly coating the throat and falling into the belly, where they meet and become one. Um...hmm...that sounds kind of odd too. Screw it! Just slurp it up, will ya?"

—**JONATHAN POGASH** is a cocktail educator, bartender, and drinks consultant. His Web site, TheCocktailGuru.com, will tell you everything you need to know about him—if you're interested, of course. And why wouldn't you be? You like to drink, right?

FOUR

I'm Just Trying to Let You Down Easy

So by this point you may have gathered that I have an issue or two. Three, max. I myself have also suspected as much. I mean, you don't have to be a Freudian scholar to guess that when it comes to people who have played pivotal roles in how I relate to the fairer sex, no one looms larger for me than my mother. Who is, as you know, stone, barking crazy. Weirdly enough, when I tell people this, a common response I get is that growing up with a crazy mom sounds suspiciously like fun. Like "let's paint the house orange and pretend we're Richard Simmons" fun (maybe this says something about the people I choose to hang around with). Anyway, it is not. It's much more like "let's go steal that cop's gun" fun. So I figured it couldn't hurt to get an expert's opinion on the matter. Which is why I solicited the services of a lovely and competent and well-meaning professional, who, to save me a giant honking lawsuit, we'll just call The Shrink. I won't bore you with all the gory details, except to say that toward the end of our first session, this exchange took place:

ME: Why am I the way I am with women?

SHRINK: Why do you think you're the way you are with women?

ME: Um, I dunno. My drinking? My mother?

SHRINK: What aspects of your drinking and your relationship with your mother do you think hinder your ability to relate to women in a healthy way?

ME: The vomiting certainly doesn't help.

SHRINK: Do you vomit often?

ME: I was joking.

SHRINK: Why would you joke about vomiting?

ME: My mother has a phobia about vomiting.

SHRINK: Are you joking again?

ME: No. She really doesn't like vomiting at all.

SHRINK: Do you resent your mother?

ME: I resent the way she acts.

SHRINK: It's important that you understand that her mood swings and manic episodes are a result of her illness, and that because of the illness, the two of you have a codependent relationship.

ME: You're getting into Freudian territory now.

SHRINK: So you're familiar with Freud's theories on mother-son relationships?

ME: Mostly from watching movies.

SHRINK: What about your father?

ME: What about him?

SHRINK: You mentioned Freudian theory. Well, Freud believed that sons are in competition with their fathers for their mother's affection.

ME: My dad wasn't around when I was growing up, so . . .

SHRINK: So how did that make you feel?

ME: Like I won the competition for my mother's affection. Kinda like being valedictorian at summer school.

And round and round we went. Questions answered with more questions. We played a game of pathological ping-pong for an hour, and then agreed to meet again to pick up where we left off—discussing my earliest experiences with women.

I don't care what Freud says; my mom isn't the only one to blame for the underdevelopment of what passes for my relationship skills. Besides her, however, few loom as large as Annette Mancini.

She was eight when I was seven, and honestly, her being an older woman didn't bother me one bit. Annette was the first person I wanted to marry. Annette was the most beautiful and intelligent girl in the entire world, and if she was destined to get wrinkled and gray and graduate fifth grade before I did, well, so be it. I yearned for her in ways my prepubescent mind didn't much understand. Still, I wasn't squeamish about openly expressing my desire. Only to her, mind you. It seemed I'd hit on this whole love business unusually early, and the other unsophisticated little punks in my grade would have (rather ironically, I might add) called me any number of synonyms for homosexual had I dared breathe a word of it to them. Truth is, mere words could not properly convey the depths of my affection for Annette, so I showed her how I felt with a simple, timeless gesture: I pulled her hair. Every chance I got. Eventually, I moved on from hair pulling and even got up the courage to tell Annette Mancini I thought she was "nice." Now, when you're a seven-year-old boy, calling a girl "nice" is tantamount to serenading her with a spoken-word version of Barry Manilow's "Mandy" at the company Christmas party. Basically, I was the biggest hetero-fag in second grade. But I didn't care, because as the fates would have it, unlike most other eight-year-old girls (who tended to regard my kind as little more than living, breathing cootie carriers) Annette didn't find my frequent displays of devotion off-putting. On the contrary, she ate it up. She delighted in knowing how radiant and incredible I thought she was. We were the perfect couple.

Ah, young love! Just like old love, only without the Botox and plastic surgery.

Today, with the benefit of 20-20 hindsight, my relationship with Annette provides numerous clues as to how I would later proceed on the romance front. For instance, the two of us played "house" all the time, though we never actually committed to living together. I now understand that had we lived together we would have come to hate each other. The sacrament that was the game of house involved feigning domestic bliss for several hours after school in Annette's basement. It was a loosely interpreted celebration of our parents and their mundane rituals—shopping, cleaning, and cooking delicious treats in Annette's Easy-Bake Oven. Of course, as would be the case in all my relationships from that point forward, my primary motivation for playing along—the only one, really—was to make Annette love me. (When I finally got around to playing house again with Summer more than thirty years later, we did so sans Easy-Bake Oven. I'm sorry to say I still miss the little cupcakes.)

I really have no other way to explain what I put myself through almost every day after school for the entirety of second grade when I should have been out playing baseball, shooting BBs at pigeons, or knocking off convenience stores like every other red-blooded American male my age. Because, with the exception of those tiny, delicious Easy-Bake Oven cakes, I didn't find house all that enjoyable. But I got chills whenever Annette called me "dear" or stood close enough for me to breathe in the dizzying scent of her Love's Baby Soft. And man, she doused herself in that stuff. The memory of it still makes me woozy.

And then one day at the conclusion of an otherwise routine session of ersatz family life, Annette kissed me. Just leaned right in without warning and pressed those long longed-for lips to mine, letting them linger there until my central nervous system blitzed my seven-year-old glands with alien signals. I still claim it was that hormonal overload that caused me to pee my Buster Browns on the spot. Or maybe I'd just had too much Yoo-hoo that afternoon. But it didn't matter. Annette had kissed me, and all the urine in the universe couldn't have doused the inferno that raged inside me. What happened immediately after the kiss, though, proved to be far more effective at extinguishing my inner fire.

"I can't play house with you anymore," Annette said matter-of-factly, her words hitting me like a blast of cruel, icy wind.

No more house? The thought of it was devastating. I involuntarily emptied the remaining contents of my bladder. Confusion quickly set in, followed by anguish, embarrassment, and, finally, some uncomfortable chafing around the groin area (soiled pants will do that to a fella). *No more house?* Those words were like daggers plunging straight into my young heart. And not just any daggers. Daggers dipped in a poisonous mixture of lethal toxins that my second-grade science teachers had yet to tell us about—the kind of stuff my mom swore would kill me if I even put in my mouth but carelessly left around the house within my seven-year-old reach anyway. *No more house?* Imagine discovering not only that there was no Santa Claus or Easter Bunny, but that your Uncle Wayne's hairy puppet Mister Willy who showed up on holidays wasn't a puppet at all. (A disturbing truth Uncle Wayne touched upon briefly many years later in a 12-step apology letter that the cynical types in the family linked to an upcoming parole hearing, but that's another story.) *No more house?* Annette had just rocked my seven-year-old world with the kiss to end all kisses, only to leave me high, not all that dry, and—to borrow a phrase—pissed off. *No more house?* Why the hell not?

"Timmy got mad at me."

Timmy? Timmy *who*? The only Timmy in the neighborhood was Timmy McFadden, and he was nothing but a common thug—a young Billy Zabka. Why on earth would gorgeous, sophisticated Annette care what a worthless punk like Timmy McFadden thought about house?

"Because he's my boyfriend," she explained. At which point I experienced a level of horror on the order of what you might feel when the transmission on your Corvette blows out in Gary, Indiana. Or when your engine overheats and it's 103 degrees and forty miles to a gas station. The only terms I now can apply to the heart-sinking despair I felt at that moment are automotive. And this was the ninth circle of car-trouble hell.

"Timmy McFadden is your *boyfriend*?" I asked incredulously. "But . . . but . . . why?"

"Because he loves me," she said, blithely twirling her ponytail and snapping her Dubble Bubble in a carefree manner that seemed brutally at odds with the staggering awfulness of the news she'd just delivered.

When I heard this news about Annette and Timmy's affair, my first instinct was to stomp him into the ground. I quickly came to my senses, however, as I determined that attacking Timmy and staying alive were mutually exclusive. The situation could not have been worse. Timmy McFadden was the baddest bully on the block, and he was making time with my best girl. For the next few months I had the exquisite agony of watching the person I desired walking hand in hand with the person I most feared. It was a lethal combination that would play out in many a failed relationship from then on.

Luckily, however, I soon figured out other, less injurious ways to quell my acute inner pain—and they have served me well (though I've since supplemented these with the obvious additional rule: Get drunk off tequila and bang a hot stripper). In any case, in the interest of all the emotionally and developmentally stunted readers like me out there, I present these three tips for coping with hostility born of heartbreak:

How to Express Your Rage at Your Thwarted Romantic Ambitions When You Are Seven Years Old

1) Get it on paper.

Sure, it was as painful as a paper cut on the eyeball at the time, yet I'm actually eternally grateful to Annette and Timmy for tearing my heart out and making me feel as disposable as a sorority girl's panties after the spring formal those many years ago. See, that's because they inspired me to pen my very first journalistic work, "Timmy McFadden Is a Stupidhead That Stinks So Bad." And lo, a scribe was born. While not without its shoddy sentence structure and excessive navel-gazing—lifelong writerly traits, as you'll surely attest— "Timmy McFadden Is a Stupidhead That Stinks So Bad" might be my most persuasively argued and aggressively punctuated work to date. It's certainly the most heartfelt.

2) Take it out on someone whose ass you actually can kick.

Looking back, I suppose it wasn't my cousin Dennis's fault that Timmy McFadden purloined my lady. And I guess you couldn't blame the poor kid for being so frail and pummel-able. Nor, for that matter, should he have been made to pay so dearly simply for showing up at my house for a scheduled sleepover just a few short hours after I'd had my heart ripped from my chest. But you see, that's the beauty of being seven—at that age, high-minded ideals such as fairness and mercy have yet to take hold. At seven, you're operating on raw instinct, which compelled me to give my cousin the atomic wedgie to beat all atomic wedgies. I'll admit I didn't feel a whole lot of remorse at the time, but better late than never, right? So now I'd like to offer a public apology: I'm sorry, Dennis, I really am. For what it's worth, you did not endure humiliation along with agonizing pain in your testicles and anus in vain. On the contrary, you suffered nobly so that one emotionally devastated little boy might somehow find his way again. So I guess you could say that by wrenching your Fruit of the Looms up over your ears, I made you a hero. A savior, even. You can thank me later, Dennis.

3) Eat an entire box of Count Chocula in one sitting.

Actually, copious amounts of any breakfast cereal or food item with an alarmingly high ratio of artificial to real ingredients will do. This time-tested road to emotional healing is all about getting so jacked-up from mainlining processed sugar that you temporarily develop attention deficit hyperactivity disorder, so that you'll become occupied with activities like, say, bouncing off the walls and trying to regulate your breathing, and thus will have little time to ponder matters of the heart. Of course, the shock to your system could also lead to permanent health and/or behavioral problems, in which case I ask that you not tell your parents I recommended you do this in the first place. It'll just be our little secret.

Not Husband Material

Back in chapter 1 I told you that playing house with Summer was as close as I've ever been to living in a committed relationship. So it might shock you to learn that I almost got married. Yup, that did happen. And it happened in Vegas, as those kinds of things tend to. And let's be clear: By "almost married" I don't so much mean vowed to spend the rest of my life with someone in sickness and in health, blah blah. I mean I actually did pop the question.

"No!" Alison yelled (hastily, I thought) over the noise and bustle of a busy nightclub.

I was confused. "Do you mean 'no' as in 'no, you don't need more time to think about it' or 'no' as in 'no, I don't want to marry you'?"

"'No' as in 'no-fucking-way-in-hell-ever-no-thank-you-no,'" she said stolidly.

Painful memories of the Annette Mancini incident came flooding back.

"But why, Alison? I mean, marriage is what you said you always wanted. It's what you *all* want, really, right?"

"Oh! Of course I want to get married! I'm a woman! We're all exactly the same, right? With the exact same wants and needs and goals, and the same pussies and G-spots, yeah?" Then her sarcastic tone abruptly shifted to the one most people reserve for telling young children that their beloved puppy isn't gone, he just went to live with a family that has a bigger yard. "Sure I want to get married, Dan," she said. "Just not to *you*."

Now I was utterly bewildered.

"It's because of my career, isn't it?" I asked.

"*Career*? You're a professional drunk."

"Journalist," I said automatically.

"Whatever," she scoffed. "What do I tell my friends? My family? My fiancé travels the world and gets fucked-up for a living?"

A cocktail waitress approached the table. She was topless.

"Hey, Dan," the waitress said.

"Oh, hey, Marlene."

"Can I get you guys anything?" she asked.

"No, I think we're cool," I replied.

"OK," she said, bouncing away.

It's worth mentioning here that Alison was also topless. Also that this conversation was being conducted smack dab in the middle of a gentleman's club.

"But you're a stripper!" I protested.

"Exotic dancer. And only until I graduate from med school." She snarled. "And I can't believe you proposed to me at work! No ring, no flowers, no romance? Would you do that if I were a lawyer or a schoolteacher? Do you think I have low standards just because I take my clothes off for money?"

"No, of course not," I said, trying not to be distracted by a guy across the way getting a lap dance from a pair of twins. "I really don't understand where this hostility is coming from, Ali. I thought we were in love."

At this, her eyes showed the tiniest sign of welling up. "I did too ... for a while there. But it's just ... it's just ..."

I held my palms out, as if to say "What?" Alison drew a deep breath and reached into the purse slung across her chair. She pulled out a folded-up piece of paper and tossed it onto the table. It lay there like an accusation. A summons. A warrant.

"What? What's this?" I asked.

Alison stormed off, fighting back tears.

"C'mon, baby. We can work this out! Ali?" I got up and followed her, unfolding the page as I walked. Ah, shit. It was a column I'd written for *Playboy* about how to score women who are out of your league—one in which I may or may not have shared with my loyal readers a story about how I'd managed to repeatedly nail Miss Minnesota. I marched over to the next table, where Alison had found a client who bore a striking resemblance to George Burns.

"OK, so you read this column. What's the problem?" I demanded.

She looked at me incredulously. "What's the fucking problem? The fucking problem is that you wrote it while we were dating!"

"I told you, Alison, it's my job! And part of my job is pretending to be a single guy who scores chicks. It's acting! Pretend you're dating an actor, and I'm in a movie where I have to kiss other girls. It's kind of like dating Brad Pitt!"

"Fuck you, and fuck Brad Pitt, too!" she shouted above the booming bass of some bad Aerosmith tune.

The old man on the receiving end of the lap dance was starting to seem confused, and a little frightened.

"We should give this relationship a chance," I pleaded.

"You do whatever you want. I can't handle the freak show."

How did she not see the irony in this? I wondered. "Baby, you carve up cadavers by day, and by night you ..." I gestured toward the old man. "Freakiness is your thing, baby. Freakiness is my thing. We can get past this."

"Would you like me to leave?" The old man gasped.

Alison grabbed him by the head and buried his face in her cleavage.

"Sweetheart," I started, but she cut me off.

"No. Forget it. My rotations end in two months, and then I have my residency interviews. And I . . . I need to focus. I *don't* need some drunk-ass womanizer in my life."

"You're being dramatic," I said.

"No, I'm not," she told me. "I'm just trying to let you down easy."

And with that she dismounted the dumbfounded old man, snatched the singles out of her pants, and beelined toward the backstage dressing room. I followed, my ego in ruins.

"Alison, wait. Alison!"

A burly doorman moved aside as Alison approached the backstage door, where she wheeled around and delivered the coup de grâce: "You're a nice guy, Dan. A lot of fun. But you're not husband material. Besides, we both know that your dick has attention deficit disorder."

"What?" I scoffed.

"Oh, c'mon. Remember two weeks ago? That bullshit excuse you gave for standing me up for dinner?" she said.

"I told you that I—"

"—that you couldn't remember, riiight," she said, the sarcasm in her tone as thick as the wad of sweaty bills in her hand. "A blackout! How convenient! Just another part of your job, right? The sad part is that you must really think I'm that stupid."

I opened my mouth to speak, but the words, for once, did not come.

"I gotta get onstage. Have a nice life." With that, she disappeared through the door. I instinctively tried to follow, but the doorman blocked my path.

"Sorry, brotha."

I returned to the table, stunned. It was like the Timmy Mc-Fadden bombshell all over again. But this time I needed an emotional salve a lot more powerful than Count Chocula. I grabbed my bottle of Dos Equis and tilted it back comptempla-tively. That's when my eye caught the label, with its trademark double *X*. Didn't that also stand for something else? Then it dawned on me. Two *X*s—the chromosomal mark of the oppo-site sex; the genetic stamp of the T&A that had just left me DOA. *Dammit to hell,* I thought. *I should have ordered a Corona.*

Tragic as this episode was, I'd hate to have suffered it for naught. So in the hope that *something* good might come out of it, I've decided to share with you the very article that got me into all that trouble. You can thank me later.

How to Date Out of Your League

I met Miss Minnesota at a book signing.

Fortunately it was *my* signing, because otherwise Miss Min-nesota probably wouldn't have given me the time of day. If you're curious, it was 7:42 p.m. on a Thursday at Book Soup on Sunset Boulevard in Hollywood. You never forget a moment like that.

She was, by any credible metric, entirely out of my league. I don't even think we were playing the same sport. She had lush, shiny, blond hair like women have in shampoo ads. In fact, I would later learn that she'd appeared in several Revlon com-mercials. Her body was as good as or better than any of the ones you were ogling here [did I mention this appeared in *Playboy*?] before stumbling on this column. If she'd been around in Bot-ticelli's day, she'd have made a perfect model for another mas-terpiece. In my mind it's *The Birth of Venus 2: Electric Boogaloo.*

Our dalliance lasted but a few short weeks. Turns out, not only was Miss Minnesota a voracious reader, she also had—just my luck—excellent taste in literature. When she realized that as an author I had more in common with Tucker Max than Ernest Hemingway, it was I for whom the bell tolled. Last I heard, she was trolling coffee shops on Manhattan's lower west side in the hope of bumping into Malcolm Gladwell.

Oh, well. It was great while it lasted. Plus, Miss Minnesota kept my streak intact. Annually, for ten years running, I've dated at least one woman who is so far out of my league that otherwise proud men get on their hands and knees and beg me to share the secrets to my scoring success.

But the secrets of how to date beauty queens and Playmates are actually quite easy. Here ya go:

1) Have a beer.

You already know to never let 'em see you sweat. And there are few better ways to stave off unsightly perspiration than with a frosty beverage. But there's more to it than mere refreshment. You see, hot chicks dig guys who drink real beer. I'm talking mass-produced, middle-American-made, all-afternoon-drinkin' brewskis. Cold boys. Pounders. None of that unpronounceable craft-brewed shit from Oregon. My ex-out-of-leaguer Kelli was a model from Georgia who I met in some dive in Hollywood. I sidled up beside her at the bar and ordered a Genessee Cream Ale. This caught her attention, so I ordered her one too, without asking if she wanted it. Never ask. Just give it to her. If she takes it, you're golden. If she walks away, hey, you got two Genessee Cream Ales all to yourself. Still golden, baby.

2) Be willfully oblivious to your ordinariness.

Look, you know you're a schmuck. Your friends and family know, too. In fact, everyone you've ever met no doubt thinks you're a bit of a lost cause. But Miss Rod-Busting Hotness has yet to make that wonderful discovery. As far as she knows, you could be James Bond … albeit with a party-ball gut instead of six-pack abs. So when that fleeting window of opportunity opens you need to play the part and tap into your inner badass. Believe it or not, it's still there somewhere, buried beneath layers of doubt, self-loathing, and belly fat. So pull out a gold-plated cigarette case and fire one up. Be sure to blow the smoke out of the corner of your mouth, real cool-like, before draining another martini. And yes, I'm aware that smoking is forbidden in most bars and restaurants in the developed world. Who cares? You're James Motherfucking Bond. Own it. When they're showing you the door, chances are she'll be right behind you.

3) Quit joking around.

You know how hot women always claim that what they're really looking for in a guy is someone who can make them laugh? It's bullshit. Actually, it's even bigger bullshit than when they say guys never hit on them in high school because they were ugly. Uh-huh. Chicks who look like Playmates didn't get that way overnight. They have been hot for a long time, and they get hit on constantly. And while they probably appreciate a good laugh now and again, what they really want—what they're tragically, frustratingly, and utterly attracted to—are guys who will make them cry. Of course you don't want to be that guy either, but pushing your image toward Frank Sinatra and away from Jerry Lewis can only help you. The night I met Lexie Karlsen (Miss March, 1999) I told her one joke, and one joke only. It went like this:

"Knock, knock."
"Who's there?"
"It's me … and I'm a total dick."

We dated for several weeks after that. No joke.

4) Focus.

You can't be everything to every woman, so figure out your strength and work it hard. Did you spend the best years of your life climbing the corporate ladder so you could afford a killer house in the Hollywood Hills? You're in. That line about how she doesn't care about money and wants to date someone her age? More bullshit. The male-model bartender may have you beat on years and looks, but that's no match for your Beemer. Or maybe you're an unemployed dope-smoker who plays video games until it's time to hit the bars. You, my friend, are "creative." So tell her about some interesting "projects" that you're "working on." Your firm laid you off nine months ago and now you've had to resort to taking a job at Burger King? Great—you can say you work with children. Or maybe you're a neurotic, immature, borderline alcoholic from a dysfunctional family whose business card reads "Public Menace." On paper you're a pathetic loser. Unless you wrote a memoir about your sorry life. Now you're a tortured artist … say hello to Miss Minnesota!

Of Course She'll Say Yes, You Dick

All my friends seemed to think it was a good idea for me to get more serious with Alison the stripper/med student. The only guy who tried to talk me out of it was Randy. I went to college with Randy. He was never great shakes with the ladies back then. Today he's a rotund almost-middle-aged man whose strawlike hair and beady, close-set eyes underscore the enormity of his overly freckled, moonish face. Oh, yeah, and he also has a yin yang tattoo on his left biceps, and the other arm is emblazoned with a rather impressively detailed image of two women having athletic and improbable sex. In short, he is not what most sane, sighted people would call a physically attractive human being ... at least not outside the adult-baby fetish community. He does have one thing going for him aesthetically, however—an extremely well-formed nose. Turns out that one good feature—oh, and about ten million dollars in the bank—is enough to get even the most unfortunate-looking (sorry, Randy) of us laid.

Randy is an Internet porn mogul. Or, as the local church groups prefer to call him, a smut king. Randy hates that. Cheap, easy labels have always bugged him. Plus, he considers himself more evolved than most of the other people in his profession. Case in point: He once wrote and directed an X-rated version of Franz Kafka's "Metamorphosis." One scene in particular stood out to me:

> "Mr. Samsa, what happened to you?" says the female lead to a well-hung stud sprawled on a bed dressed like a giant insect.
>
> "Help me," he cries. "My legs don't work!"
>
> The actress looks him over and gasps as her line of sight reaches his crotch. A sly look crosses her face, and she licks her lips. "It looks like something works," she purrs. They then make sweaty bug-love for twenty minutes.

Anyway, the point of this story is that Randy was in Vegas to accept an AVN Award, which is the porn equivalent of the Oscars. In his acceptance speech, Randy quoted immortal costume rocker Gene Simmons, who once said that porn "makes the world a more exciting place," then went on to claim that what he and his colleagues produce for the enjoyment of the horny masses is as harmless as a pillow fight (announcing this to a roomful of pornography professionals is kind of like preaching to the choir, but whatever). "So drink up and enjoy yourselves," Randy said, moving into the finish and raising a Champagne glass. "And here's to many more years of continued success in the porn business . . . at least until we all find Jesus and start making sites for Christian youth camps. Cheers!"

After his speech he was holding court with a gaggle of admiring, artificially enhanced women. Randy's game had apparently improved since college, when someone started a rumor that he was the brother of a notoriously corpulent comedian known for such cinematic gems as *Canadian Bacon* and *Uncle Buck*. Unfortunately, the physical resemblance between the two was uncanny, and a month later most people on campus believed he really was named Randy Candy (that's where his nickname "Big Candy" really comes from, no matter what he tells his dates). But despite his pulchritudinous limitations, the big guy has charisma in bunches, though the bunches of money don't hurt either.

"Yes, it is my original nose," Randy was telling one of the babes as I waved him over. He excused himself and joined me in the banquet room foyer.

"Randy, what if I told you I was going to propose to Alison?" I asked.

"I'd tell you that you're a fucking moron, then take you through the five stages of grief: anger, denial, bargaining, substance abuse, and, step five, ass-whupping."

"I'm serious, man," I said.

"I know you are, you fucking moron," Randy barked, before taking a big pull from a bottle of Korbel Brut. He took a deep breath, made me promise I wouldn't punch him for what he was about to say, then proceeded to tell me what a giant heap of unimpressive he thought Alison was and that he had it on good authority she fucked at least three members of the Phoenix Suns basketball team . . . purportedly all in one night, during All-Star weekend. There was a long uncomfortable silence, then Randy inexplicably doubled over with laughter, tossed an arm around my shoulder, and spun me around to face the revelry inside the banquet room.

"Alison's OK and all, buddy, but just remember, you'll have to keep it in your pants around *that* for the rest of your life," he said, referring to the scantily clad bevy of loose women.

"I know what I'm doing," I lied.

As we headed back into the party, Randy asked, "Do you think she'll say yes?"

I was answering before he was done speaking. "Of course she'll say yes, you dick."

"B.B.G."

CREATED BY BOBBY "G" GLEASON

1 1/2 oz. Jim Beam Black Label bourbon
3 dashes Angostura bitters
Ginger beer or ginger ale
Lemon wedge or twist, for garnish

Build over ice in a tall highball glass. Garnish with a lemon twist or wedge. Fill with ginger beer or ginger ale.

"If you want to give the impression that you have class and know what you want, you should treat bartenders and cocktail waitresses with respect, order exactly what you want, and make damn sure you can taste the difference between good bourbon and shit whiskey. Ordering a bourbon cocktail lets people know you're a drinker with some balls. And because bourbon is the only true American spirit, when you drink it you're doing your country proud. Unless you're not from America, that is."

—BOBBY "G" GLEASON is the master mixologist for Beam Global Spirits & Wine. He lives in Las Vegas and knows someone at almost every hot spot in town, yet—somewhat suspiciously—always seems to be "away on business" whenever Dan rolls into town.

FIVE

If the House Does Not Want You to Win, You Do Not Win

ow, my Vegas stories all start out pretty much the same way. It goes a little something like "Hey, Vegas, let's have a near-illegal amount of fun!" The endings, however, differ wildly. But I can still break them into three main categories: (1) heartbreak or depression (see chapter 4); (2) detached bemusement and head-scratching at the idiocy that surrounds me; or (3) complete, unmitigated disaster.

Category threes tend to be less dangerous to my self-esteem than category ones, though more hazardous to my physical being. Still, they both make detached bemusement sound like hitting the lotto. This next story is an example of what I like to call a category-five category three.

Back in 2009 I hit town with a high-ranking media relations executive from one of the world's largest spirits companies. For once, though, we weren't just there to drink and gamble (though that inevitably happened); we were there to enjoy the third most quintessential of Vegas activities—a boxing match. And this wasn't just any boxing match, mind you. It was a world lightweight championship fight at the MGM Grand. And we weren't just a couple of unruly assholes joining the ranks of the drunken rabble in the nosebleed section. We were a couple of unruly assholes sitting ringside in some of the most expensive seats in the house.

I won't say which brand this executive—who we'll call Rob—works for, nor who the fighters were or when this went down, because I really like Rob and I'm pretty sure what transpired that night is fair grounds for being fired. I, on the other hand, rarely worry about getting in trouble for getting in trouble—my corporate masters expect such recalcitrant, unprofessional behavior out of me. It's right there in my contract, between the clauses regarding designated drivers and sexual harassment (which are tied in to my year-end bonus).

Anyhow, Rob and I had spent most of the day drinking at the adults-only "European-style" pool at the Moorea Beach Club at Mandalay Bay. What they mean by European-style is that women are free to go topless, an invitation many of them are happy to accept after their inhibitions have been sufficiently doused in alcohol. Which flows freely in the form of sugary iced concoctions that taste like a mango smoothie and kick like a mule. Now, like most men with spare time, a computer, and Internet access, I probably see twenty-four to twenty-five bare breasts every day. And usually these breasts belong to strangers. All of which would lead you to think that me getting my drink on with a bunch of topless tourists in Vegas would be old hat, right? Just a typical day in the life. However, it turns out that no matter how many unclad pointer sisters a guy sees daily on the Internet or in magazines (or on the Internet pages of magazines he works for), boobies never cease to be fascinating. Consequently, bearing witness to bare titness in a social setting is unnerving even for the seasoned funbag connoisseur. And this manifests in a certain demonstrable behavior: When I see a sexy stranger in the buff in the real world (as opposed to in the fantasies that consume the bulk of my waking hours), even I tend to behave like a freaking bozo.

So when, in the midst of telling me about the time she and her friends met Dave Matthews at Lollapalooza, Marie from Minnesota suddenly peeled off her bikini top in the pool at the Moorea Beach Club, I was almost guaranteed to blush, stammer, sweat, fidget, laugh nervously, and have every sane thought suddenly rush out of my head—which I did. Unfortunately, my difficulty in finding something to say in the next ten seconds was compounded by the fact that in the short time we'd been chatting all I'd managed to gather about Marie was that she likes lame music, drinks vodka sodas with a splash of cranberry, and teaches math to second graders in St. Paul. Everything else about her, including her motivation for flipping out her floppers right there in front of me at that particular moment—*especially* that, actually—was a tantalizing mystery. My mind raced at the possibilities. So to deal with all this confusion, I did what any guy hanging out in a Vegas hotel pool with a topless math teacher would do—drank heavily.

Anyway, all of this goes to explain why, by the time Rob and I arrived at the MGM Grand that night for the fight, we were only slightly less pickled than the sandwich menu at Jerry's Famous Deli.

We knew little about either of the fighters vying for the championship belt, but that didn't stop us from wagering serious bank on the outcome. I even promised Marie from Minnesota I'd bet a few hundred on her behalf and, gentleman that I am, covered the nut myself. The fighter we randomly chose to hitch our financial fortunes to hails from Cuba and, wouldn't you know, they happened to be selling cheap nylon reproductions of the Cuban flag at concessions stands in the MGM lobby. So we had to have one. Duh. That turned out to be our first mistake.

When we arrived at our seats, the first two things I noticed were attached to a voluptuous young platinum blond seated in the row in front of us (OK, so we weren't *literally* ringside, but we were close enough). Where had *she* been all my life, I wondered aloud. This got her attention. She was alone, and seemed bored, frankly. We struck up a conversation. Mistake number two.

"What brings you here?" I said coyly (or, at least, drunkenly, with intent to be coy).

"I'm here with some guy," she replied matter-of-factly.

"Some guy, huh?" I said. "Boyfriend? Coworker? Brother?"

"Just a guy," she said, popping her gum. "I don't know him."

Because I was drunk and more than a little woozy from overexposure to the sun and bare stranger breasts, it took a while for it to register why a gorgeous gal like that would be sitting ringside at a championship bout with a total stranger in Las Vegas.

"She's a real looker," Rob whispered in my ear. Or it might have been "She's a real hooker." Either way, he was correct. I then determined it would be a good idea to sidle up next to the lovely young working girl to get a better feel for our romantic prospects. It was not. A good idea, that is. On the contrary, it was my third mistake.

"Nice flag," she said. "What country is it from?"

"Cuba," I replied.

"That's in South America, right?"

"Yes, it is," I answered. Close enough.

The blonde's "date" arrived less than a minute after the first fight on the undercard began. He was dressed entirely in black and looked like Michael Clarke Duncan in *The Green Mile,* only significantly larger and more menacing. I should've put my money on him instead of that joker from Cuba.

"You mind moving over?" He glared at me.

"Oh, sorry, we were just talking. My seat is right there, in the row behind."

"Why don't you get the fuck back there, then," he said, snarling. Not a good sign, this snarling business. Nor did I feel very good about the fact that he was wearing an all-access badge. So not only was he a very large, angry man, in all likelihood, he was a made man as well. Using my vaunted powers of ratiocination, I instantly determined the best course of action was to keep my mouth shut and to do what he said.

But before I did so, I couldn't resist putting one last nail in my coffin. I winked at the blonde. Big Black saw it too, and shot me a ferocious look letting me know that imminent death or dismemberment was a distinct possibility. But at that point, I wasn't too worried. Though it was clear he could easily and irreversibly rearrange my facial features in a matter of seconds, odds were he wouldn't dare do so in front of thousands of witnesses and a date he'd obviously spent a pretty penny on.

Rob and I stepped outside for a smoke after the first fight. This proved to be mistake number—are we up to five?—because, as fate would have it, the blond bombshell was out there all by her lonesome and in search of a light. No sooner had Rob flicked his Bic for her than Big Black came storming out the door. He grabbed her by the arm, pulled her away from us, and dressed her down something awful in full view of at least fifty future lung cancer victims.

Then came the glare, directed at us again, only this time he followed it up with a fiendish grin.

"What was that all about?" I said.

"What?" Rob replied.

"That fiendish grin," I said.

"It looked like he had something stuck in his teeth."

"Yeah, like someone's head, perhaps."

Anyhow, back inside, the main event was about to begin. Big Black and the blonde had moved even closer to the action, further proof that he was a big swinging dick in this town. Multiple sets of ringside seats aren't easy to come by at sold-out championship bouts.

At the end of round one Big Black got up and lumbered menacingly in our general direction. Instead of accosting us, however, he sat down nearby, next to a female security guard who looked to be in her fifties. They both watched us intently as he whispered something in her ear and she nodded. I pretended not to notice. Rob didn't have to pretend. He was lost in the booze and blood.

When Big Black returned to his seat after one final death stare in our direction, the security guard dutifully got up, strode over to our section, and sat down in a chair directly across the aisle, a scant three feet away. As she fixed her penetrating gaze upon us I got that prescient feeling I so often get in such hostile situations involving lots of booze and a very large man whose "date" I have evidently tried to hit on, that things were about to break bad. Still, I pretended not to notice that the guard was staring at me like a lioness crouched in the weeds eyeing a herd of delicious lunch meat. Hey, I could take her. To prove just how blissfully unconcerned I was about the security guard's presence, I jumped up, waved my Cuban flag, and shouted some encouraging words to the pugilist upon whom I'd wagered next month's rent money.

"Stop waving that flag!" she barked. Suddenly she was standing over me, practically foaming at the mouth.

"Why can't I wave my flag?" I asked. "Look—they're all

waving *their* flags," I said, gesturing out at the crowd where, literally, hundreds of other fans were doing just that.

"You're bothering the people in front of you," she snapped.

"Am I bothering you, man?" I asked the young Latino dude seated directly in front of me.

He shook his head no, but the security guard was unmoved. "Don't wave that flag again," she warned. Then she returned to her chair and resumed her icy-stare routine.

That's when I started to get angry. Why was I being singled out? Everyone else in the damn arena got to wave flags without being scolded like a restless first-grader at naptime. Was it something about Cuba? *The Cold War is over, lady,* I felt like screaming at her. But I didn't, because I knew the reason she was *really* riding us. It was sitting a few rows away, next to a hooker. A hooker I'd just minutes ago hit on. But, hey, it was a free country, wasn't it? This wasn't, say, Cuba, for chrissakes. Boy, I was getting angry, and it was drunk angry, too. The worst kind.

At the conclusion of the fifth round, I looked over at the security guard and demanded, "You don't like me, do you?"

Without hesitation she said, "No, I don't like you at all."

I smiled mischievously. Then I turned my attention back to the bloody action inside the ring.

"Excuse me," I said to her at the end of the sixth and—for us, at least—final round, "but can I ask you something?"

She said nothing, just stared at me dispassionately.

"We're guests here, sitting in very expensive seats, trying to enjoy this fight that we flew a long way to see. And for the life of me, I can't figure why the hell you felt entitled to sully the experience by insulting me with an unprovoked assault on my character. Can you explain this to me, please, miss?"

"OK, that's it," she said. She marched off, and a moment later two male security guards—significantly larger than her in stature—and two Las Vegas "peace officers" with billy clubs were standing over us, looking anything but peaceful.

"Let's go, gentlemen, you're out of here," said one of the guards.

Rob suddenly snapped out of his booze-induced stupor.

"What the fuck?" he yelled.

That's when one of the cops grabbed him by the arm and hoisted him out of his seat. "Let's go. Now!"

Once we were out in the hall, we demanded an explanation.

"A member of our security team witnessed you throwing an ice cube at another guest," the guard explained.

"An ice cube? Bullshit! I don't even have a drink, so where did I get the ice?" And shockingly, this was true. I didn't have a drink. Neither of us did. At a boxing match in Vegas! I think we have uncovered the real injustice here.

"That bitch security guard said I did that, right? Where is she?"

"Where she is, is none of your business," the guard said. "All you need to know is that you're leaving the MGM Grand now, one way or another."

"Do you know who the fuck we are?" Rob shouted. I winced. Look, no matter who you think you are or why you feel it might possibly matter, it is never a good idea to pose that question to anyone, at anytime. Even the most out-of-control, arrogant, self-absorbed celebrities know this. Asking someone you clearly deem beneath you whether they know who the fuck you are is like asking for permission to take a dump on their head. It's just not going to garner a favorable reply.

"We're with the fight's biggest sponsor!" Rob shrieked. "Without us there wouldn't be any fucking fight!" Which I suppose is true if you think about it in a metaphysical "tree falls in the forest" kind of way. But Rob had forgotten the first law of Vegas: The house always wins. It doesn't matter who you are; if the house does not want you to win, you do not win (case in point: our guy, the guy with my money in his shorts, got knocked out cold in the ninth round).

At this point, it was clear we'd run afoul of Sin City's karmic overlords, as the cops loomed above us with expressions of consternation I could only interpret as indecision over whether to incarcerate us, beat us silly, or both.

Next thing we knew, we were against the wall being "searched" by a gang of thugs in a small windowless chamber somewhere in the bowels of the MGM Grand. And let's just say they were thorough. Hell, I'll never associate the word "cavity" with dentistry again. Then the leader of the thugs rammed a gun into Rob's mouth and glared at me.

"What's the smallest country in the world?" he barked.

"H-huh?" I stammered, shooting a panicky look at Rob, whose eyes were suddenly wider than a two-time divorcée's ass on a singles cruise.

"Name the fucking smallest country in the world or I'm pulling this fucking trigger, fuckface!" the thug raged.

"What? Are you serious, man?"

"And guess who's digging the fucking grave out in the desert?" he said, and snarled. He looked possessed. Barking, raging, snarling mad. "Five . . . four . . . three . . ."

"Wait, stop!" I implored him. "We were just waving a flag and flirting with a hooker, for chrissakes!!!"

"Two . . . one . . ."

"Monaco!" I pulled out of the air.

And with that the thug turned, looked at me with what appeared to be high regard, and eased his finger off the trigger. I couldn't believe it. I'd done it. I'd saved Rob's life. It was a miracle. I mean, Monaco? Where'd that come from? I barely passed geography in high school. Clearly it was divine intervention, though lord knows—excuse me, the Good and Most Gracious Lord knows—I'd done nothing to deserve such a blessing.

Rob was sweating like Robin Williams in a sauna, and from the stains on his pants and the stench in the room I gathered he'd pissed *and* shit himself. But even with the business end of what appeared to be a Walther P99 semiautomatic pistol still in his mouth, I could tell he was smiling the most grateful smile ever. It dawned on me at that moment that I would never have to spend another dime on a bottle of booze again.

"Wait a minute," one of the other thugs chimed in, browsing the Internet on his iPhone. "This says Monaco is the *second* smallest country, behind Vatican City."

"Oh, that's right," said the lead thug. "Forgot about the Pope's place."

Then he blew Rob's head off. And let me tell you, digging that grave in hundred-degree heat damn near killed me, too.

OK, not really. Truth is, after getting muscled out of the arena we avoided any serious trouble, saved (as I have been in more situations than I'd like to admit) by strategic deployment of my *Playboy* business card and a fraudulent invitation to the next Midsummer Night's Dream Party at the Mansion. Which I have never attended, nor probably will I ever.

But we weren't totally out of the woods yet. As we trudged, tails between our legs, down Las Vegas Boulevard, Rob, finally sober enough to intuit that getting forcibly removed from a very public venue while he was, technically speaking, on the clock wasn't necessarily the best career move, got on the phone with his company's regional sales director to attempt some damage control. But the more time that passed between Rob and his last cocktail, the more determined he became to exculpate himself from the mess at the fight (I'd given him permission to throw me under the bus in the event it became necessary to save himself, but to his great credit, he dismissed that idea outright).

In the end it wouldn't matter. We didn't get our faces bashed in by MGM security, nor were we gang-raped by Clark County Jail inmates. Rob didn't even get fired. Nobody at MGM really wanted to make any more trouble for us. We were tourists in Vegas, for chrissakes. The city's survival depends upon our fucking up. And forgiveness is what keeps the roulette wheels spinning. Cuban flag? What Cuban flag? C'mon on in and try your hand at Pai Gow!

Plus, Rob works for a liquor company—his betters understand only too well what their product is designed to do. They sponsor boxing matches, for chrissakes. It's unclear whether his boss bought his vehement declarations of unaccountability or just didn't give a shit, knowing this kind of thing comes with the territory. If your job is to be constantly surrounded by drunk, rowdy people, then hey, you're going to be one of them yourself from time to time. At least that's the line I use to get out of trouble on a regular basis.

Personally, I chalk the whole incident up to something Larry, a Vegas cabbie I know, once told me. He said, "One thing's for sure about Vegas. When you come visit, you're gonna get fucked before you leave. One way or another, you *will* get fucked. Sometimes you get fucked good, and sometimes you get fucked bad. You might get ass-fucked or mouth-fucked or wallet-fucked. You'll probably get fucked-up too. The one constant is the fucking. That always happens here, no matter what. So the key to enjoying Vegas is that you gotta like getting fucked ... and you should always carry rubbers, too."

He's a font of wisdom, that Larry.

At Least a Few Every Night

"I'll tell you what," Larry growls as we inch down Las Vegas Boulevard en route to the Encore Hotel and Casino (Steve Wynn's two-thousand-plus-room bauble in the heart of the strip). "A lot of people in this city are clueless about how much fuckin' trouble this country's in ... and they don't even fuckin' know it, either."

That's what I love about Vegas—the cabbies here can provide you with just about anything, from poker tips to where to find the nearest tattoo-removal joint. In the time it takes to traverse the short distance from the Mandalay Bay to the Bellagio, you can even get unsolicited observations about America's flatlining economy from a Jim Cramer look-alike with what appears to be a wicked case of Tourette's. Of course this was mere months after the housing bubble burst and half the country realized their homes suddenly weren't worth the paper their mortgages were printed on. Not Larry, though. Larry owns his place outside of town outright. It's his fucking whoremouth nut, apparently. According to Larry, they'd have to drag him out of there feet first in a pine, nun-diddling box. Right on, brother! Larry's been driving a cab eighteen ass-fucking years. Suffice it to say, he's seen a lot. After we paid him, all he said was "People are fuckin' strange, man."

Indeed.

Anyway, it's 11:45 p.m. on a Saturday—barely happy hour by local standards—yet inside the Encore a crush of young humanity is already bum-rushing the entrance to the casino's opulent new forty-thousand-square-foot playpen, the XS nightclub. It's early April and there's still a slight nip in the air, but most of the girls here are wearing next to nothing. So, actually, strike that; there's an immense amount of nip in the air. But while the ladies look amazing, their male counterparts are decked out in desperation-casual, which smells a lot like cheap suits, bad cologne, and hair gel, set off by a top note of tragic bluster. It's a scene playing out all over the city right about now: guys who reek of body spray and flop sweat, begging and pleading and lying their way onto a deafening and choked club floor. Offering bribes to burly doormen. And dropping names to supercilious pricks holding clipboards and lists. Those who finally do break on through to the other side pay thirty dollars (ladies ten bucks less), and a couple of rounds of drinks later, most of these hombres are out more than they pull down in a week, without even gambling a penny.

Like Larry said, clueless.

Then again, tonight I'm one of them. But I'm here strictly on official business, which is why I left Rob back at the hotel. In the shape he's in, he'd be doing me no good. Instead, I have Marie from Minnesota and one of her girlfriends with me, both of whom seem duly impressed that not only are we "on the list," we have a VIP escort to boot. I look at them, all done up in their tiny little dresses, and wonder if perhaps I can parlay this starlike treatment into a threesome later on. Hey, a man's gotta have dreams, right?

As we reach the top of the stairs, my eyes are drawn to an illuminated outdoor pool and island bar, over which hangs a huge rotating chandelier. The place is awash in rich gold, black, bronze, and brown, with dance poles designed to look like lanterns interspersed throughout. The publicist who invited me here had explained via e-mail that the club's design was "inspired by the sexy curves of the human body," and while I'm not really sure I see it, it's clear they had one specific body part in mind when they set the prices on the drinks menu: the asshole.

"We actually sell a lot of them," says our waitress when I inquire about the "Ono," a Champagne and cognac–based cocktail that sells for $10,000. "At least a few every night," she adds.

OK, so maybe I'm the asshole.

Tables are at a premium here, but thanks to extremely professional conduct on the part of the publicist, we're shown to one in a prime location and presented with a bottle of Ketel

One vodka (for which I would like to thank Steve Wynn and all the wonderful folks at XS nightclub) and a four-pack of Red Bull for my lady friends. (The Imbiber's official stance on vodka–Red Bull is "just say no.") Upon inquiry we ascertained that any subsequent bottles of booze would set us back $485 a pop, plus an additional $9 per Red Bull. I shudder to think of the barrage of profanity Larry would unleash if he knew what the hell was going on in here.

But hey, garish nightclubs that cater to the rich and fool-hardy are nothing new. Hell, back in 1977 throngs of wannabes would routinely line up around the block outside Studio 54 to pay a then staggering $8 for the privilege of seeing Bianca Jag-ger and Halston do the Hustle. (Fun fact: I have it on good au-thority that Brooke Shields attended the opening-night bash at Studio 54. She was eleven, and nobody gave a rat's ass. If she wanted to, she probably could have shot heroin and driven herself home in an NYC police cruiser.)

Then again, the seventies weren't quite such screwed-up economic times as these, and the incongruity between what I'm witnessing in here versus what is happening out in the real world is becoming more jarring by the second. I know no one comes to a shiny city in the middle of a massive desert where buildings are modeled after pyramids and pirate ships and you can't go five minutes without running into a fake Elvis be-cause they want to embrace the real world, but all the same. This place has the feel of someone flooring it when they know they're running on fumes. Then again, why the hell not? This is where you come to surf the American Dream. The real Ameri-can Dream, where you can shop, eat, drink, fuck, and gamble away your life savings without ever having to see a ray of day-light. Was it Jim Morrison who said he'd get his kicks before the whole shithouse went up in flames? Let it roll, baby, roll.

I'm in my head trying to recall the middle lyrics to "L.A.

Woman" when an Ed Hardy boy with three hotties in tow taps me and says, "Dude, looks like you've got some room. Mind if we join you? I'll buy the next bottle."

The platinum card slaps down and I see no need to mention that, with the Ketel killed, we'd been seconds away from blowing this joint for the $4.99 buffet at Binion's. "Sure," I say, settling back into my seat, "but you should definitely order their signature drink as well—it's called the Ono."

Like shooting fish in a barrel.

Before we leave, a voluptuous VIP hostess comes over and gives me a black trucker's cap emblazoned with an electric red XS logo. The brim is covered with a glittering orange flame design ringed with silver. If Liberace had chosen a career path that involved tooling around in an 18-wheeler instead of tickling the ivories, this would surely have been his headgear of choice.

"A little something to remember us by," the hostess says with a wink, having clearly mistaken me for someone devoid not only of any fashion sense, but of dignity. Nonetheless, she's hot, so I thank her for her generosity and slip her my card on the way out, with an invitation to call me in the event she's up for some fun after she gets off work. I toss the XS cap in the garbage as soon as I'm out the door. Hell, I'd just as soon whack my nuts with a mallet than don something that garish. Indeed, when it comes to collecting clothing from nightclubs and bars, I consider my taste to be impeccable. Which tells me it's high time for another set of my invaluable pointers.

How to Cultivate a Kick-Ass Collection of Drinking Memorabilia

I was once at a party in Venice Beach where a guy showed up wearing a T-shirt from a pub in Portsmouth, England, called the Sociable Plover. When I asked about it, he explained that it's the only bar in the world named after an endangered species, apparently a member of the lapwing family of birds. I almost began to turn a very unattractive shade of green, until I remembered that I am myself in possession of one of the world's great collections of drinking-establishment clothing. In fact, that very evening I happened to be wearing a cap from none other than Kung Fu Tap & Taco. How do you like me now, Mr. Save the Rain Forest? KFT&T is a biker bar in Des Moines, by the way, where only two beers are served on tap: Hamm's, and the one they'll beat the crap out of you for drinking.

Like any hobby, there are rules to collecting bar gear. Problem is, most serious drinkers have trouble remembering any of them at the very moment when the opportunity to procure such an item generally presents itself. Fortunately, as a professional, when I'm out boozing I always carry a notebook for the very purpose of having this kind of information (and other stuff too, like what hotel I'm staying at, or the name of the girl I'm with) on hand when I'm too drunk to remember it. Here, then, I bequeath to you the guidelines I've devised for amassing a bar-wear collection that falls on the badass side of cheesy.

1) Anything with the word "dick" on it is funny.

The jewel of my collection is a T-shirt from a roadhouse in central Alaska called Skinny Dick's Halfway Inn, which has—without a doubt—the single best taproom name in America. What makes this even cooler is the fact that it's no cheap marketing ploy: There really was a Richard "Skinny Dick" Hiland, a notorious hell-raiser who passed away a few years back at the ripe old age of eighty. If you ever happen to find yourself at the midway point of the highway that runs between Nenana and Fairbanks, I'd highly recommend checking out his popular beer and burger joint. Why do the Skinny Dick's T-shirts they sell in the gift shop feature an image of two bears humping? It's a cheap, innuendo-laden marketing ploy.

2) Avoid cheap, innuendo-laden marketing ploys (unless they involve the word "dick").

My kid brother is an aspiring collector who owns no fewer than three T-shirts from a place in Ocean City, Maryland, called the Bearded Clam Bar. He thinks it's hilarious. He's twenty-three.

3) Get your story straight.

Bar gear can be an excellent conversation starter, as there's no better way to impress a drunk chick than with a colorful story about the origin of whatever it is you're wearing. So if you don't know the colorful story behind it, be sure to make up a good one. For instance, drinkers who know what they're doing in Ocean City, Maryland (my kid brother not being one of them), get a visor from the waterfront nightclub Seacrets. They're perfect. I own two. Now, I have no idea what the actual history of the place is, nor do I care enough to find out. So I just tell people my version, which is that Seacrets was opened in the early 1980s by two friends named Barry and Chuck. Barry owned a tanning-salon chain, while Chuck was an assistant manager at Chess King who also played in a fairly popular synth-pop cover band. Chuck's girlfriend at the time, Krystal (who would later become Barry's third wife after Chuck OD'd), was the one who came up with the name. She thought it sounded exotic, like one of those all-inclusive nudist resorts she and Barry liked to go to in the Caribbean. Hence the visors. This story is complete bullshit, yet amazingly, not a soul has ever questioned it. (Bonus tip: There's also a nightclub in Ocean City called Scandals. Alas, I don't have any clothing from Scandals, but if you're ever there, pick something up. That crap writes itself.)

4) Be secure in your manhood.

I own a black cotton T-shirt from a place called the Back Door. It reads, COME IN THE BACK DOOR! in bold pink lettering. By far the most entertaining thing about this shirt is the faces people make when I wear it around Orange County.

5) No mail order, no exceptions.

OK, so *you* don't actually have to have been to the bar featured on your shirt—gifts from a friend or family member are acceptable. But for it to count—and this is a hard-and-fast rule—it must have been purchased for you *on-site*. eBay and other online purchases are bullshit. You get your Seacrets visor the hard way, or you don't get it at all.

6) Dare to dream.

Just because a place like, say, McDrunk Fuck's Fake Tit Emporium and Organic Car Wash doesn't actually exist is no reason to abandon hope that it might someday. Bust out your scanner, a stack of magazines, and your Photoshop skills, then head to CafePress or Zazzle (or whatever idiotically named purveyor of customized crap exists in your area) and make the dream happen. The more nonimaginary apparel you create for your imaginary joint, the more real it becomes. It's like magic!

7) Charity is good for the heart.

Buying bar wear for yourself can make you self-conscious, and it's often cooler to be the guy who bought his buddy a shirt from the Foaming Head than the guy who bought it for himself. So remember your pals next time you're in a bar with a funny name. Which reminds me, if any of you happen upon the Walk Her Inn Roadhouse in Milwaukee, Wisconsin, I'd be much obliged if you'd pick me up something from the gift shop. Hell, I'll be your best friend.

Oh, and in case you're wondering, the hoped-for threesome with the gals from Minnesota? Didn't happen. In fact, last I saw them they were both sucking face with the Ed Hardy boy on the dance floor. It couldn't have gone down any other way, really. It doesn't matter who you are; in Vegas, if the house does not want you to win, you do not win.

"Up Yer Bum" (WHICH ALSO MEANS "CHEERS" IN SOME COUNTRIES)

CREATED BY NATALIE BOVIS

1 sugarcube

3 dashes Peychaud's bitters

Maraschino cherry

2 oz. London dry gin

3/4 oz. dry vermouth

Ice

1 ounce lube*

Douse the sugarcube with Peychaud's bitters in the bottom of a mixing glass. Toss in the cherry and muddle. Add gin, vermouth, and lots of ice. Stir well. Strain into a chilled glass.

"As you're about to discover in this rather, uh, *revealing* chapter, there's something to be said for a gal who can handle her booze—at least to the extent of not letting some guy stick it to her in the keister behind a Dumpster after a few shots too many. Like Dan, I'm a 'spirits professional,' which means I'm a good-timing broad who drinks for a living. I am also a free-thinking Cosmogirl who respects that strippers, *Playboy* Playmates, and prostitutes fly their own flag of liberated femi-

---

*DO NOT put the lube in the drink. You can use your imagination on that one.

nism. That said, a girl in a bar has to watch out for herself. Especially when a lot of liquor is involved. And guys like Dan.

"This drink is created in honor of the wayward women out there who stoke the fire of the 'bros before hos' philosophy, and here's hoping they find themselves a good shrink and a pile of break-proof condoms."

—**NATALIE BOVIS** (aka The Liquid Muse) has more than two decades of experience in the hospitality industry, in one form or another. She writes cocktail books, teaches cocktail classes to the everyday guy or gal, and does live mixology demos at events around the United States, as well as on TV and radio shows. The only thing she loves more than a well-crafted cocktail is sipping it in a far-flung locale, so she can blog about local talent all over the world. Drink with her at TheLiquidMuse.com.

SIX

We're All Little People

My parents may have urinated into several unfortunate parts of my gene pool, but there's one area where they did me right: at least I'm a decent-looking guy. I'm not going to be on the cover of *GQ* any time soon, mind you, but based on the fact that over the years I've managed to attract more than my fair share (at least according to my friends) of good-looking women-folk, I must not be too hard on the eyeballs. But good (or good-in-one-area) genes will carry you only so far when it comes to attracting the ladies; especially as you get older and find that more and more of you requires carrying. My profession certainly doesn't make staying fit particularly easy, either. Maintaining a thirty-three-inch waist and just the two chins *and* a career-mandated nonstop bender is no easy task. Something's got to give. In my twenties, drugs and cigarettes were enough to stave off serious weight gain. Then in my thirties I fell on hard times and couldn't afford to stick to my self-styled and rather pricey "health" regimen. Once my cash flow had slowed to a trickle, meaning no more Marlboros and not nearly as much blow, I knew I had to try something new to stay in shape. Something different. Something radical. Something free.

And so I run. Sounds unlikely, I know. I run to keep the love handles at bay, and I run to commune with the great outdoors, but mostly I run to make the incessant yapping in my head stop. Yapping about my career, my relationships, my inexplicable inability to master the skill of swirling wine in a glass with grace and elegance.

Still, despite what I shrug off as "a few hang-ups," I've always considered myself to be a relatively happy individual. Turns out, however, that my happiness has almost always been entirely contingent on some form of self-medication: booze, sex, drugs, and now, in a somewhat startling development for someone who by all accounts should wake up hungover most mornings, losing myself in the knee-pounding, sweaty oblivion of the jogging path.

And so that's how it happened that I was at Will Rogers State Park in the Palisades pounding my way down a narrow trail that cuts through dense foliage and overlooks the Pacific Ocean (another benefit of living near the beach), when I got to thinking about the particular utility and excellence of that most fundamental of men's by-laws, "bros before hos." Now, see, just me bringing it up probably makes you think I'm some kind of mouth-breathing asshat frat boy. I am not. I use this phrase for its efficiency, not its cultural connotations. It is simple and it is clear and it is correct. And in a world when so few things fit all three of those descriptors, I think it would be a shame to abandon this phrase for the sake of political correctness. It does not mean that I think all women are "hos" (or, in common parlance, loose women). It does not mean that I regard all men as "bros" (which is to say, awesome dudes). What it does say, however, is that when it comes to women, men should heed the prior research done by their fellow right-thinking men (which is to say, the bros). And if one of these right-thinking men has had a particularly odious experience with a particularly vicious member of the opposite sex (for the sake of this exercise we'll call them hos), then it is advised, for the sake of both the original bro's feelings and his fellow bro's future, that his buddies steer clear of the lady in question. It's etiquette and common sense rolled into one. Just look at the logic: "My friend is a good dude. He had a hard time with this lady. Either my friend is secretly an asshole or this lady is trouble." Not a hard equation to pick up on. Yet the fact remains that the simplest and most effective way of communicating this truth is culturally insensitive. That doesn't mean "bros before hos" is any less true.

Why was I pondering this particular eddy in my mental stream that morning? Because of some unfortunate news I'd just received—that Summer is now dating a friend of mine named Art, a commercial director who played a prominent role in the penultimate chapter of my previous book, *Nobody Likes a Quitter (And Other Reasons to Avoid Rehab)*. As a result, as far as I am concerned, Art has been summarily de-bro-ed. And he will remain so until such time as his priorities come back into line with societal norms. Or until I find out that I'm actually the asshole here.

Forty minutes and two gallons of sweat later I got back to my place and checked my voicemail.

"You have two new messages. First message: Dan, it's your mother. I need to tell you something about how you were conceived. I was—"

I punched a button.

"Message erased. Next message: Dan, this is important. The

president of the Philadelphia City Council and agents from the Vatican are all coming to—"

"Motherfucker!" I shouted involuntarily.

"Easy, bro," came a voice from behind me. Randy had apparently let himself in.

I showered quickly, after which Randy and I retired to the rooftop deck to throw back a beer and smoke a bowl. As the sun went down, he talked me into taking a drive along the coast in his new Audi, which he claimed I needed to take two hits of Ecstasy in order to appreciate properly. I know, this all sounds very romantic. *Bros before hos, eh,* you're probably thinking. Well, fuck you. Truth is, I was really glad to have Randy there, even if he *did* give me some static for not snapping out of the Summer mess already. Actually, his words on the topic were only slightly less colorful than the Pacific Coast sunset (on E). As I recall, it went something like "Jesus Horse-fucking Christ! If you don't cheer up soon I'm going to shoot myself in the goddamn face!" This left me no choice. I took the pills. Which of course led to a whole lot more talking.

"OK, I get that you're pissed at Art, but I'm just saying maybe he isn't the problem. Maybe you might want to entertain the idea of shying away from the crazy women for a while," Randy said.

"I don't go for crazy chicks!" I lied. "Name one!"

"Forget it," Randy said, stomping down on the accelerator as the Santa Monica Pier began to turn all sorts of colors not normally found in nature. The pills were kicking in.

"No!" I replied, pounding on the dash. "You're the one who said I go for crazy chicks. You have to name one." I paused. "A recent one." I paused again. "Not Summer."

"Ellie Haven."

I started to protest, but that name—which I've changed here to protect the not-at-all-innocent—stopped me in my tracks. Indeed, Ellie Haven is crazy, and for a long time I admit I had it bad for her. She was the relationship right before Alison, though "relationship" might be overstating the nature of our unholy union. We met in New York's East Village, at the dingy, graffiti-covered kind of bar that neighborhood specializes in, got pissed as farts, and eventually wound up making hysterical monkey love in the alley behind the joint. Slightly unsanitary, but also shockingly salutary. And straightaway, despite several rather obvious red flags, I got it in my head that Ellie was my soul mate. Red flag number one appeared right after said first sexual encounter, when she feigned embarrassment and claimed, far too vehemently, she'd never done it next to a Dumpster with a stranger before (what was that line from Shakespeare about protesting too much?). "Yeah, me neither," I mumbled, but the truth is, she wasn't my first hasty screw in proximity of garbage. And I knew damn well I wasn't hers. Even if she hadn't been so quick to deny it, all the signs were there. Women who really truly never do it on the first date don't carry multiple condoms in their purses. And on that fateful night Ellie was packing more jimmies than an Irish phone book. Plus, the kind of woman who makes a man wait for it would never dream of ducking into a dark alley under the pretense of smoking a joint with a total stranger. And she damn sure wouldn't let him do anal.

"You know what, Don, I get you," she told me as we stumbled up the uneven sidewalk of Avenue A toward where my out-of-town actress friend was letting me crash.

"Dan," I said, tapping my chest instinctively. "Me Dan. But yes, I believe you *do* get me," I concurred, giving her rump a gentle pat to punctuate the notion. I still recall being profoundly aroused by the little lipstick smudge on her cheek and how her excess mascara clumped all her eyelashes together.

"So you wanna hang out with me at my friend's apartment for a while?"

"Is he there?" she asked pleasantly.

"She. Her name's Debbie. And she's not there this week, and even if she were she wouldn't give a shit."

"ARE YOU FUCKING HER?" she suddenly snapped.

"Who?" I said, taken aback.

"Donna!" she spat. "You're fucking Donna, right? Figures!"

This chick was clearly not very good with names.

"Whoa, easy," I said. "It's Debbie. And we're just friends now."

"Don't lie to me," she hissed. "I'll bite your dick off when you're sleeping."

Somewhere, from far in the back of my head, I heard a faint voice telling me to run away very, very fast, but it was being told to shut the fuck up by my incipient hard-on. And this just fifteen minutes after our Dumpster sex. *She must be joking around,* my hard-on said. *She gets me* that *much! Plus, someone as hot as Ellie doesn't let just* anyone *fuck her behind a Dumpster in an alley. In the ass, no less.* Something special was definitely happening between us. It would be insane to throw it all away over one silly little disagreement.

"I'm not lying," I lied. Truth be told, from the beginning, Debbie and I had had what polite company calls a "friends with benefits" arrangement.

Ellie stopped dead in the middle of Twelfth Street. "Look at me!"

I did as directed, eyes locked on that tantalizing lipstick smudge.

"I want you to slap me in the face," she said.

"Huh?"

"Smack me," she said. "Hard."

"I'm not going to slap you," I replied, glancing around nervously.

"Oh, you *will* slap me," she insisted. "If you ever want to see me again, you'll bitch-slap me right across my fucking face right here and right now. And then you'll swear on everything that's righteous and holy that you will never, ever, EVER hurt me like that again. Do you get what I'm saying to you?"

I didn't entirely get it, but I was more than a little soused, let's remember. And I *did* want to see her again. I wanted to do a whole lot more to her than just see her. So I smacked her. I smacked her hard. I'm not proud of this, but at that moment my cock demanded it. And sometimes you have no choice but to give the cock what it wants.

"OK, then," my soul mate said, her cheek as red as Stalinist Russia. "I'm all yours, Donnie Boy." And indeed she was—for four whole weeks. Four glorious weeks of wall-to-wall Olympic-level screwing. I'd been optimistic about getting to nine and a half weeks (just a little personal competition I have going with Mickey Rourke), but by the time week four rolled around, I couldn't take any more (like I said earlier, years of professional boozing can take their toll on a guy physically). So I ended it . . . carefully, I might add. Over the phone. After I was a safe distance from New York City. After all, this was the woman who once threatened to chomp off my penis. Like I say, I give the cock what it wants, and in this case, what it wanted was continued attachment to my body (that said, even if it was me who ended it, I'll nonetheless go to my grave believing God owes me five and a half more weeks of monkey sex with Ellie Haven).

I have neither seen nor heard from Ellie Haven since, but I'm pretty sure she's not dead. Like vampires, women like Ellie never die; they find some other poor schmuck to suck on. Not that it matters to me. I'm so over her. OK, maybe I'm not completely over her. Sometimes I'll think about the way things went down and get a little misty-eyed. OK, maybe not misty-eyed so much as mildly annoyed. And a little turned on.

"You picked Ellie up in a bar, right?" Randy asked, jarring me out of my reverie. He was weaving with a pleasurable fluidity through dense traffic on Sunset Boulevard.

"Yeah, something like that," I nodded woozily. *What happened to the coast?* I wondered. And how long had we been driving? *Oh, look, it's Kate Beckinsale in her underwear on a giant billboard. I love billboards. Like a lot more than I ever really thought about . . .*

"I gotta say," Randy drawled, "you are good at that. Talking to strangers in bars. Not just chicks either. You have a gift, my friend. I've watched you work a room."

Now, I'm not going to say he was wrong. Making conversation in bars is a skill, and I've got it. In spades, actually. So once again, generous soul that I am, I share with you my professional advice.

How to Master the Barroom Conversation

It's been observed that there are only seven unique plotlines in the world, and that all books, movies, and plays are just variations on those themes. The same principle holds true for barroom conversations, except there are only five. (There used to be six, but when Charles Bukowski died he took one to the grave with him.) Now, as someone who gets paid to go out to bars, I've had plenty of opportunities to study these archetypes closely. And since I'm on the road a lot of the time, usually alone, I often have the rabid curiosity to talk to strangers. I'm not looking to become best friends with these people, or even necessarily to fuck them in the alley behind the bar. I just want to hear the crazy things that come out of their mouths once I (and five whiskies) get them going. Which is why I dedicate this list of how to master the five most common bar conversations to all the crazy fucks I've sat next to on bar stools over the past ten years. You people are insane.

1. The Boy Meets Girl

There is a big difference between picking up a woman in a bar and *meeting* a woman in a bar. Any idiot willing to shell out a couple of bucks on a vodka cranberry can do the former. But the latter—always a more rewarding experience in the long run—is more of a challenge. The most important thing is to stay off the rehearsed lines and open with some genuine, off-the-cuff banter. Keep it breezy, and never mention the weather. But you can't just dive right in, or even the most clever opening line will come off sounding like some variant of "Come here often?" The trick to a well-received opener is to lay the groundwork before the conversation starts by becoming the most popular person in the bar. How? The first thing you need to do is build what I have termed a Coalition of the Thrilling. Which is to say, a third-party group that can validate how awesome you are to the object of your ardor. This means becoming what I call "Liquor Fabulous." It all starts with the bartender. Introduce yourself when you walk in, write his or her name on your hand, and tip well. Really well. (This does wonders for helping a barkeep remember your name.) Now you just need to strike up conversation with the other well-lubricated patrons around you (see conversations two through five below). Once you have a decent Coalition built, by the time you get a chance to chat up the hottie who just walked in, everyone in the whole place will know your name and think you're the funniest bastard who ever lived. She'll never know what hit her.

2. The Alter Ego

When out drinking, everyone wants to be somebody. Somebody else, that is. Somebody a lot cooler than you. For instance, a few months back I had a grand old time in the lobby bar at the Morrison Hotel in Dublin, regaling the locals with the story of the time I was forced to turn back just five hundred feet from the summit of K2. My tone grew somber as I recounted how rapidly and unexpectedly the weather conditions had deteriorated, just as the peak came into sight. Tears welled in my eyes as I continued to tell how, when my Sherpa lost his footing and broke his ankle, I had no choice but to strap him to my back and turn around.

"Now keep in mind it was no easy task securing Tenzing to my back, given that I was already carrying little Timmy," I said bravely, tossing back the remainder of a tall glass of Redbreast whiskey.

"Little Timmy?" someone asked, wide-eyed. I think her name was Siobhan.

"Yes," I whispered, my voice cracking ever so slightly. "From the Make-A-Wish Foundation."

And then the tears came. Oh, how those tears came. Not a dry eye in the house. And not only was it terrific fun, I'm pretty sure I got laid that night.

3. The Say What?

Between all the noise in the joint and all the spirits in its patrons, bar conversations tend to drift miles from their intended destinations. Let them. Life is too short to not find out what's out there in left field. One time, while hunkered down at Ye Olde King's Head, my favorite pub in Santa Monica, I got into a debate over who would win an imaginary fight between a drunk and a stoner. Not the most fascinating conversation (nor, sadly, was this the first time I'd had it), I'll admit, which is why I was happy when it went off the rails. My dance partner in this mess was a spiky-haired, twentysomething Club Dude who had apparently ingested a bunch of E earlier in the evening. No doubt this contributed to the conceptual slipperiness of what followed.

"Before considering this question we must first establish the identities of the parties under the influence," I said, in as professorial a manner as I could, given my level of intoxication.

Club Dude nodded in agreement. "For instance," I continued, "take Chris Robinson, frontman for the Black Crowes. Total baker. Dude weighs about a buck-oh-five soaked in bong water. Let's put him up against a drinking Crowe, say, Russell. My bet is Chris would wind up on his back faster than a one-legged hooker."

Club Dude concurred. "Russell Crowe definitely throws down the booze. I partied with that guy once at my buddy Todd's place in Malibu. Kept rambling on about what a badass he was cuz he wrote *Fast Times at Ridgemont High*. I mean, what the fuck ever, I went to high school too."

"Sounds like a nasty scene," I parried, "but I will say one thing for Cameron Crowe, he knows how to write a tune," I added, picking up this rapidly spiraling out-of-control football and running with it.

"Yeah, what's that song, 'Mister Jones'? I love that shit," he replied, revealing a taste in music as appalling as his taste in hair product.

"Yeah, I'd do Sheryl Crow in a hot minute," I fired back.

"Me too, bro," he said and laughed, tossing an arm around me, as onlookers stared at us in utter bewilderment. "Me too."

4. The Parasite

This is perhaps the most difficult maneuver of the bunch. Even seasoned tavern talkers have a hard time pulling it off consistently. I'm talking about the delicate black art of injecting yourself into two strangers' conversation (level of difficulty goes up considerably if said strangers are two hot women). If you dare to give it a go, note that your success relies almost entirely on brevity and timing. When you butt in uninvited, you've got a window of five, maybe ten words with which to make a good enough impression that you'll be invited in. And if they're not delivered at precisely the right moment, you're toast. Just swoop in and hit them with a nugget of knowledge like "Hey, David Bowie wore tights," lean back, and say no more. Worked like a charm for me once with a couple of British magazine editors in Budapest. Although I tried something similar in Miami and fucked it all up trying to quote the chorus to "Velvet Goldmine." Again, brevity and timing, my friends.

When you attempt to butt in on other people's conversation, just don't forget what a raging bitch karma can be. Do this enough and you're bound to find it coming back at you from the other direction. When your conversation is the one being butted in upon, it can either be the beginning of a beautiful friendship or the end of a potentially magical night, so if you sense it might be the latter, you'll have to run some interference. Just hit the interloper with these magic words: "Before we get into your story about your lush hag of an ex-wife, can I tell you about my personal relationship with Jesus Christ?" Works every time.

5. The Boy Meets Fight

Now, these methods don't come without their attendant risks. After all, engage in enough conversations with drunken strangers, and trouble is eventually bound to rear its ugly head. Maybe you made an impolitic remark about the Mets' chances in this year's World Series, and now the biggest Mets fan in the world has strong opinions about the manliness of your shirt. In fact, he'd like to butch it up a bit by decorating it with, say, your blood. Admittedly, this is not a conversation that bodes well for your physical well-being, but there are still a number of ways to achieve a nonviolent resolution:

a) Apologize and try to backpedal. As in, "Sorry, what I meant to say was that the Mets are a big bunch of boozers, not losers. So was Mickey Mantle, and who doesn't love the Mick, right?" If he sees through this admittedly lame tactic, offer to buy the next round. This should settle things down, at least momentarily. Hell, if plied with enough free booze, one of his friends may even concede that you have a point about the Mets sucking, that this *could* be the year the Royals finally turn things around (the added advantage of this is that now Mets guy may redirect his rage and frustration over his team's twenty-five-year losing streak to someone else). That said, don't let the fleeting feeling of brotherhood lull you into a false sense of security. You need to get out of Dodge at your earliest opportunity, because eventually Mets guy will forget all about that conciliatory whiskey you bought him (ironically, he'll forget *because* of that whiskey you bought him) and remember that you referred to his hero David Wright as "a poor man's A-Rod."

b) Follow the steps outlined above, and excuse yourself to take a leak. Then sneak out and stick them with the tab. A strategy for the thrill-seeker.

c) If all else fails and you have no line of escape, try throwing up on yourself. It'll be messy and embarrassing, sure, but think about it—not even Mike Tyson would hit a man who just puked on himself. And take it from someone who knows: Your lunch will wash out a lot easier than blood.

Is That by Any Chance Love's Baby Soft You're Wearing?

So, where were we? Oh, right, me and Randy, high as kites, cruising down the Pacific Coast Highway. Next thing I knew, a valet parking attendant was opening my door. It was dark now. There were people everywhere. And everything was very bright. And very loud.

"Good evening, sir," the valet said into an invisible megaphone. "Welcome to Mood."

What the fuck? I thought to myself. *When did it become evening? Where the hell did the ocean go? And who the hell are all these people? I want my ocean back.*

"We're at Mood, baby!" Randy chortled. "C'mon, let's tear it up."

Though my brain seemed to be rolling down the sidewalk, I was somehow able to confirm that we were, in fact, standing in front of one of Hollywood's trendiest hot spots, where the usual doorman drama was playing out in front of the club's ornate exterior. I hate going to nightclubs. And while I usually tell people that it's because nightclubs are cheesy and too expensive and the people are fake and the music's bad, the truth is, I'm too old to enjoy them anymore. Also, I'm too old for anyone who goes to nightclubs to enjoy me. I don't have the right clothes or drug connections, and I'm neither rich nor famous enough to pull young club chicks (the *Playboy* connection gets me in the door, but after that I'm generally on my own). My membership to the cool-kid club expired around the time Right Said Fred went careening off the popularity cliff. When young ladies in the clubs catch me checking them out now, they don't see a devastatingly attractive stud they can take home to have a rip-roaring one-night stand with; they see a too-old-to-be-out-at-four-in-the-morning dude trying to eyeball whether their severed head will fit in his freezer. I am no longer in bloom, friends. True, experience has my back. Time, however, does not.

Yet somehow, when Randy exhorted me to "tear it up," it sounded like the single best idea I'd ever heard in my life. I wanted to be inside Mood. I wanted to hug it and squeeze it and stroke it and never let it go. Never let the mood go.

Randy bro-clamped a burly doorman and motioned for me to slide on inside past the throngs of frustrated would-be patrons, all at least ten years my junior, clamoring for entry (experience: 1, youth: 0). Inside we moved through a wilderness of gorgeous, drug-addled women and their horny suitors, doused in overpriced cologne. *That was easy,* I thought. *Too bad we don't have a . . . Where did this booth come from?* As it turned out, we had a booth. A booth smack dab in the middle of the action, with bottle service and attractive women already in it. How did we get here? How did this happen? Then I remembered Randy. Duh. Randy makes things like this happen. Or maybe they'd heard about the time I was forced to turn back just five hundred feet from the summit of K2.

"You having a good time, hon?" Randy asked the young lovely sitting next to him. She looked like the prom queen of a high school for wayward trailer park kids. I would later learn that her name was Gwen and that she had recently made her adult-film debut in one of Randy's productions. Obviously.

"This place is off the hizzy!" Gwen tittered. "And you, like, know, like, *everybody.*"

Randy smirked as he topped off her Champagne flute with Veuve Clicquot. "It's my job to know everybody, baby. Stick with me and before you know it, you'll know lots of people too. How's the Champagne?"

She giggled. "Really good, I guess. I've never had Champagne before. It's bubbly."

Randy waved his hand in the direction of the flood of young hot humanity shimmying on the dance floor. "See those people out there? Pretty soon all of 'em are gonna want a piece of you, Jade."

"But my name's Gwen."

"Yeah," Randy said, tilting his Champagne glass toward hers, "but let's stick with 'Jade' for now, OK? Jade is gonna be gold for us!"

And with that, Randy led Gwen out onto the dance floor. But not before sliding me another hit of Ecstasy, which, genius that I am, I took.

After pouring a fresh, absurdly strong drink from our four-hundred-dollar bottle, I stroked my glass for a while, my drug-addled brain held captive by the beads of condensation rising to the surface. Then I got up out of the booth and tottered slowly out across the dance floor. Passing a delectable young redhead, I stroked her hair. Some distant part of my brain told me this was socially unacceptable, while a much louder one smothered it with universal love.

"Astounding," I said. Or something along those lines.

Before she could slap me, I ambled on, stopping every so often to do some small jig with random women who may or may not have been aware I was dancing with them. I shimmied across the dance space and into a lounge area. As I scanned the unfamiliar but fascinating faces in the crowd, I amazingly happened upon one I was pretty sure I knew. A female one, no less! My eyelids fluttered furiously as I tried to focus, to will myself toward clarity. She had reddish blond hair, and eyes that looked like electrified green Skittles. Pale skin. She seemed like a good person. Built like a dancer. Even better person. Was she one of Randy's girls? Nah, too put together for that line of work. Wait a minute ... did I know her from college? Yes, yes, college! I stared at her and smiled a big stupid smile.

"Jennifer," I whispered to myself creepily. "Yes. Jennifer. Jen Topping." (Her real name, by the way, is not Jen Topping, but that's a good pseudonym, isn't it?)

She was looking at me now, curiously.

"Dan? Dan Dunn?" she said finally. Then she was hugging me, and my knees nearly buckled.

"Are you OK?" she asked.

"I'm good," I mumbled. "Really, *really* good."

"Jesus, Dan, it's been forever. Have I seen you since graduation?"

"Could be, could be," I said, bewildered. And the only thing that made any sense was hugging her, so I did it again. See, when I was in college, Jennifer Topping was on a very short list of women that I deemed "untouchable." Women I considered too smart, too cool, too lovely, or too together to mess with. This was before I learned how to date out of my league (see chapter 4).

I took her back to the booth. "So, what happened to you? Did you ever write that great novel you were always going on about?" she asked.

"No, you first," I said. "Please, Jen Topping, tell me about *you* first."

"OK," she said. "I'm in publicity, at least until I finish grad school." She gestured to a nearby booth where a young white rap-rocker decked out like a ghetto-fab pimp sat surrounded by a sizable entourage.

"My agency is handling his concert tour," she continued. "If you want, I could probably get you good seats for the show."

"Shh . . . yeah, that would be cool. I'm into that whole white assimilation thing," I said. "And I dig his midget."

I waved playfully to a scruffy little man seated next to the rap-rocker.

"His name's Tyler," she said. "And I think the PC term is 'little person.' "

"We're all little people," I said, and sighed, repeating the words "little people" softly to myself.

Apparently intuiting that the weirdness quotient had yet to reach critical mass, I leaned in and took a big whiff of her.

"Is that by any chance Love's Baby Soft you're wearing?" I whispered.

"What? No. What am I, in second grade?" She laughed. "Are you OK, Dan? You didn't turn into a club fiend on me, did you?"

"Well, I'm on the prowl for my friend Randy. He should be lurking around this wilderness somewhere . . . with the girls," I said.

"The girls?"

I leaned in close. "Yes, the girls. I feel it's time for total honesty between us, Jen. I'm not a novelist. I'm a booze columnist. For *Playboy*. And lately I've been hanging around with hard-core pornographers."

"Really? That's funny."

"What kind of funny? Like, there's something seriously wrong with me funny? "

"I don't think that. Do you?"

"I have no idea," I said, "but you'd be surprised how many so-called respectable people in your life suddenly become scarce after you tell them that you drink professionally and that you pal around with a dude who peddles shaved vaginas for a living."

"I think you should do what makes you happy," she said.

I smiled a boozy smile. Then my eyes rolled back slightly and I nearly passed out from pleasure. I quickly recovered, though, and leaned in to whisper in Jen's ear. "Can I talk to you about something?"

And talk I did. Told her the story of Annette Mancini, my first love, followed by a complete oral history of my ill-fated dalliance with Summer. I continued to share what was, looking back, some incredibly embarrassing personal information about my relationship with my parents that I could tell, even in my tripped-out state, made Jen more than slightly uncomfortable. I only managed to salvage the conversation by steering it back to Alison's rejection of my marriage proposal. I was beginning to grasp that that one's always good for a laugh.

"She dumped you? Just like that? Over a column you wrote?" she said.

"Yes. Is that history's all-time biggest bullshit overreaction or what?"

"I don't know. What was in it?"

"Nothing! I dunno. Everything," I said.

"Everything could be a lot," she said. "You were always a dog in college, Dan Dunn. Charming, and fun at parties, but distinctly canine."

For a moment, my Ecstasized mind drifted back to my college years. A rapid, staccato montage of images danced in my head: breaking up with a girl, consoling her as she cried, offering her a hankie, then promptly leaving, walking into a bar, hitting on a different girl, finding the hankie in my pocket, throwing it away before leaving the bar to go bang the new girl . . .

"You're right, Jen. I was a cad," I said, the memory of my asshole past hitting me like a punch in the gut. "But I've changed, I really have . . . except for the pornographer friends and booze-writing gig at *Playboy.*"

"Are you always this forthright with people you haven't seen in years?" she asked.

"Apparently yes," I said. "Truth is, I've taken a lot of Ecstasy tonight. Like, Timothy Leary–level doses."

"I had a pretty good idea you were rolling," she replied.

I struggled to compose myself. "Jen, what am I going to do? Lately I've been feeling like my head is gonna just fly off my neck and skyrocket up into the ozone layer and burst into flames or something."

"I think that's the Ecstasy talking. Listen, have you thought about seeing a therapist?" she said, taking my hand and softly kneading it.

Enraptured, I closed my eyes. My jaw dropped involuntarily, and for a moment I thought it was gone. And I was OK with that.

"I am seeing one," I whispered softly, childlike. "We talk about my parents a lot and stuff."

"That's good. You need to work all that shit out," she said. "This could be a wonderful opportunity for you."

I opened my eyes and perked up. "You know what, Jen Topping, enough talking. Let's dance! Let's dance like trailer park prom queens."

And so we did.

"The Internal Upgrade" (AKA THE ROOFIE MARTINI)

CREATED BY BEN REED

3 miniatures of any hooch you can charm off your trolley dolly, preferably gin

A cup filled with ice

1 stirrer

2 cans of European lager (room temperature preferred)

2 mg of Rohypnol (or any of the following: Xanax, Ambien, Vicodin, Codeine, Stilnox, or any prescription drug whose name ends in "pam")

A bag of pretzels

1 lemon slice

1 eye mask

1 large napkin

Pour gin into cup of ice; leave to stand. If beer is not warm enough, place between legs, under seat, in shoe, until warm. Stir gin. Open one beer and drink quickly. Stir gin. Use second can to crush up meds on in-flight magazine and siphon into chilling gin. Stir gin. Eat bag of pretzels ('cause you ain't gonna be awake for the meal). Drink second beer, quicker.

Stir. Consume quickly. Suck lemon (your neighbor may appreciate this).

Tie large napkin around neck (there's a strong likelihood of drooling).

Apply eye mask and shut down.

Disclaimers:

1) For the lowbrow nature of this cocktail I blame global terrorism and understocked drinks trolleys.

2) The warm-beer thing isn't a Brit thing. Warm beer drunk at pace perfectly replicates that bloated end-of-session feeling your body needs to recognize before properly shutting down for the long haul.

3) Due to the transatlantic nature of this piece, certain meds mentioned above may not be locally available . . . or strictly legal.

"The beauty of drinking hard on a plane is that most of the side effects you're trying to avoid when drinking on the ground (inability to stand, walk, speak, or remember anything) are exactly what you're looking to embrace in the air. If, like me, you travel around the world, mostly at the expense of a client, and your enjoyment of the journey is often at the mercy of their goodwill (and your day rate), then trust me, you're going to need this cocktail.

"The many air miles I've accrued are seldom spent in first class; if they were, the trip would go down like a tepid martini back home at Chez Reedo. So I've learned that on the odd occasion you are told firmly (and often forcibly) to turn right rather than left upon entry to your assigned aircraft, something a little creative is often required to numb the senses and propel you instantly to the place that, were you in business or first class, you would be gently (and expensively) reaching somewhere over a large water mass. This is your escape route to aviation oblivion."

—**BEN REED** is British and demented. And not necessarily in that order. A former bartender at the famed Met Bar, Reed is the author of the best-selling tome *Cool Cocktails.*

SEVEN

Dude, Where's My Celebrity Teammate?

Standing on the rooftop deck of New York City's plush Kitano Hotel, Seann William Scott put a hand my shoulder, looked me in the eyes, and vowed, "Dude, I'm gonna win this race." Then Seann—the guy best known for playing the incorrigible Stifler in *American Pie*—fired up a smoke and ordered a couple of bottles of wine to take with us in the limo to the airport.

We were on our way to the Drambuie Pursuit, an adventure race that takes place annually in the picturesque Scottish Highlands. Spoiler alert: Seann did not win this race. Point of fact, Seann did not finish this race. But we'll get to that in good time. First we had to get across the pond on a big old jet airliner.

Most people think flying in a post-9/11 world sucks donkey

balls, but I beg to differ. As a seasoned jet-setter who still actually enjoys commercial air travel, I'm part of a dying breed, and I believe my capacity to derive pleasure from circumstances others deem intolerable can be traced directly to my close personal relationship with alcohol. Booze, I find, has an amazing power to take the sting out of endless delays, mile-long security lines, and hours spent 35,000 feet in the air in a pressurized germ-filled death trap packed with disgruntled airline employees and edgy civilians. As with most things in life, when it comes to flying, the difference between enjoyable and unbearable is all in the execution. And by execution I mean drinking. Thankfully, the air-travel experience is designed to offer myriad opportunities to numb the stress and anxiety of flying with alcohol (which, when you think about it, is pretty damn smart of the air-travel industry). The trick, of course, is to drink enough to forget about the fact that you're 35,000 feet in the air in a pressurized germ-filled death trap packed with disgruntled airline employees and edgy civilians (and maybe even catch a few winks of sleep), but not get so blotto that you lose your luggage, vomit on your seatmate, or board the wrong plane and end up in some remote, frightening destination, like Milwaukee. Lucky for you, however, while my many travels as a booze columnist may not have made me any more cultured or well-rounded a human being, they sure as hell have made me a bona fide expert at drinking while airborne. Therefore, I present my time-tested strategies for maintaining the perfect buzz for the full duration of the air-travel experience.

How to Drink While Flying

1. At the Terminal

The first thing you need to do when you arrive at the terminal is rank your preflight worry on a scale of one to five. (A one means you're slightly apprehensive; a five means you'd rather have unprotected sex with everyone in sub-Saharan Africa than get on that damn plane.) This number also happens to be the number of alcoholic beverages you should order at the bar near your departure gate. I find that a couple of glasses of wine take the edge off nicely. But if you're not a wine person, or feel foolish ordering a glass of pinot noir at Rick's Skybox Sports Bar (as well you should), beer works too. I'd stay away from anything sweet, fruity, or liable to make your breath smell like the bathrooms at Grand Central Terminal (this rule, incidentally, does not apply only to flying). One other thing: There is no inappropriate time to drink at an airport. I don't care if your flight is at nine a.m.—if the bar is open, it's not too early. Everyone knows that airports exist in their own time zone, and as far as I'm concerned, in that time zone it's always happy hour.

Hopefully you're traveling business class, in which case there will be some warm nuts waiting for you when you get on the plane. Warm nuts make everything better.

2. Boarding

The most critical part of boarding—especially if you scored high in step one—is not to exhibit any behavior that might draw the attention of a stewardess prior to takeoff. Examples include slurring, wobbling, drooling, flatulence, dropping your carry-on bag on another passenger's head, unwanted sexual advances (which experience has taught me is pretty much all sexual advances during boarding), off-color remarks about warm nuts, and, of course, using the word "stewardess." (The dude stewardesses are particularly bitchy about that one.) Remember, most airline personnel are criminally underpaid and terminally unhappy. (Get it? Terminally? See why they hate me?) Also, the overwhelming majority of them are menopausal women who have been deputized by the U.S. government to forcibly remove anyone on the plane who pisses them off. Become the focus of their ire, and you may find yourself being rerouted to Totally Fuckedville. Just read your magazine and pretend to be normal until they shut the cabin door. After that, they're stuck with you.

3. Beverage Service

Assuming you've handled your liquor well up until this point, you'll get airborne and graduate to the best part of any flight: the drinks cart. When ordering, a number of variables need to be considered. Is it before ten a.m.? A Bloody Mary will get you 30 percent less stinkeye than a triple tequila. The general rule when en route to a business meeting or conference is to stick with Jack and Coke; it won't make you as drowsy as wine or beer. Of course, if you're in the insurance, accounting, or medical equipment sales business, you can get as drowsy as you like and nobody will notice. Headed to Vegas for a bachelor party? Pack in a few vodka and Red Bulls with some sugarcubes to give your central nervous system a preview of what's in store for the next forty-eight hours (not that *I* would ever drink this shit, mind you). On the way *back* from Vegas I favor a beer or two, just enough to get that warm "I think I'll just settle in for a touch of a nap" feeling.

Jetting off to see relatives is a different animal altogether and calls for something with far more numbing capability than usual, especially if you happen to be traveling with (or near) one or more of those sippy-box-toting hellspawn known as children. Of course, if your kids are in tow, Xanax and scotch could be construed as irresponsible. As would making it a double. Just be sure to let one of the kids drive when you get there. Do rental car companies still install boosters in the driver's seat?

A fun exercise for any amateur mixologist on an airplane

is to try to concoct as intricate a cocktail as possible using items available on the in-flight menu. Something containing at least five ingredients is very respectable. (To accomplish this, it helps to have a mobile-phone drink-recipe application such as Cocktails Made Easy for iPhone or EasyBartender on the BlackBerry—or, always travel with this book.) For instance, I once was on a flight that offered Beefeater gin, Chambord, and Champagne, so I set about making a variation on a Gin Buck called the Pearl S. Buck, created by my pal Jonathan Pogash, beverage director for the Hospitality Holdings group in Manhattan.

Pogash's recipe calls for the following:

> *1/2 oz. Chambord*
>
> *1 oz. Beefeater gin*
>
> *1/2 oz. fresh lemon*
>
> *1/2 oz. simple syrup*
>
> *1/4 tsp. minced ginger*
>
> *Splash Moët White Star Champagne*
>
> *Lemon, for garnish*

Directions: Shake all ingredients except for Champagne and strain into ice-filled highball. Top with Champagne. Garnish with a lemon wheel.

I substituted Billecart-Salmon Champagne since they didn't carry Moët, and I whipped up some simple syrup using hot water and sugar packets. I thought I might have to go without the ginger until I noticed a sushi sampler on the starters menu and—voilà!—spice, with some decent yellowtail to boot.

(Please note that when playing master mixologist while

airborne, it's important that everyone around you—the crew, in particular—is aware that you're simply making a drink and *not* carrying out orders from al-Qaeda high command. People see you behaving like a mad scientist without warning, and the next thing you know you're getting suplexed by a tile salesman from Toledo while a tax attorney from New York smacks you upside the head with a MacBook Pro.)

4. During Layovers and Delays

Perhaps the trickiest travel-drinking situation is the layover. Overdo it on the initial leg of the journey, and the many, many hours in an overheated, airless airport terminal could wreak holy hell on your nervous system. Trust me, it's not fun to go from being drunk to sober to hungover to drunk again before even getting halfway to your destination. Same goes for missed connections and delays. For God's sake, pace yourself, or you may be too wasted to get on that plane once it arrives. Or you might get too loose and give the overly sensitive Hollywood star you're traveling with an honest assessment of the artistic merits of *Mr. Woodcock* and the *Dukes of Hazzard* remake. I'm happy to say Seann William Scott took it pretty well, and against all odds all seemed right in the world by the time we arrived in the UK ready to do some racing and some drinking . . . not necessarily in that order.

Let's Get Drunk and Dance

Legend has it that back in 1746, while on the lam from British troops, Bonnie Prince Charlie gave the recipe for a honey-sweetened, spice-infused whiskey to a cat named John MacKinnon as thanks for providing the rebel prince sanctuary from the redcoats. Whether that part of the story is true or not, it's been verified that in the nineteenth century the

MacKinnon clan passed the formula on to James Ross of the Broadford Inn on the remote Isle of Skye, where the locals dubbed it *an dram buidheach,* which translates as "the drink that satisfies." Ross went on to combine this new grog with Skye's most popular whiskey, Talisker, and thus the esteemed cocktail known as the Rusty Nail was born. (Technically, since ice cubes weren't generally available at that point, what Ross was serving back then is now known as a Straight Up Nail.) By 1910, Drambuie (*an dram buidheach* being a bit of a mouthful) was being sold commercially throughout Europe, and the rest—as people say when they want to get back to their awesome boozy celeb story—is history.

Anyhow, after an epic twelve-hour delay at Gatwick Airport we finally boarded a connecting flight to Inverness on a value-priced regional carrier called Flybe. Now, I don't hold it against Flybe that its name sounds like a personal grooming product sold on QVC. And it's possible I was a touch out of sorts thanks to all the Rusty Nails they force on you at Gatwick's bars. Still, I was a mite pissed to discover that (a) my seat wouldn't recline; (b) none of the seats on the entire plane reclined; (c) there were no TV monitors on board (d) or headphones; and (e) a bottle of freakin' water cost £1.20. I figured the Marquis de Sade and Josef Mengele were probably up in business class— flying free as design consultants for the airline. Then I found out there is no business class on Flybe. Lucky for them, my anger was tempered by the knowledge that I was on my way to Inverness, the Cooperstown of single-malt scotch.

The events kicked off late on a Saturday with an archery competition. To my utter surprise, Seann William Scott proved to be nearly as adept with a bow and arrow as he is at portraying party-hearty wiseasses. Which is to say he hit the bull's-eye several times. At that point I officially decided he deserved that second *N* in his first name.

Sunday's first stage was a Zapcat race. This was basically an aquatic race during which a bunch of scotch-soaked idiots like me held on for dear life while professional speedboat drivers whipped them around the water off the shores of Kyleakin. While, amazingly, no one was injured out on the water, another notable C-list celebrity race participant—Dan the Song Parody Man from the Howard Stern show—suffered a strained tongue trying to pronounce Kyleakin.

Next up came the event hereafter referred to as "Dude, Where's My Celebrity Teammate?" It consisted of a grueling hike up a steep hill called Boc Beag. Three quarters of the way up, though, Seann's will to compete—sorry, his back—apparently gave out. And believe you me, nobody was more disappointed about this turn of events than Seann William Scott. Do you know how hard it is to maintain a busy groupie-banging schedule with a critical lumbar injury? Oh, the humanity.

Somehow the games continued on, however, and even though (because?) the injured Seann was forced to sit out of a number of the remaining events, his team managed to finish a respectable fourth out of thirteen. I was bummed, though, because I really wanted to see the actor attempt the whitewater raft ride that nearly killed Dan the Song Parody Man. Call it schadenfreude, but I also would have enjoyed watching him navigate the wood-planks-over-water section of the mountain bike leg that nearly killed me and everyone else. There is video of this, by the way. Look up my YouTube channel (my handle is "thefunhog").

The trip culminated with a ceilidh—which is apparently Gaelic for "let's get drunk and dance"—featuring a stunning nouveau-traditional Scottish band, the Red Hot Chilli Pipers. Following dinner, Seann delivered a touching valedictory about teamwork and friendship that damn near moved me to tears. I told him as much afterward. And again he placed a hand on my shoulder and looked me in the eyes. "Dude," he said, "let's get drunk." It's called commitment, friends. You can't teach that in acting class

You Can Mix Gin with Just About Anything. Even Cereal.

Now, the preceding events seem like fun, and believe you me they were. But they are also an example of how success in the booze-writing life can be your worst enemy. Most of my esteemed fellow journalists on this trip drank tons of Drambuie and tons of scotch for three days, then passed out hard on the six-to-ten-hour transatlantic flight home and presumably spent at least the next couple of days detoxing. I, however, have risen to a certain pinnacle of the booze-writing trade. Which apparently also turns you into a moron. Because I drank with them, then passed out for the four-second hop back to Gatwick, where yet another European booze trip was commencing. I had barely enough time to recover from a bad kiss, let alone a four-day bender.

On the plus side, I was about to enjoy the subtle and beguiling pleasures of gin, the least understood bottle in the bar. On the minus side, my body was very literally threatening to give out on me. See, on the soggy shores of England, gin flows only slightly less freely than stupidity on the set of *The Hills*. So, hungover as I was, I spent four more days there soaking it in with the folks who understand it best. (On a side note, I also made an important philosophical discovery during my time in England. Contrary to popular belief, if a drunk falls in the middle of a forest, it does make a sound. That sound is a sort of keening wail followed by repeated requests for my mommy. Granted, when I tripped and fell over what must surely be the most poorly situated bench in the whole United

Kingdom, I wasn't in *the* woods, rather *a* wood. St. John's Wood, to be exact, a posh enclave at the north end of London. And while I can't tell you with any degree of certainty what I was doing staggering around that area alone at three a.m. on a Wednesday, I suspect it had something to do with gin. That, or I just really needed to have another good cry at the Abbey Road zebra crossing. That place really gets to me. Anyway, the great tragedy of the fall wasn't the nasty gash I sustained on my left hand, though I must say it made typing columns a bit unpleasant for some time thereafter. What really hurt were the indelible bloodstains that now adorn my very favorite Ted Baker button-down of all time—the shirt I fondly refer to as the Lady Killer. For two years it's been my go-to garment for when I absolutely positively *had* to get some action. And now, to my great and utter dismay, the Killer has been laid to rest ... by my own hand, no less—which has gotten considerably more use since the best weapon in my seduction arsenal has been eliminated.)

But we were talking about gin, which though now heavily associated with the UK was actually invented by the Dutch. They dubbed it "jenever," a name that was promptly shortened by a drunk Englishman. It's kind of the same thing the Brits did when they co-opted Madonna and started calling her Madge. The only difference is that gin doesn't adopt foreign babies or look like beef jerky.

Also unlike Madonna, gin is sophisticated, despite its secret shame that it's actually the world's original flavored vodka. That's right, ladies and gentlemen, it's a neutral grain spirit that's distilled a second time with juniper and other botanicals to add an interesting bouquet of flavors. The diverse mix of botanicals is what makes each brand a rare and delicate flower. And you know how I like flowers.

Look, there's a reason that in *Casablanca*, Humphrey Bogart doesn't lament about all the "passionfruit-flavored vodka joints in the world." In the days before pansy-ass, annoyatini-drinking *Sex in the City* fans took over the bar scene, gin was the most popular clear spirit on the planet. It's classic. Timeless. And if you give it a chance, it's likely to surprise you. Taste some Hendrick's alongside Plymouth and see for yourself just how different one high-end gin can be from another. Note how the former shows sweetness up front, yet is absolutely dry at the finish. And the Plymouth, well, it's sharp and citrusy and complex through and through.

On top of that, gin and tonics have been scientifically proven to make women hornier than a certain famous now-British songbird at a Hispanic dance club. Trust me on this. I've done the research. Makes 'em feel like virgins. Touched for the very first time. Just like those sweet, innocent nymphs on *The Hills*.

To get the lowdown on the best way to use the stuff (the whole purpose of this ill-timed visit) I went to Nick Strangeway, who, in addition to having the coolest name in the Western world, was crowned International Bartender of the Year at the 2008 Tales of the Cocktail Festival in New Orleans (the adult-beverage industry's Oscars). Strangeway plies his trade at a London steakhouse called The Hawksmoor, and his specialty is punch. So I went there. I drank his punch. I was moved to tears. The man, he has a gift. Plus, England makes me a tad weepy.

One of Strangeway's favorite brands is Plymouth, the only gin in the world that by law may be produced in only one place (what is known in the booze industry as an *appellation d'origine contrôlée*)—within the city of Plymouth, in southwest England. Strangeway tells me the water there is what makes Plymouth so tasty. Apparently the River Dart runs through peat over granite, imparting interesting mineral content. Plus, they use excellent juniper berries that grow wild on Italian hillsides. Here's a great gin-based recipe from Nick for the next time you want to get a large crowd drunk in your house:

Nick Strangeway's Signature Punch

Mix:

2 parts Beefeater Dry

1 part lemon and bitter orange sorbet

1 part fresh lemon juice

1 part pineapple syrup

3 parts chilled Sencha green tea on ice

Top with 2 parts Prosecco or demi-sec Champagne and garnish with sliced lemon, orange, and pineapple. Gorgeous.

In the interest of furthering my research, I also spent several pleasant hours boozing at the improbably well-stocked bar in the cozy offices of IP Bartenders in Notting Hill. IP stands for "International Playboy," so you can see why I would be drawn to such a place. It was also a chance to kick it with Ben Reed, one of the UK's most charismatic and munificent bartenders. Ben made a name for himself in the 1990s running the Met Bar, where Liam Gallagher and Kate Moss used to get caught behaving badly. He then went on to write the fantastic drinks book *Cool Cocktails,* host a spirits show on the BBC called *Shaker Maker,* and pen the "Barfly" column for the Saturday *Times.* You should see this man shake a cocktail.

While whipping up his favorite gin-based concoction, the Self-Starter (1 oz. Beefeater, 2 tsp. Lillet, 1 tsp. apricot brandy, and three drops of Pernod shaken over ice and strained into a cocktail glass), I ask Ben what he likes most about gin. He says it's all about the mixability. "You can mix gin with just about anything," he says. "Even cereal. Want some?"

This is when I realized, *Christ, I've got to get the hell out of the United Kingdom*.

I Gotta Do a Samurai Flick

Upon my crapulous (yes, crapulous) return from the UK, I visited Randy at his production studio in Van Nuys, where we wound up tying on an afternoon load while lounging on two huge leather chairs that flanked a four-poster bed in an otherwise unfurnished warehouse. Porn aficionados might recognize the trademark bed from some of Randy's more popular films. And the extremely informed reader might realize that the chairs we were sitting on were the same ones a hot Asian chick once pushed together to create a "special report" for her boss in a picture called *Secretary Something-or-Other*. The boss was played by a guy with a monster cock who, I'm pretty sure, later killed some people in Big Sur. Great business, porn. Good people.

Randy doodled on a sketchpad, and I flipped through a photo album containing stills from porn shoots.

And we talked, of course. About how men were obdurate creatures who all wanted the same thing out of life: that which they did not have. In my estimation it wasn't merely a case of the grass always being greener on the other side; it also smelled fresher over there, was easier to mow, and looked hotter in a bikini. My envy wasn't limited to sexual partners, either. I was perpetually jealous of other guys' careers, friends, physiques, hobbies, homes, cars, and cable packages. And don't even get me started on penis size. The bottom line is this: For the bulk of my adult life I agreed with Thoreau when he said most men lead lives of quiet desperation, even though in my personal experience, my desperations weren't quiet in the least. Not once did I ever entertain the notion that the life I was leading was the one I was truly meant to have.

I glanced over at what Randy had wrought on the sketch-pad. It was a drawing of a Buddhist monk laying pipe with a geisha.

"I gotta do a samurai flick," he said.

I took a long pull off my beer. "You know who I reconnected with on Facebook?"

"Who?"

"Nicole Van Buren."

"From college? No shit?" said Randy.

"Yep."

"You guys were kind of serious, if memory serves," he said. "Until you dumped her."

I nodded. "She lives near New Orleans now. Married. Kids. From the tenor of some of her Facebook posts, sounds like she's a Bible-thumper. I'm thinking about going to visit her."

"Why?" he asked, raising an eyebrow.

"Well, I'm headed to New Orleans anyway to cover the Tales of the Cocktail Festival," I said.

"And conflating a work trip to the world's biggest cocktail festival with a visit to a married ex-flame from college is a good idea *why*?

"I dunno. I'm on a quest," I said, warming to the topic. "A road trip into the meaning of my existence; a chance to see this poor girl again and smooth out any misunderstandings; maybe achieve a bit of that closure once and for goddamn all."

"Wow, a real live Soji Yang," Randy said.

"Come again?"

"A Mongolian warlord who visited the families of his vanquished."

"Gotta love History Channel," I said.

"Look, I appreciate your wanting to get your spiritual house in order, but are you sure you're not just after some ex-sex?" Randy asked.

"C'mon, man," I protested. "I told you she's married."

"Name one time when that has ever stopped you!"

I had to think about that one for a moment. "Now," I said finally. "It'll stop me now."

"Don't say that, my friend," Randy smiled. "You're a man on a mission. There ain't *nuthin'* gonna stop you now."

"The Punch in the Mouth"

CREATED BY JEFFREY MORGENTHALER

1 oz. bourbon

1/2 oz. Bacardi 8

1/2 oz. maple syrup

2 oz. half and half

2 dashes vanilla extract

Cinnamon, to taste

Nutmeg, to taste

Shake ingredients with ice and strain into an ice-filled Old Fashioned glass. Dust with cinnamon and nutmeg and sip in place of anything resembling a nutritious breakfast.

"Drinking in New Orleans requires the constitution of a warrior. You're up until the wee hours, deep in the knowledge that you'll be starting all over again before you've had more than a few hours to compose yourself. Drinking in New Orleans with Dan Dunn requires a little creativity, as he's a hard-charging sonofabitch boozer with a bottomless expense account. In order to keep up with Mr. Dunn, whose appetite for trouble seemingly knows no bounds, I've found it essential to fortify my belly in the morning. So I came up with this seemingly innocuous libation based on the great-granddaddy of New Orleans breakfast beverages: the Brandy Milk Punch. Dan and I have spent many a morning in bars all over New Orleans sipping this one in lieu of, say, that case of beer by the pool with the nymphomaniac bikini models that he's always promising. It's probably for the best, anyway; everyone knows bikini models can't hold their liquor . . . or, at least, Dan and I know it."

—**JEFFREY MORGENTHALER,** of JeffreyMorgenthaler.com, is a writer, philosopher, and overall great guy who manages the bar at Clyde Common in Portland, Oregon. Jeffrey's recipes and wisdom have appeared in the *New York Times,* the *Wall Street Journal, Wine Enthusiast, Playboy, Wired,* and *Imbibe.* In 2009, Playboy.com named him one of the top ten mixologists in the United States.

EIGHT

There's Enough for Everybody, and You Can Never Get Too Much of It

I was fresh into town and still feeling human as I hunkered down at the Carousel Bar off the main lobby of the Hotel Monteleone, in New Orleans's French Quarter. By force of habit, I did a spot survey of who I was drinking with. I always like to check out my temporary family before I get soused with them. The guy sitting one stool over was in his mid-fifties, wearing a tie-dyed T-shirt that read LOVE SUCKS, TRUE LOVE SWALLOWS. From the brown stains slightly obscuring the lettering, I put him on Jack and Cokes. As I soon confirmed, he was downing two for every Louis Armstrong song. And Louis Armstrong is all they play at the Carousel Bar. It was ten a.m. on a Wednesday—pretty close to this guy's bedtime.

He turned and looked at me, or at least tried to. His pupils were swimming in opposite directions. The old reverse cross-eye. I'd seen this before, of course, sometimes in the mirror. Call it an occupational hazard.

After taking a long contemplative drag off one of the two Marlboros he had going simultaneously, he croaked, "If alcohol kills millions of fuckin' brain cells, how come it never kills the ones that make me want to drink?"

This turned out to be an entirely appropriate introduction to the 2009 Tales of the Cocktail Festival, the annual bacchanal that puts representatives from the world's biggest liquor brands in the same room with the world's biggest celebrity bartenders and the industry's most notorious journalists/ charity cases (still not sure which side of that equation I fall on). It's the place where the big business of big booze gets done, over many, many libations.

And while the ninth annual Tales event promised to be the biggest yet, the fashion-impaired degenerate next to me felt like a harbinger of some heavy shit to come. Nearly four years after Katrina, New Orleans was still damaged goods, friends. Plus, the second Great Depression and its gut-punch to the tourism trade hadn't helped the local recovery effort. But there we all were nonetheless, thousands of folks from all over the world, tied together by a common interest in the promotion and consumption of luxury adult beverages. But hey, why *not* New Orleans, right? It's not like people are getting killed there. What's that? They *are* getting killed? Three in this neighborhood last week? I see.

Despite my twitchy mood, I managed to have a hell of a time—at least as far as I can tell from my trusty notebook and voice recorder (in this profession you learn to live like that guy in the movie *Memento*). I was apparently blotto for five days straight, no doubt because there were people handing out sample cups of alcohol damn near everywhere you went. Hell, what else is a professional booze writer to do in the Big Easy at a spirits festival? My *Playboy* editor's answer to that question, by the way, was, "Oh, I don't know, Dan. Attend a seminar? Interview someone? Be a, you know, journalist?"

He's so cute when he's angry.

According to my trusty voice recorder, here's how things went down.

WEDNESDAY

10 A.M.—I'm hanging out at the Carousel Bar off the main lobby of the Hotel Monteleone with my new vision-challenged friend. You've heard this part before.

10:30 A.M.—Roll into a panel discussion (take that, Editor McAsshole!) called "Big Trends in Cocktail and Spirit Service," featuring Jim Meehan of New York City's PDT, who went on to win American Bartender of the Year a couple days later. Also speaking were Michael Waterhouse of Devin Tavern and Dylan Prime, and Simon Difford of Sauce Guide Publications. Heavyweights all. Meehan says flavored vodkas are on the way out. Waterhouse adds that just because vodka is distilled twenty times and filtered through diamond dust and baby hair does not necessarily mean it's good vodka. Difford claims he's using less and less vodka in the recipes he develops. Duly noted.

10:32 A.M.—I spot a guy sitting in the front row wearing an Absolut cap. Bet he feels like a dick.

10:34 A.M.—Down sample cup of a cocktail made with Tommy Bahama rum. No, wait, turns out this is not a cocktail at all, rather just a plain old shot of Tommy Bahama rum. While conceptually impoverished, it tastes woody. Smooth. Almost nutritious-breakfast-like. Woof.

10:44 A.M.—Difford opines that cocktails made with fruit are out and that classic cocktails are where it's at these days.

10:45 A.M.—Jim Meehan counters that he's all about cocktails made with grapefruit, blood orange, kiwi, and pineapple. Difford, in turn, threatens to drown Jim in the pool. Wait, maybe it was "Wow, Jim, you're cool." Frickin' British dudes and their hard-to-understand English. For the record, I'm with Meehan on the fruit thing, mainly because he was kind enough to lay an easy-to-make-at-home recipe on me:

There Will Be Blood

BY PDT BARTENDER JOHN DEBARY

2 oz. Old Grand-Dad bourbon (100 Proof)

3/4 oz. Godiva Original Chocolate Liqueur

3/4 oz. blood orange juice

Blood orange twist, for garnish

Shake over ice and strain into a chilled coupe. Garnish with a flamed blood orange twist.

Some would say a flamed blood orange twist doesn't exactly fall into the easy-to-make-at-home category. I say these people lack an appropriate commitment to their drinking life. Anyway.

11:22 A.M.—Waterhouse just referred to cloudy apple cider as a great "lengthener" and quipped that size matters when it comes to ice cubes. I can't handle this sort of sexual innuendo before noon. Time to get out of here.

11:23 A.M.—Down another sample cup of Tommy Bahama rum for the road. I'm not even halfway through the first day and every trace of shame has left my body.

11:36 A.M.—Back in the Carousel Bar for a few rounds of Bacardi daiquiris with an impossibly hot spirits-industry professional. Try out new pickup line about how love sucks and true love swallows. The shame returns.

11:38 A.M.—Impossibly hot spirits-industry professional has to run. Literally, apparently. I decide to stay a while and keep the daiquiris company.

1:45 P.M.—Walking down Chartres Street toward my room at the posh W Hotel French Quarter. Wait, what's this in my hand? Why, it's my perfectly legal to-go cup of daiquiri! All the places in me that were filled with shame a moment ago are now filled with love for this town.

2 P.M.—I have discovered that my room overlooks the courtyard pool. As luck would have it, several bikini-clad spirits-industry publicists are catching some rays as I sip my perfectly legal daiquiri and surreptitiously observe them through the slats of the wooden blinds. Good thing that stupid shame stuff got the hell out of Dodge.

4:44 P.M.—While having a late lunch of Maker's Mark, Red Stripe, and a fried shrimp po'boy at a watering hole called

Coop's Place, I meet a local woman with tar-colored hair, moonish eyes, and plasticine skin. She looks like the daughter on *The Addams Family*, except with a decent personal trainer and great boobs. She swears she's a real vampire, and while she certainly looks the part, I don't buy it. So she offers to bite my arm and suck my blood. I tell her that's way too weird for me. As if to illustrate my new shame-free existence, we make out instead.

6 P.M.—Turns out the Monteleone is something of a home base here at Tales. I'm back there again and heading into a seminar called "You Need to Get the Fuck Out of Here Before You Make an Ass of Yourself." Wait, no, that's just what I wrote in my notebook for this time frame. In lieu of an actual seminar I bump into "King Cocktail" himself, Dale DeGroff, perhaps the world's most famous mixologist, and begin telling him about how I just made out with a vampire.

6:01 P.M.—Dale has to run. I'm beginning to notice a pattern.

6:03 P.M.—Down sample cup of something . . . could be a rum punch.

6:04 P.M.—Down another one to be sure. Yep, seems like rum punch. Rhum Clement? This requires further investigation. Another sample cup.

6:05 P.M.—I realize my powers of deduction are paramount. It reads RHUM CLEMENT PUNCH right on the side of the sample cup. I celebrate with another.

6:10 P.M.—Headed back to my room for a power nap.

THURSDAY

8:30 A.M.—That was one powerful goddamn nap. I feel like a new man.

12:45 P.M.—I've finally discovered a type of moonshine worth drinking. In fact, I've discovered two: Junior Johnson's Midnight Moon and Catdaddy Carolina Moonshine. They go for twenty dollars a bottle, and both are triple-distilled from corn at the only legal distillery in North Carolina. The Catdaddy's a little sweet, with a hint of spice. The Midnight Moon tastes a lot like vodka and I love it. Which is to say, "Suck it, Jim Meehan!"

2:55 P.M.—I'm wondering if anybody else finds it ironic that the average age of the attendees at a seminar called "Port: Not Just Your Grandpa's Drink Anymore" seems to be about sixty-seven.

5:30 P.M.—The Cocktail "Carnival" Happy Hour at the historical Presbytere on Jackson Square is hands-down the most impressive gathering of mixological all-stars I've ever seen. I turn into a very drunk version of a twelve-year-old girl at the MTV Movie Awards.

5:32 P.M.—Look, it's David Wondrich, author of *Imbibe!*

5:35 P.M.—And there's the Modern Mixologist, Tony Abou-Ganim.

5:37 P.M.—"Hi, Dale! Over here, Dale. Dale!"

5:38 P.M.—"Dale? Dale?"
   Can people in this town run or what?

5:44 P.M.—Hey, I know that dude. It's Marcos Tello of the Edison. Best bar in L.A.

5:51 P.M.—Oh, dear God, it's Jeffrey Morgenthaler of Clyde Common in Oregon. Whenever I spend time with Jeffrey, I wind up blackout drunk, in jail, or both. So naturally I rush right over and ask him how the bar business is going up in the Pacific Northwest.

"In this economy? We're all fucked," he says, handing me a sample cup of absinthe. We nod solemnly and slam 'em. We have just created the official drinking game of Tales '09. It goes like this: "We're all fucked! Hey, I know, let's get even more fucked."

7:12 P.M.—I take a stroll down Bourbon Street to sober up—which speaks volumes about how much of an ass-kicker the Tales Festival is—and pass at least three other guys sporting the LOVE SUCKS, TRUE LOVE SWALLOWS T-shirt.

8:14 P.M.—Suddenly I'm feeling nostalgic about the days of old when my dad used to wear a shirt that read MUSTACHE RIDES, 5 CENTS. I drop into a T-shirt store to look for one, but the old bearded guy behind the counter tells me they discontinued that rude stripe of misogynistic casualwear years ago.

"Besides," he adds, shaking his head ruefully, "you can't get a mustache ride for five cents anywhere anymore."

I fear he's correct. The impact of the economic shit storm is definitely evident on Bourbon Street, where women are now getting IOUs instead of beads for flashing their tits. Near the famed Old Absinthe House I run into an executive from a luxury vodka brand who claims the idea that the booze business is recession-proof is a bunch of bullshit. I'm not surprised he's scared shitless. The guy's peddling the good stuff at a time when people are saying peace to the high-end hooch in favor of Georgi or even Kirkland (for those of you who don't buy their toilet paper in bulk, Kirkland is Costco's house-brand vodka).

"Everybody's scared things are going to get worse," he says. "And nobody really knows what to do about it."

I suggest getting drunk.

And with that, we head back to the Monteleone in search of sample cups. After all, they're free.

FRIDAY

Apparently I called in for a radio segment with Danny DeVito on Playboy Radio's Morning Show today. I know this because there is a tape. Other than that, however, I have very little in the way of evidence of what happened Friday. Wouldn't be the first time.

SATURDAY

8:30 A.M.—I wake up to discover that some asshole has vomited all over my bathroom. Since I'm alone, the conclusion is obvious: It was housekeeping. I'll be keeping an eye on them from now on.

10:30 A.M.—At the Martin Miller's Gin tenth-anniversary tasting party, the incorrigible Limey mixmaster Ben Reed is going drinko-a-drinko against America's own Jon Santer, president of the San Francisco chapter of the U.S. Bartenders' Guild. It's standing room only. Everyone is drinking and hooting and hollering and drinking more. I haven't even had my coffee yet. This town is going to kill me.

11 A.M.—And the winner of the America versus UK mix-off is . . . me! See you later, hangover! Welcome back, buzz! Oh, buzz, my oldest and dearest friend, how I missed you.

11:15 A.M.—Martin Miller himself, a legendary British entrepreneur and inveterate playboy, is telling the crowd how fortunate he feels to be celebrating ten years in the gin business, particularly in such a grim economic environment. On cue, everyone in the room nods solemnly and downs a sample cup. My drinking game is catching on.

12:23 P.M.—Run into fellow spirits scribe Jenny Adams. Ask her what she's been up to lately. Not much, she says. Work has been hard to come by. I grab Jenny by the hand, lead her to the Carousel Bar, and order two shots of Jägermeister.

"What's this all about?" she asks.

Drinking game, I tell her. Don't ask questions.

She nods, and we slam the shots.

12:40 P.M.—I've never been a huge fan of Xanté, a liqueur made with pears, vanilla, and cognac. Until now, that is. Because now I've just been introduced to Adele Nilsson, the Swedish goddess who owns the brand. Right about now, pears, vanilla, cognac, and Adele Nilsson are damn near all I can think of, not necessarily in that order (and not necessarily the pears you're thinking of). Indeed, as one of the world's foremost authorities on spirits, and despite the fact that Xanté is sweet and girly, I can say without equivocation that it is the single greatest alcoholic beverage ever invented.

12:45 P.M.—It's become clear I have no chance of ever making time with Adele Nilsson. It's possible I may need to rethink my position on Xanté.

1 P.M.—Vampire Girl calls and says she'd like to get together for a cup of coffee or something. I tell her I wish I could but that I'm a professional on assignment for *Playboy* and that I need to attend some seminars, interview some folks, and, you know, be a journalist. She, in turn, says she doesn't need coffee and that all she really wants is to get laid. I decide there'll be plenty of time to be a journalist later.

1:10 P.M.—My suspicions about housekeeping and their secret regurgitators have been confirmed. While I was out the sneaky mothers snuck in and cleaned up the evidence. Make no mistake, I will be writing a strongly worded letter to the management. I consider this a public service. They should know about any predatory hurling happening on premises.

1:15 P.M.—Vampire Girl just called to say she can't make it after all. Some crap about not being able to go out in the sun.

1:17 P.M.—I'm lying down for a quick nap.

SUNDAY

11:15 A.M.—OK, nap ran long again. But Christ, I needed it if I was going to walk out of this town alive. Besides, my work here is done. I have taken the temperature of the industry (remind me to wash my thermometer). Now I've got bigger fish to fry.

What, you ask? I'm bringing back the five-cent mustache ride. All proceeds will benefit the Imbiber Home for Wayward Spirits Publicists. You can tell the Nobel people to forward the prize to my *Playboy* editor. That poor bastard deserves it.

"Lost in Oaxaca"

CREATED BY STEVE LIVIGNI

2 oz. Del Maguey Santo Domingo Albarradas Mezcal

1/2 oz. lemon juice (fresh)

1/2 oz. lime juice (fresh)

1 oz. egg whites

2 bar spoons of superfine sugar

Ice

Jalapeño, sliced, for garnish

6 drops Miracle Mile Bitters Co. Chocolate/ Chili Bitters

Combine all ingredients in a cocktail shaker and dry shake (no ice) with a thin slice of jalapeño pepper. Once you get a nice froth, let the contents rest.

Add ice (preferably one big cube) and shake lightly until the shaker is too cold to handle.

Add one big cube into a double Old Fashioned glass (9 oz. is a nice fit).

Strain the contents slowly into the glass.

Garnish with a very thin slice of jalapeño (no seeds) and 6 drops of Miracle Mile Bitters Co. Chocolate/Chili Bitters.

"As this chapter will reinforce, you never really know what to expect from people, or from cocktails for that matter. I've come to expect certain things from Dan Dunn: an unsurpassed thirst for all things fortified, brewed, or distilled; solid stories (including the ones that actually give me a legitimate reason to buy *Playboy* for the articles); and the kind of joie de vivre that turns a painful eight a.m. call time for his Playboy Radio segments into, say, a full-blown coffee-cup wine tasting in a Glendale, California, studio green room. The 'Lost in Oaxaca' is one of those things you don't expect to be delicious. Mezcal's worm reputation scares people, raw eggs have gotten NYC bartenders fines from the health department, and jalapeños can definitely burn. Yet when these things are mixed in the right proportions, you get a delicious blend of sweet, spicy, smoky, and savory, with a serious buzz ... kinda like Dan. Enjoy, and *Salud!*"

—**STEVE LIVIGNI** is a lifelong booze enthusiast and barman (what's a cubicle?). Steve is half of Top Notch Beverage Consulting and can be found almost every day running La Descarga in Los Angeles or drinking Gibsons at Musso and Frank.

NINE

Would You Have Come If I Had Told You Ahead of Time?

Nicole Van Buren (my college ex turned Facebook friend) invited me (via Facebook, natch) to the small movie theater she owns and operates about a half hour's drive out of New Orleans. When I entered the weathered building, the lobby was empty save for Nicole and two teenaged boys after my own heart who, I soon gathered, had been caught sneaking liquor into the theater.

Nicole looked remarkably similar to the way she did in college. Eerily so, in fact. With her black hair up in a ponytail, her chemise dress, and her pink retro eyeglasses, she had always had a 1950s pinup girl thing going on that I was powerless against.

"I'll let you go without calling your parents or the police on one condition," she said to the boys.

The teens eyed her nervously, unsure what to do or say next. Nicole continued without their input.

"Christ can help you with this," she told them. "I'd like you to say the Lord's Prayer with me."

The boys looked at each other, confused. Then one of them asked, "Which one's that?"

Nicole smiled and said, "It's the one that begins 'Our Father, who art in ...' "

And with that, she led them in prayer, helping them through the parts they didn't know, adding special emphasis to the part about temptation, and ending with an unsettlingly enthusiastic "amen." When they were through, she made the sign of the cross over their heads and showed them out.

OK, I guess she *had* changed since college. As she reentered the lobby I caught her eye and saw in her face a spark of recognition (or was that horror?). She bopped over for a hug.

"Hi, Dan!" she said.

In that instant I flashed back to a moment in college when Nicole, wearing the standard sorority-cute uniform of baseball cap and ponytail, had sauntered over to my table in the university commons where I was having lunch with Randy.

> *"Oh, hey, Nicole," I said uncomfortably, flinching as she bent down to give me a kiss.*
>
> *"Last night was fun," she said.*
>
> *"Yeah. Totally."*
>
> *"I'll talk to you later tonight, OK?" she said, smiling knowingly, shooting a dismissive glance at Randy.*
>
> *"Sounds good, Nic."*
>
> *Nicole sauntered off, letting her hand trail over my arm as she left.*

"What was that about?" Randy hooted.

"Disaster, man. Flat-out disaster." I groaned. "We were monkey-fucking last night, see, and I was so into it . . . so Calgon'd, that it just came out."

"What, your load?" Randy asked.

"No, the words."

"You fucking moron. You told her you loved her?" he replied, incredulous.

"Just shut up."

Later that day, back at my apartment getting high, Randy was still in disbelief.

"Dude, that shit is so fucked-up," he said in his best bong hit–holding voice.

"I meant to say: I love this. *I love THIS! Y'know, sex!"*

"It's not a total disaster," Randy said. "You can take it back."

"You can't take shit like that back! You can't go: 'Excuse me, allow me to clarify. I don't really love you, but I seriously dig fucking you.'"

"So what do you do? You've got to dump her, right?"

"I guess. The thing is, she's a real australopithicus in the sack." I was taking anthropology at the time. Also, I was kind of a tool. I took a hit, coughed, and laughed. "Whatever. Hey, are you going to Lollapalooza with us next week?"

"Oh, yeah. We're so going," Nicole said, changing a reel in the projection booth and jolting me out of my reverie. She was putting on the full-court press, trying to get me to go to a big rock show with her the next day. "It's going to be great," she said.

"Who's playing?" I asked, dubious.

"A bunch of great bands," Nicole said. "Some local, some national. It'll be a lot of fun. I'll pick you up at your hotel tomorrow at noon, OK?"

"OK, cool, sounds like fun," I said, kissing her cheek and making a quick exit. It was at least beer-thirty, or maybe even beer-forty-five, at this point. I walked out, hoping I could find a decent bar close by. Then I remembered I was in Louisiana. There were three between the theater and where my car was parked.

Louisiana is located in what's called the Deep South. As a Philadelphia native, in the Deep South I am what's called a Yankee. And not the kind people like to watch play baseball either. Now, some folks—not everyone, mind you—some in the Deep South don't take too kindly to people from Up North. We Yankees don't mind. Everyone's gotta hate on someone. Personally, I hate jugglers and Bulgarians. But suffice it to say that when I'm in the Deep South I don't always wear my Philly roots on my sleeve, because why stir up trouble? I know we'll all probably get along just fine, and we don't need a little something like the marriage laws in Massachusetts to come between us. When entering the sort of place that serves the kind of clientele for whom second cousins are acceptable members of the dating pool, and you want to have a good time, it is crucial that you modulate your behavior appropriately. (If you're looking for trouble, of course, feel free to walk in and shout "Where the white women at?") Fortunately, over the years I've visited many a bar below the Mason-Dixon Line and west of the Delaware Water Gap, and therefore have mastered the art of . . .

How to Be a Yankee and Survive a Bar in the Sticks

1) Say as little as possible.

As we all learned in first-grade math class, zero is as little as possible. And if getting away with not speaking in a bar were possible, I'd recommend it, given that the easiest way to out yourself as a Yankee is by opening your mouth. To a Southerner, a Northern accent is like a bee sting on the nuts—hard not to notice. The problem is, at a bar you will need to order a beverage. And this means that if you don't want to blow your cover you must be able to utter at least one syllable while affecting a believable drawl. That syllable is "Bud." As in the King of Beers (that microbrew shit don't hunt in the boonies). Don't fuck around and try to tack on the "weiser" or a "please" (or, God forbid, "light") either, because if Tom Hanks taught us anything in *Forrest Gump,* it's that even the finest Northern-bred actors can screw up a Southern accent if they try to say too much.

2) No glasses.

Pour your beer into a glass and you may as well be wearing a skirt, heels, and a cock-ring necklace. Also, don't wear glasses. Makes you look like you read.

3) Once you've ignored rule one (which you will), watch where you roam.

Let's face it, you're drinking here. And drinking tends to lead to social engagement. So you're going to end up talking eventually. But if you've flown under the radar for long enough, and seem to be a good sort, they might not care that you talk a little funny. That does not mean you can just start shooting off about whatever comes to mind. For instance, it's probably best if you stay off the topic of family relations. Hey, what happens between two cousins should stay between those cousins. And their kids. Also, avoid religion, for reasons that will become clear later in this chapter. Sports are also tricky. If you can figure out some of their allegiances and not cross them, you might be OK. But on no account should you enter into a discussion about college football. These people may never have seen the inside of a college classroom, but you can bet your ass that they can sing the Ole Miss fight song backward, and the fact that you can't could be interpreted as an act of aggression. Oh, and France. Whatever you do, don't mention France. What you *should* do posthaste is discuss the weather. Southerners are calmed by a mutual interest in all things hot, cold, rainy, and dry. Be careful that this conversation does not stray into global-warming territory, though, because as we all know, that is a myth fabricated by East Coast liberals in France. Another good idea is to establish some geographical connection to the Deep South. Maybe your grandmother is from Georgia and your dad, her Bubba Boy, had to move up North because that faggot Bill Clinton didn't nuke that sand nigger Obama bin Laden when he had the fuckin' chance. I don't know; have fun with it.

4) Remember, those girls have brothers. And those brothers have shotguns.

Women are gorgeous everywhere in the world, from Papua New Guinea to North Cackalacky. But in some areas they are touchier about being hit on by dudes who are demonstrably NLU (Not Like Us). Now, I've met Southern women so beautiful that the stomping you'll get for smiling at them seems worth it. Just make sure it's worth it, because these girls not only have brothers, their brothers have friends, and their friends are in the bar (because where the fuck else are they going to go?), and these fellas are all *big* fans of the Second

Amendment. So if you must hit on that pretty magnolia sitting by the jukebox, do so with caution. When you approach the Vision (and you will, because you're drunk), lead with your best shot. Try not to smile right away, as having a full set of teeth may mark you as an outsider, or a fag, or both. Ask her which NASCAR driver she likes, and nod when she answers. If somebody notes that you probably know more about sucking cock than you do about NASCAR, just sigh deeply and say you lost all interest after Dale got killed. And he "got killed." He didn't "die" or "crash" or "pass on." He got killed that time. Never mind who Dale was.

5) Buy drinks.

From time to time, buying a round for the house, or at least the aforementioned brothers, can also buy precious minutes. Minutes in which you can quietly slip out to the "bathroom." And by that I mean out the bathroom window and then as far away as your little Northern legs can carry you.

6) Don't do this:

When somebody calls you a pussy, respond with "Well, you are what you eat, Big Dick."

7) Stay butch.

If you've ignored rules one through six and things remain calm, you're in a gay bar. You should still order Bud. But enjoy the Harley tats. And the attention.

If all else fails . . .

8) Exit in glory.

If things are starting to look dicey, loudly announce that you have to leave because your mom just called and said your brother is coming back from Iraq next week and can finally resume his efforts on the LSU football team, where he was a walk-on last year before signing up to defend freedom. A toast to the American military *and* Old Glory! Then leave twice what you figure you owe and get the hell out of Dodge.

If rule 8 fails . . .

9) Know the fight rules.

Once you're actually in a fight, remember that the Deep South is an honor-driven society. Which means your foes are unlikely to make the first dirty move. Head-butting is virtually unknown south of Atlanta, and a knee to the groin is considered gauche (which is to say, French). Bear in mind that your use of one of these time-honored defensive techniques will incapacitate only the first responder. But they will be considered an open invitation for others—including people you might not think would get involved, like girlfriends or cops—to stomp you. Also, it's important to remember that Southern fights don't end when Northern fights end, like, say when somebody is beaten bloody and blacks out. In the Deep South, this is known as merely the "boot-shining" phase of the altercation.

If You Can't Stand the Sex and Drugs, Get Out of the Rock and Roll

Anyway, where was I? Oh, yes, soaking up some good ol' Southern culture with my college ex, Nicole.

"Take me now, JC!!!" the guy in the row behind us was screaming, his face contorted in the sort of rock and roll ecstasy usually associated with either seeing Led Zeppelin in '74 or crapping your pants. The GOT JESUS? T-shirt was a nice touch, though. I looked at the woman next to him, whose eyes were closed in a similar fervor; she was sporting SMILE! YOUR MOM CHOSE LIFE! on her chest. I'd seen someone selling both these numbers on the way in, along with shirts that read CONFUSED? READ THE DIRECTIONS! next to a picture of a Bible, and one that said GET STONED LIKE PAUL, STAND YOUR GROUND! I think my favorite was GOD'S LAST NAME IS NOT DAMMIT! Which is true; everyone knows his last name is "I Love Fucking You."

We were at Jesus Jam. I figured out it wasn't a typical concert around the time we rolled into the parking lot and I spotted a bunch of people dancing around a gigantic inflatable crucifix. Now we were halfway up the stands in a packed-to-capacity outdoor stadium. Weirdly enough, apart from the lack of pot smoke and the preponderance of Christ-alicious T-shirts, the vibe was eerily like that of a real rock concert.

"Would you have come if I had told you ahead of time?" Nicole asked, noting me noting everyone's T-shirts.

"Yeah, but I wouldn't have snorted quite so much angel dust first."

Nicole smiled indulgently as I paged through the concert program. "I don't need to read T-shirts to have a good laugh, you know." I was winding myself up. "The band names are enough: Revelation, Salvation, Final Piety. Final Piety?! Seriously? I figure whatever you're doing stops being rock and roll as soon as piety gets in there. Let alone Final Piety. What does that even mean?"

As the words left my mouth, it dawned on me that I knew exactly what Final Piety meant. It meant marriage. More specifically, marriage without any precursory sexual contact. Which, really, when you think about it, is just an incredibly bad idea all around. Not to mention that if you take the sex out of rock and roll, you also remove most of rock and roll's reason to exist. Early detractors said rock music would turn its listeners into wanton, sex-crazed freaks. And if you're doing it right, it still will. As Randy has reminded me time and again, "If you can't stand the sex and drugs, get out of the rock and roll." We're talking about an art form predicated on the exact opposite of piety. For the love of God, it's about trashing hotel rooms, overdosing, sleeping with models, and punching people for no reason, not the love of God!

"Christian rock is my truth," Nicole replied, undeterred.

"But see, 'Christian' and 'rock' cancel each other out. It's an oxymoron, like 'premium vodka.'" I hoped I was getting at least a tiny bit under her skin. I'd been trying ever since she picked me up.

"Behave," she replied. "I don't come to your office and quote Bible scripture."

"And thank Christ for that! You know what I do for a living?" I asked.

"You write about getting drunk for a boobie magazine," she said. And then she added dryly, "And to think I let you get away."

All right, the lady wants to mix it up. "So, is your church really badass?" I jabbed. "One of those youth-oriented places with a JumboTron and a four-piece band, right?"

"There is a band, yes." She chuckled.

"When did this happen? It wasn't your scene in college by a damn sight."

"I guess I got tired of playing demolition derby with temptation," she replied. "You know what I mean?"

I wasn't sure I did. As far back as I could recall I'd had a "strangers on a train" relationship with religion. I don't mean that in a homicidal way; I just mean that for me, "higher power" meant the unbelievably hot specimen on the subway who doesn't know she's pretty but could be convinced by your tender caress; you can't help but fantasize a whole life together for the two of you, down to what your grandchildren would look like, but then, a minute later, the train stops and she gets off and you never see her again because you have to truck all the way the hell up to the Bronx to take a meeting with an obscure absinthe maker. Nobly, however, you convince yourself it's a good thing you never met her because you would have wanted to help her with her self-esteem issues, even though you know you're actually exactly the kind of guy she should be staying away from. So it's really better for everybody this way. And then you feel just a tiny bit sad, but you chase the feeling away with nicotine, caffeine, or alcohol. Or all three.

So I've never had what those in the conversion business call a "personal relationship with God." It was more like He and I have a few mutual friends who get together every once in a while at weddings and funerals. And while my parents may not have been ideal, I can thank God for one thing: They also weren't overly religious. My mother preached the gospel of live and let crazy, but it didn't veer into Jesus territory much, and when I finally reconnected with my dad when I was a teenager, the closest thing to religious wisdom he imparted was what would prove to be an even more valuable lesson about the merits of tolerance: "To the broad-minded flock the broads, son."

Suddenly, the Jesus Jam crowd erupted as a five-piece heavy-metal band bounded onto the stage, flashing halo signs to the crowd. They looked like the second coming of Judas Priest, which was somewhat fitting since Nicole told me both the bass player and keyboardist were studying to become clergymen. The spiky-haired lead singer with the giant tattoo of the Virgin Mary across his exposed chest sauntered up to the microphone, sneering like Billy Idol. "Hello, Louisiana! We are Proc-lo-ma-tion! A one, a one, a one-two-three-four!"

The band burst into a speed-metal number, and the singer belted out the lyrics:

My heart of hearts is burnin'
I unwrap the Shroud of Turin
My faith is aflame with fiiiiiire!

His Billy Idol affectations aside, the singer looked like a shorter, less hirsute version of David Lee Roth, swinging the mike stand around as the guitar player bodysurfed atop a sea of revelers. So this is what happens when the secular youth scene collides with the convulsive power of the Holy Spirit. Rebellion meets Revelation. Fuck-You Fundamentalism. Baptism by mosh pit. Even I had to admit that martyrdom was punk as fuck.

After Proclamation's set, a muscular, heavily tattooed motivational speaker in his mid forties strode out to center stage with a purpose, grabbed the mike, and began battering the audience with high-volume tough love. Think Henry Rollins, high on sweet JC, with a side order of faith-based rage.

He was warming up nicely now. "It's a *war* out there, and you better believe Satan is busting out the heavy artillery," he shouted. "I know about war. About drugs, prostitution, and booze. I did all that. And then I got turned. By a secret agent of God. An agent named Jesus."

I looked around at all the people holding hands and hugging and nodding while listening to the sermon. I couldn't decide if it was beautiful or pathetic. I leaned in close to Nicole.

"Didn't you say your husband was going to be here? Doesn't he care that we're out together?" I asked.

"Paul? Oh, he's here. He's with his youth group. We'll meet up with them afterward."

"How many of you brought friends today?" yelled tattoo guy from the stage. "Raise your hands!"

To my horror, Nicole did just that.

"Give them a big hug!" Nicole did that too. And that felt a lot less horrible. The bystanders screamed like somebody had just kicked a field goal.

"When you came into my theater I *knew* Jesus sent you," she whispered in my ear.

"I, uh . . . you're scaring me a little, Nic."

"Change *is* scary, Dan. It always is."

"Bring them out!" yelled the aggro emcee. "Onto the field! Into God's bosom! Come to Jesus!"

"C'mon!" Nicole said, grabbing my hand and tugging me toward the aisle. I pulled back immediately.

"It's not my thing, Nic."

"How do you know?"

A fair question, I suppose. And in the elongated moment of decision that followed, I explored it.

How did I know that Christianity wasn't the real deal? Jesus was a cool dude, right? But then his followers all seemed to get caught up on crazy stuff like banning sex and gayness. Just too much horrifying weirdness for me, I think. But then again, couldn't I do it without being crazy? It was actually strangely tempting. There was something nice and floaty and serene about being told exactly what you need to do to be a good person—must be kind of like spiritual heroin. And you can get a fix 24/7, without the needles. All you have to do is close your eyes and pray.

Plus, let's face it—I'd be a chump to pass up an opportunity this weird.

"Fuck it, let's go," I said, standing up and running down the stadium steps like a star quarterback at a high school pep rally. The faces I passed looked familiar, like the kids I used to see spinning in circles outside Dead shows, now grown-up and into the next high. We hopped the field-level fence and charged onto the infield grass, which was packed with worshippers on their knees, drunk on religious fervor. When we got to the foot of the stage, Nicole dropped to her knees, which immediately made me think of blow jobs. Guilt-free college blow jobs. With a bong and a hammock. And then making naked grilled cheese after. Jesus, she looked incredible.

"Oh, yes. Jesus!" she moaned, pulling me down.

Exactly. But I didn't want to kneel. I also didn't want to be the only one standing up. Nicole gripped my hand tight and my knees buckled.

"Do you feel the love, the infinite love?" she cooed. "It's not like money or land or food. There's enough for everybody, and you can never get too much of it!"

Over Nicole's shoulder, I spotted a woman genuflecting on the grass, her arms extended toward the sky. A stranger stumbled upon her and dropped to his knees, and they hugged. I closed my eyes, weirdly intoxicated by all the love going around.

"I almost got married," I whispered.

"When?"

"Last year in Vegas. To a stripper."

Nicole squeezed my hand still harder. "Don't worry. You can find happiness. I mean, it's not like you're gay or anything."

"My, that's comforting," I mumbled to myself. The warm glow of my Jesus buzz was fading fast and this place was starting to look seriously twisted. I suddenly realized I was kneeling in a field with fifty thousand strangers who had just begun singing Creed's "Higher" in eerie unison. I craned my head around and scanned the crowd in disbelief.

When I finally looked back toward Nicole, there were hands blocking my view. Big, tattooed hands. It was the alternapastor from the stage, piercings and all, reaching toward me for a laying-on of hands. Unfortunately, that was the moment my finely honed fight-or-flight instinct kicked in, and before I realized who he was I panicked, ducking and swerving away from the sudden threat. Once I got to my feet I stumbled a few feet back, then looked up to see the guy glaring at me. He had nothing on the people around me, though. I was getting looks of anger, reproach—and was that disgust? I realized immediately that for all these folks, being touched by the guy I'd just shunned was the next best thing to being touched by the hands of God himself. I started to sense anger in a couple of them. Which is when I started to laugh. This did not seem to help matters. I mean, I'm not immune to a little hero worship now and then. There are people I idolize beyond all reason, often despite their rampant douchery: Mick Jagger, Bono, Lady Gaga. But this guy? This cheap peddler of pseudorighteous Kool-Aid? This alterna-tard who couldn't handle the hard-partying life of real rock and roll and so decided to corrupt innocent young minds with this Jesus crap instead? How much was he getting paid tonight, anyway, to pretend to feel things SO FREAKING HARD? Suddenly I didn't feel like laughing anymore.

I caught Nicole's eyes as I backed farther away. Then I saw an echo of that same look she'd given me fifteen years earlier when I'd taken back the L-bomb, telling her what I'd *meant* to say was that I really loved her tits.

"Look, Nic, I should go. I have a lot of sinning I have to get to."

Bye, Dan, she mouthed, the sound lost in the crowd's roar as another band—Jars of Clay, maybe?—took the stage.

You're Saying I'm Conflicted?

The Sunday morning after I proposed to Alison I met up with Randy at our regular meeting place of the past few months. It's a gently rolling, semi-treed hunk of grass alongside the 101 freeway in Hollywood. When I rolled up he was sitting on a plastic lawn chair sunning himself, as were about two dozen other guys, all wearing bright-orange jumpsuits emblazoned with L.A. COUNTY DOC. Several had unzipped the suits to facilitate upper-body bronzing. Off to one side near two huge, matte-black Mad Max buses stood a group of shotgun-toting guards staring off into the center of the grassy knoll with their backs to Randy's group. I grabbed a bright red cooler out of the back of my 4Runner and wrestled it toward Randy, who came to help.

"You're late," Randy fumed.

"Good morning to you too," I said. "It's L.A. Nine means ten . . . and besides, some gratitude! Any of your other buddies ever show up so you ain't out here all alone with these murderous, raping bastards?"

"Nope. Just you, buddy." Randy smiled, grabbing a handle to help with the cooler. "And I doubt half these guys could rape their left fist. Most of them are stockbroker yuppies. The weekend DUI plea-bargain chain gang just ain't what it ought to be."

"What about the other half?"

"Regular Los Angeles County inmates on work release. Kill you as soon as fuck you."

"Great," I said. "Next time use my lawyer."

"Wouldn't help. I'm a third-time DUI offender in California, man. Even the child molesters look down on me. Easier to get off on an underage porn rap, although let's hope I never have to prove that."

"Don't even joke about that shit."

We put the cooler down and Randy dragged over two chairs. One of the largest black men I had ever seen—even bigger than Big Black in Vegas—walked over. "Hey, Shawshank," he said, digging a beer out of the cooler. "How's it goin'?"

"*Other*-half guy, I'm guessing?" I said as the man walked away with three Buds. Randy nodded. "I think so. His name's Titan. I'm afraid to make eye contact."

I sighed. "Life is shit. I feel like a goddamn floating piece of shit."

"Yeah," Randy said. "I got that from your fourth or fifth voicemail last night. If I'd been answering my phone instead of spending the night breaking commandments, I'd have told you that there's just one constant in the universe, and it's suffering, my friend. That's the wheel of life."

"Do tell."

"It was really stupid to propose at the strip club."

"Yeah, I'm a dick. I got cocky," I said glumly.

"Marriage and G-strings," Randy said, shaking his head. "They represent opposite sides of the human instinct—light and dark, yin and yang, Hall and Oates. It's always bad news, like when they mix matter and antimatter on *Star Trek*. Or like crossing the beams in *Ghost Busters*. Or like when Steve Martin had those two heads—"

"Got it!" I cut him off.

Randy quickly drained his first beer. "Best thing about drinking on community service is I know I've got a designated driver." He nodded toward the buses. "Hang on." He fished out two six-packs and walked over to the group of guards. They were staring into a dip in the grassy knoll where, amid relative privacy, two of the porn industry's finest young performers were re-creating their roles from *Phi Beta Lesbo*. Randy nudged one of the guards and handed him the beers, and wordlessly the six-pack made its way around the circle without any of them shifting their eyes from the girls.

A car zoomed by and a young guy hanging out the window screamed "Nice tits!" The car slowed until one of the guards waved it on with an abrupt but purposeful sweep of his shotgun.

"So, are you, like, upset about this Alison thing?" Randy asked. "Is it like 'my pet hamster died' upset, or 'my pet hamster was murdered by the local bully and he made me kiss its severed head on the playground' upset?" For a moment my thoughts turned to the girls on the grassy knoll. I wanted to say something clever, or maybe stupid, about the fact that the only litter-free piece of California Interstate was actually filthy. I wanted someone to laugh, even if they were laughing at how stupid my joke was. But right then everything seemed to lead inexorably back to The Problem. There didn't seem any point in delaying it.

"OK, it's the second one—it *does* kinda feel like the playground bully thing. I mean, Ali was perfect for me. Hot, smart, disease-free as of last month's test. Got together with other chicks. Knew the difference between a cock ring and my European wristwatch. I really blew it."

"Nah. It's karma, bro. You had this one coming," Randy said.

"Yeah, maybe. So you know what Alison told me right before she kicked me to the curb? She told me my dick suffers from attention deficit disorder."

This elicited barrel laughter from Randy. "You're a professional boozehound for *Playboy*! What did she expect? Your cock is not just a pleasure device, it's a divining rod."

"You should talk, porn czar," I countered.

"Sure, but I'm not dropping marriage offers around town like campaign buttons. You see, women are sharp; they can see my lack of internal conflict a mile off. *That* is what makes them want a taste of the Big Candy," Randy said.

"You're saying I'm conflicted?"

"I'm saying you drink a lot and you think with your dick. Women are going to want to have fun with you forever, but who wants to marry your shit?"

"Is that a yes?"

"If you want to settle down with someone there's a way you can totally do it, though."

"How?"

"Easy. Just stop being you."

"Lyceum"

CREATED BY ALLEN KATZ

1 1/2 oz. American rye whiskey

1/2 oz. cognac

1/2 oz. Yellow Chartreuse

3/4 oz. pear liqueur

2 dashes orange bitters

Orange peel

Shake ingredients over ice and strain into an Old Fashioned glass with one large ice cube. Garnish with a wide orange peel.

"If you are going to drink, well then, drink. This is a sturdy little number for the study, the library, the smoking room, the bathtub, wherever you care to entertain—the drink, that is.

"Dan's brilliant rules ('Don't shit where you eat') and other marked pieces of advice ('If you can't afford to tip, you can't afford to be here') are more than words to live by. They are words to nap by, at least while contemplating the ethics of Aristotle and the nature of human well-being.

"I imagine Dan wrote this chapter after research and contemplation at one or more of the nation's finest universities. These insights are of such value that you will want to immediately share them with your friends, workmates, and fathers-in-law. If you have fathers-in-law, pay particular attention to rule 3 under 'How to Not Ruin Your Life While Drinking.'"

—**ALLEN KATZ** is the director of mixology and spirits education for Southern Wine & Spirits of New York, the president of the New York chapter of the United States Bartenders' Guild, a lecturer, a consultant, and an all-around cocktail aficionado. He hangs out with Martha Stewart too, which is pretty cool.

TEN

I Used to Drink It with Quaaludes. The Vomit Was Technicolor.

The less fortunate, my grandma used to call them. Those folks whose grimy, impecunious fingers clung to rungs beneath ours on the economic ladder. Which is to say, homeless people and cockroaches. Because when I was growing up in northeast Philly, even the economic ladder we clung to was metaphorical. We couldn't afford a real one.

Still, for as bad as things were back then, Grandma never let us lose sight of the fact that the less fortunate were out there, hungry and tired and available for her to look down upon. Ah, bless her heart. She could always find the silver lining. Right up until the day she got hit by that bus on her way to Horn & Hardart for the $1.29 early bird special. Grandma never really was the same again after that. She stopped doing all those little grandmotherly things. Like breathing.

Now, I'm well aware that during the adorable little economic shitshow of the late aughts, the ranks of the less fortunate swelled to enormous proportions. Luckily this hasn't drastically affected my line of work. After all, when times are tough, do people stop drinking? No! If anything, they drink more! But they do start drinking cheaper, some turning to concoctions that, while cost-efficient, really have no business being put into the human body. On one particularly insolvent sunny afternoon in August 2009, even I, someone who drinks for a living and most definitely knows better, resorted to something called a White-Trash Russian. If you've yet to have the pleasure, this is a toxic combination of Bowman's Virginia vodka and Yoo-hoo that I'm almost certain did irreparable damage to my stomach lining and quite possibly my central nervous system. Seriously, I walked with a limp and talked with a Southern accent for several weeks before I was right again. Then again, it did the job. I got so fucked up that for an entire six hours I forgot how broke my ass was.

But it got me to thinking—is there such a thing as a "good" poor man's cocktail? Surely not every cheap drink out there tastes like Sterno and makes you piss blood, right? When I see guys in tank tops drinking out of Styrofoam cups while munching on pigs in a blanket and cheese puffs at the local municipal park on Saturday afternoon, they look so goddamn happy. What's in those cups?

I knew of a few varieties. The Poor Man's Margarita—tequila and Squirt—is a popular one out West. And in some Eastern cities, large parties of paupers used to get by on Purple Passions—Welch's grape juice and grain alcohol. But then I heard that Blue Lagoons—whatever that blue sports drink crap is, plus grain alcohol—was becoming the budget beverage of choice in some circles. I've also heard that some folks in Denver mix up the delightfully named concoction Pee in a Cup—Mountain Dew and vodka (or Everclear), served warm for verisimilitude, of course. Some of the curb-sitters in my old neighborhood in Philadelphia used to specialize in what was known as the Colt Python (which delivers a wallop similar to that of its eponymous handgun) by adding a few shots of whatever cheap whiskey was on sale at the state store to a half quart of Colt 45 malt liquor. Then, naturally, there's the mecca for white trash everywhere, the Jersey Shore. My brother Brian used to go to parties "down the Shore" that served Skippies. These are made by stirring up a bottle of rotgut vodka, a case of Natural Light, and lemonade mix in a trash can or beer tub with ice. Add fake tan and stupidity and you've got yourself a party.

Sound strategies, all. But I wanted even more options, so I put out a query to my network of alcohol operatives.

Terry Sullivan, who penned *GQ*'s "Mixology" column for years, back when it counted, reported that cash-strapped drunks in Chicago swear by Muddy Bottoms, a potent combination of Green River "gourmet" soda and cheap bourbon.

Ashley Perkins out in Salt Lake City told me she loves her some Trailer Park Sangria. "Buy the cheapest box of red wine available," she instructed. "Some places even take Food Stamps. Drink some wine to make room in the box. Add grape juice." Smooth.

Playboy's former assistant editor Rocky Rakovic said his favorite cheap drink is the Pabst-Smir, "a shot of Smirnoff dropped into a glass of Pabst." Bear in mind, however, that he was quick to warn me: "You can't drop your own shot; someone else needs to 'administer' it to you." You stay classy, Rock.

Ashley Rodgers from Culver City, California, is of the opinion (and I'm not going to say she's wrong) that a pint of Popov vodka and a Slurpee get the job done.

And don't challenge Carole Parker from Marina Del Rey to a drinking contest anytime soon. Her broke-ass hooch of choice? Grape-flavored Boone's Farm. "I used to drink it with quaaludes," she said. "The vomit was Technicolor." Thanks for sharing, Carole!

Once I'd gathered enough intelligence (or rather, lack thereof), I did my own reconnaissance mission. I hit the liquor store closest to my house, Davey Jones Liquor Locker in Venice Beach, which isn't so much a final resting place for dead seamen as it is the killing fields for homeless people's livers. Vlad behind the counter told me the cheapest drunk in the store was a tie between a pint of Popov vodka (way to call it, Ashley Rodgers!) and an abomination called Kessler American Blended Whiskey, which bills itself as "Smooth as Silk." I'd venture it's more of a silk-burlap blend. In the interest of science (and because they were only five dollars a pop), I bought them both. However, after some brief experiments with the Kessler, I lost all interest in science and instead became fascinated by something written on the side of the bottle of Popov: NOW! UNBREAKABLE BOTTLE. Seems like a handy trait in a product that makes people lose the coordination required to carry things. Plus, I like the sense of urgency generated by the caps and the exclamation point. It's as if they're daring you not to start drinking as soon as you hit the parking lot. In my lubricated state, however, I saw this less as a service to the consumer than as a prideful boast. Which is how I ended up dropping a bottle of Popov off my fourth-story balcony. And why the cops now know where I live. Which is how I came to make a video in which I dropped a NOW! Unbreakable Bottle of Popov off a four-story building. Check it out on YouTube. And what's my handle again? You got it—thefunhog. Amazingly enough, however, while the Popov did lose structural integrity in the fall, let's just say it'll break you before you break it.

And so, impoverished boozehounds, remember, there's always hope. It's just that hope is trying to get out from under a bad mortgage, so it's going by an assumed name these days. The clever alias? Popov vodka. Sure, it may not be as invincible as the fancy happy juice—I once heard about a case of Ketel One that survived an airplane crash—but at least you can rest easy knowing that even if you do manage to break a plastic bottle of Popov, you can still drink out of it without fear of slicing up your small intestine with shards of glass. How's that for a silver lining, Grandma? So call me less fortunate if you will. Hell, call me anything you'd like. I won't be listening. Because I'm pretty sure the Popov made me go deaf.

If You're Drinking to Forget, Please Pay in Advance

Say what you will about the classlessness of the above, about its buzz-at-any-cost mentality, but it's how a lot of people drink in the real world. And this is one of those uncomfortable facts usually conveniently overlooked by people in my trade. We booze journalists like to tell ourselves that we're arbiters of some kind of high-minded gourmet sensibility because we explore and elucidate, say, the subtle distinction between strains of yeast used in malt fermentation or the sophisticated chemistry of how to infuse flavors into recipes. But the truth is the only reason we write about the good stuff is because rich people like to get fucked-up on the good stuff, and they need someone to tell them about it. Most people, however, will settle for just getting fucked-up. And the place I learned the most about people just wanting to get fucked-up was P&J's, the Philly joint my dad used to take me to when I was seven.

I had plenty of time to learn, because while technically my old man and I went there together, we didn't get much in the way of quality time, at least not once we got inside. See, booze was always hanging out there, and Dad had been friends with booze a lot longer than he'd known me. So they'd talk for a while, privately. And I never knew what kind of mood he'd be in afterward. Best to steer clear just in case. Then after a little while booze would usually meet some chicks and introduce them to Dad, and they'd all start talking. I sure as shit knew not to interrupt him then. It sounds bad, but looking back on it now, I can't honestly blame him for all this. Dad was young and single and had a drinking problem. What else was a guy like that expected to do in a bar except drink and hit on women? The geniuses among you might point out that he might have started by not taking his kid to the bar every day, but I honestly think it didn't occur to him not to. Anyway, I don't believe I suffered much as a result of his actions. If anything, his questionable behavior taught me to be independent—and gave me some of the best pick-up moves in my repertoire. Plus, him being preoccupied with Jack Daniel's and Jane Doe simply meant I got to spend more time with Tall Paul.

Tall Paul was the P in P&J's—the owner, head bartender, and karmic standard-bearer of the establishment. He was a 6'7", 250-pound behemoth renowned for his kind, humorous nature and large, sledgehammer-like fists. He was a teddy bear most of the time, but woe be to troublemakers who attempted to make their trouble in his joint. Because if tempers flared and reconciliation failed, Tall Paul could kick the living shit out of anyone this side of Superman. To me, though, he was a gentle and benevolent giant who always made sure my glass was filled with Coke and that I never ran out of change for the pinball machine. He even gave me my very own extra-tall stool so I could see over the tops of the pool and shuffleboard tables. Kept it safely stored behind the giant barrel of pretzel mix, next to the men's bathroom. I used to live on that pretzel mix—until the day I witnessed a grubby old degenerate exit the bathroom without bothering to wash his hands after taking a crap, then plunge his grubby shit-digits into the beloved barrel. From that moment on, at P&J's I subsisted wholly on bags of pork rinds and Munchos.

What I remember most about Tall Paul—and the thing for which I am most indebted to him—is that he introduced me to a bar's most mysterious and magical space, the bar itself. Behind the stick. The holiest of holies. There he laid the foundation for much of what would come to matter most to me later in life, and indeed for the book you hold in your hands right now.

It wasn't playtime back there, mind you. Tall Paul wouldn't stand for anyone playing grabass behind his bar. It was a place where serious work got done, and he taught me how to do it too. He showed me how to make screwdrivers, Bloody Marys, and Rusty Nails. Actual drinks that were served to actual people who tipped me actual currency (usually only a dime but, hey, back then that was two credits on the pinball machine). It was my first summer internship, and it was beyond kick-ass. So what that my dad was too busy getting lit or trying to get laid to pay attention to me? I was the only seven-year-old in the entire neighborhood who knew how to clear beer lines and change a keg. You think that woman-stealer Timmy McFadden understood what it meant when someone ordered from the top shelf instead of the well? Or what the letters on the soda gun stood for? Or that a plastic shot cup turned upside down in front of a customer at the bar meant Tall Paul was buying his next round? Other kids my age were planted in front of TVs watching *Tom & Jerry* reruns while I was slinging gin and learning invaluable lessons about commerce, toxicology, and the oeuvres of Led Zeppelin, Rod Stewart, and Thin Lizzy.

But I think the most important things I learned in P&J's had to do with self-discipline and personal responsibility. Some of this came from watching the way people acted in there, and what happened to them when they abdicated the above. But much of what I surmised about how you should act in a bar came courtesy of a weathered set of handwritten rules tacked to the wall, right next to a framed photo of John F. Kennedy. I can still recite them verbatim.

P&J's Rules of Behavior

(Note: The following rules are nonnegotiable, unless your idea of a negotiation is getting knocked upside the head. In which case, feel free to consult the management.)

1) If you can't afford to tip, you can't afford to be here.

2) Your bartender is not afraid to stomp you into tomorrow. As a reminder, he is armed and sober. Soberer than you, anyway.

3) If we see you arguing with inanimate objects, you're cut off.

4) Men: No shoes, no shirt, no service.

5) Women: No shoes, no shirt, free drinks.

6) Pricing for fielding calls from wives:
"Just left"	$1
"Not here"	$2
"Haven't seen him all day"	$5

7) If you're drinking to forget, please pay in advance.

8) No swearing. Unless you're swearing to buy the next god-damn round.

9) P&J's does not serve women. You need to bring your own.

10) Don't put any shit in the toilet besides shit.

11) If you reach behind the bar, be prepared to lose an arm.

12) P&J's closes at 2 a.m. sharp every day, unless we close early or stay open late.

13) No dogs on the bar.

14) We reserve the right to refuse service to Cowboys fans.

Sadly, the visits to P&J's with my dad ended abruptly after my mother was released from the mental institution. Well-meaning relatives had told me she'd gone to a farm to get some rest for a few months. Apparently failing to kill yourself is immensely tiring. When she learned my dad had been taking me to a bar most days she seemed to recover her energy, going after him with a frying pan in front of our apartment building. I didn't see my dad for a few years after that.

But I did see booze. That guy still hung out at P&J's even though Dad didn't. I wandered by the bar pretty regularly for a few weeks after the summer ended. I never got up the nerve to go inside without my old man, though. I just waited out on the curb, watching people come and go, always hoping the door would swing open and Tall Paul would be standing there, smiling, with a roll of dimes in one hand and a glass of Coke in the other.

"Come on in, Little Dunn," he'd say. "Where the hell you been?"

I have a feeling that my experiences at P&J's that summer were what led me on my chosen path. They're certainly why I pride myself on not just being a student of the glorious pleasures of liquor, wine, and beer, but also a student of bars and the culture of drinking. And also why I love me some bartenders. Especially when they create custom drinks to go along with each chapter of one of my books. Anyway, in my extensive studies in bar culture, I have determined that there are eleven specific kinds of bars in the world. I call them the Eleven Barchetypes. And it's time for me to tell you about them.

Notes Toward an Ontological Exploration of the Eleven Barchetypes and the Flora and Fauna Found Therein

1. The Neighborhood Dive

If you look this one up in the dictionary, the definition actually just has a picture of P&J's next to it. The neighborhood dive is a no-frills joint owned and operated by a native son with a name like Sully or Mac (or Tall Paul). These bars are open every day from six a.m. till two a.m. (four a.m. in New York) and cater to a tightly knit, fiercely loyal clientele that revel in the camaraderie, cheap drinks, and proximity to home. Beyond being a temple of worship for local sports franchises, a neighborhood dive doesn't purport to have a "concept" or "theme" (they may serve food there, but you can be damn sure none of the regulars has ever referred to it as a "gastropub"). They don't need one. With the possible exception of replacing a worn-out dartboard or updating the jukebox selections every decade or so, neighborhood dives don't keep up with the times. They are enduring reminders that the more things change, the more working-class drinkers remain the same. It's poetic, really.

2. The Pub

Pubs differ from dive bars in that they're usually larger, cleaner, and more tourist-friendly (and when I say tourist, I mean anyone who didn't grow up within a three-block radius of the place). They tend to be cozy spots where a lot of drinking still gets done, but you're far less likely to see someone projectile vomit on their wife, get beat up by a teamster, collapse and die of liver failure, or put their shit-digits in the pretzel barrel. Most pubs offer good beer, reasonably priced drinks, and greasy cheeseburgers that taste awesome after midnight. The Cool People to Total Jagoff ratio in these places tends to hover around 10-to-1. Disregard this ratio, however, if said pub has a karaoke night. In this case the ratio reverses. In the unfortunate event of a karaoke night, you may actually want to consider downgrading this place's rating from a Pub to a Plastic Bar (see #8).

3. The High-Concept Bar

These are built upon a central idea that is sometimes clever but more often tiresome once the novelty has worn off (usually takes about a week). Such places can only exist in major metropolitan areas like New York, L.A., and Paris, where there's an ample supply of tourists looking for expensive thrills, or arrogant twits who believe they're more sophisticated than the average beer-swilling Philistine and feel the need to prove it by embracing the latest in nightlife novelties. For example, I was once dragged by a publicist—against my will, of course—to the Ice Kube Bar in Paris where, for somewhere in the neighborhood of seventy-five dollars, I got to dress up like an arctic explorer and spend twenty minutes doing Grey Goose shooters inside a bleak frozen chamber made entirely of ice. The publicist maintained that freezing my dick off just to catch a buzz was an "authentic experience like no other." Funny, it seemed an awful lot like another experience called "homeless in winter," only a hell of a lot more expensive.

While there are plenty of examples of the high-concept bar gone wrong (like the Hobbit House, a freaky Tolkien-themed joint in Manila staffed by midgets decked out like Bilbo Baggins), I will admit that there is a high-concept bar here and there that is just too crazy and original to be dismissed as a mere gimmick. For instance, the Skeleton Bar in Gruyère, Switzerland (yes, where the cheese comes from), is a magnificent, otherworldly boneyard designed by H. R. Giger, the guy who won an Oscar for production design on *Alien* and also conceived the highly controversial Dead Kennedys album cover for *Frankenchrist*. That was genius. Similarly, there's something delightfully twisted about sitting in a wheelchair sucking cocktails out of IV bags, which is precisely what goes down nightly at the Clinic Bar in downtown Singapore. And while I've not been there myself, I hear the vodka martinis at the coffin-shaped Eternity Bar in Truskavts, Ukraine, are to die for. But for every Skeleton Bar, there are ten Rodeo Bars and ten Waikiki Wally's. The bottom line is, when in doubt, stay the fuck away.

4. *The Hotel Bar*

These come in many shapes and sizes, but have one defining characteristic that unites them: Hotel bars are always located within stumbling distance of a bedroom. And that means possibilities. Not all of them good ones.

5. *The Vertically Challenged Bar*

Not just physically, of course. I'm also speaking demographically here. These bars—all located more than six feet under—cater to a specific clientele, i.e., bikers, leather enthusiasts, oenophiles, fur-wearers, midgets, furry midgets . . . oh, and fans of eighties synth-pop bands. Once, while in the Estonian capital city of Tallinn, I went to a subterranean watering hole called the DM Baar that is devoted entirely to the musical stylings of Depeche Mode. "I Just Can't Get Enough," indeed. That sentiment was put to the test at the DM Baar. To get an idea of what I mean (without trekking to northern Europe), try holing up with a group of people in a dark basement with copious amounts of vodka while *Songs of Faith and Devotion* plays on perpetual loop at high volume. When will someone snap? Turns out, if you're part of the regular clientele, never. If you're a lonely, horny, vodka-soaked booze journalist dicking around Eastern Europe, however, the answer is thirteen minutes and fifty-three seconds. I seriously considered calling the consulate and ordering a daisy cutter strike just to be sure we stopped the infection before it could spread.

6. The Full-of-Itself Bar

I hesitated before including this category because, depending on your point of view, you could potentially put this in with the Vertically Challenged Bars. But these are bars aimed at that vertical slice of humanity that enjoys liquor, and that makes them special. And when they go wrong, it makes them especially odious. Plus, there are too many of them around these days to ignore. I'm talking about the bars that purport to bring a science and purism to the creation of cocktails. Places that always refer to bartending as "mixology" and have no compunction about charging you fifteen to twenty dollars per drink. Some of the best known are New York's Death & Co., L.A.'s The Edison, San Francisco's Bourbon & Branch, and Chicago's Violet Hour. Listen, I have nothing against keeping tradition alive or making authentic cocktails. And many of these places (including the ones mentioned earlier) are wonderful if you can afford them. But it's extremely easy for spots like this to veer off the rails. And the last thing you want when you're trying to enjoy a relaxing drink is either smug superiority from the bartender or a member of the waitstaff insisting on telling you about the fair-trade origin of the drink's agave syrup. Shut the hell up and get me my drink. And turn off the fucking lounge music. And get me a comfortable chair.

7. The Nostalgia Bar

These are old-timey bars that serve classic cocktails of yesteryear (nary an appletini in sight, I assure you) and display tattered black-and-white photos and yellowing newspaper articles on the walls. I'll put it another way: If there's any place you can get away with wearing a fedora unironically, the nostalgia bar is it. My editor at *Playboy* has my eternal gratitude for not only putting up with me for this long, but also for introducing me to what is thought to be the world's first nostalgia bar, Bill's Gay Nineties on East Fifty-fourth Street in New York. Founded during Prohibition as a speakeasy, Bill's pays homage to the so-called gay 1890s, a time when alcohol enthusiasts were reported to have had an ass-pounding amount of fun hanging out in bars. Hence the name that makes my editor's wife look twice every time it shows up on his credit card bill. Not that there's anything wrong with that.

8. The Plastic Bar

My friends and I call these Karl Rove bars. Which is to say, these places have no soul. You might know them as fern bars, or yuppie bars, or "that place with the frozen daiquiri machine." But while they may not have authenticity on their side, they do have booze, so let's not get too hung up on technicalities. Treat your plastic bar the same way you'd treat a museum exhibit. Speak softly, don't touch anything, and leave as quickly as possible. You may have sex with things you find inside the plastic bar, but only once.

9. The Strip Club

Ah, where to begin? Mandatory two-drink minimums for watered-down cocktails in plastic shotglasses at fifteen dollars a pop. Or twenty-dollar glasses of fruit punch masquerading as mai tais that you're obliged to buy the stripper who's charging you twenty more for every three minutes of grinding robotically on your lap to some of the most awful music ever recorded. Throw in all manner of creeps, pimps, punks, and skanks, and what do you have? A multibillion-dollar industry that generates more money per year than theatre, opera, ballet, jazz, and classical music concerts combined. And thank fucking Christ for that too, 'cause a world in which more people would pay to see an anorexic perform a pirouette than a ripe pair of tits is not a world I want to live in.

10. The Live Music Joint

These places barely qualify as bars because trying to order a drink is a lot like trying to secure a bowl of gruel in a Calcutta soup kitchen. Be prepared to hold your own against a crush of sweaty, alcohol-starved humanity. Then there's the aural assault that is the experimental ragecore quartet (who are always friends of the friend who dragged you there), or the fucking Converse-wearing indie-rock fans who get more annoying by the second once you're over the age of thirty. Oh, and make sure you bring throat lozenges, as you'll be screaming "WHAT?" at the top of your lungs most of the evening, not just because the music is loud but because the only thing fewer people do than actually get a drink at a live music joint is shut up and pay attention to the music. Last, if you must endure this pointless exercise in feigned hipness, do not wear open-toed shoes. Especially if you plan on using the bathroom.

11. The Sports Bar

In addition to being the barchetype responsible for the second-highest number of divorces, sports bars are also a factor in a large number of DUI arrests, full-scale brawls, illegal gambling rings, and chicken-wing choking incidents. As a result, men can't seem to get enough of these places. This is because men, while occasionally cute and cuddly, are complete assholes most of the time. And with the exception of a few really raunchy sex clubs, there's nowhere a man can tap into his inner asshole more completely than a place where the menus are shaped liked goalie masks and feature meals named after ballparks and Heisman Trophy winners. Though, to be fair, I have to admit that I once had a transcendent dining experience at a Hooters in South Florida—though I have a suspicion that it owes something to the fact that the Eagles were winning against the Giants in a divisional round play-off game, and that our waitress Sandra insisted on sitting in my lap every time she came to check that we had enough beer. It's possible those things made me elevate my pasta testaverde with marinara sauce and peppers to legendary status. But Mamma mia, what a meal!

Learn how to handle these eleven types of joints and you can get drunk in any city in the world. But while we're on the topic, I will point out an anomaly I've noticed. By any credible metric, New York is one of the top two or three drinking towns on the planet. This is a place that has every barchetype in the world, plus some genetically mutated hybrids. Want to choose from a selection of more than two hundred vodkas while eating greasy cheeseburgers in a hotel lobby? New York's got you covered. Or maybe you'd rather sip a Pink Lady while getting your nails done beneath a vintage chrome-dome hair dryer—no problem. If you're more in a mood to drink Burgundy out of baby bottles while eating fondue, that can also be arranged.

But New York's drinking life does have a flaw: sports bars, or rather, the lack thereof. Sure, there are plenty of cozy joints where you can knock back cheap drinks and watch the Yankees win, the Knicks lose, and the Rangers play that funny sport on the ice with sticks (curling, is it?). Those exist, and they're lovely. In fact, if I had to choose a city outside Europe in which to watch a soccer match, NYC is head and shoulders above the competition. But I'm talking about the modern sports bar, those expansive palaces of beer and sweat with high-def flat-screens everywhere you turn blaring every sporting event in the western world, as well as a few pretenders (I'm looking at you, cricket). In these, the Big Apple is sorely lacking. And no, the ESPN Zone does not count. Any activity that makes you enter the soulless hellhole Times Square has become comes at too high a price for this particular imbiber.

Then, like a visitation from an angel, in the fall of 2009, New York got the Ainsworth—a six-thousand-square-foot pleasure palace in Chelsea that boasts more TVs than a Best Buy show-room. The folks who own the place will tell you the Ainsworth isn't so much a sports bar as it is a gastropub that caters to sports enthusiasts. You say tomato, I say it's a fucking sports bar . . . an upscale one, sure, with its rustic-chic décor and pork chops drizzled with apple chutney and a balsamic reduction, but it's a sports bar nonetheless. It's the best place I've found in the city to watch virtually any sport and any team at any time . . . like my beloved Phillies.

The problem is, in addition to its TV collection, the Ainsworth (which sits at 122 West Twenty-sixth Street, between Sixth and Seventh avenues) also has one of the sexiest bar and waitstaffs in Manhattan. Why is that a problem? Because at the very goddamn top of my ironclad laws of how not to ruin your life while drinking (which we'll get to in a later chapter) is "Don't shit where you eat." And by "shit" I mean "have or attempt to have sexual relations with the staff," and by "eat" I mean "get drunk and eat chutney pork chops and watch the Phillies."

The awful truth is that putting the moves on a waitress at your favorite bar never, ever works out in your favor. Ever. As a mistake, I'd rank it up alongside such drinking no-no's as getting behind the wheel of a car or singing karaoke. If it doesn't go south out of the gate, the chances are stacked astronomically against you that things will work out in the long term. Partly because even good relationships have hard times. And where do you go when your relationship is having a hard time? Your favorite bar! Where the Phillies play! And where you can eat balsamic-drenched pig. Whether it's your shame reflex, the management, or a restraining order, bang a waitress at your favorite spot and you can kiss your little sanctuary good-bye. Now, I'll admit that my life revolves around drinking more than most, but for me, losing a favorite bar is like losing a great friend.

And if there's one thing in this life you should hold on to with all your might, it's a great friend. I overheard Tall Paul tell my dad that once at P&J's. And my dad said he couldn't agree more—you never want to lose a great friend. And I recall feeling really, really happy then, because I was sure they were talking about me.

"Buck Naked"

CREATED BY TONY ABOU-GANIM

3 oz. white wine (a sexy white with floral notes and
essence of honey, peaches, and freshly cut grass)

1 1/2 oz. Belvedere citrus vodka

1/2 oz. Aperol Aperitivo

1/2 oz. St-Germain elderflower liqueur

1 oz. freshly squeezed lemon juice

1/2 oz. simple syrup, to taste

Chilled seltzer water

Orange and lemon spirals, for garnish

Shake above ingredients over ice until well blended. Strain into an ice-filled Collins glass. Spritz with chilled seltzer. Garnish with spirals of orange and lemon, and serve with a swizzle stick.

"It seems that it is always the simplest indulgences that bring us the greatest pleasure: a wonderful meal shared with friends and family; a great glass of wine, or in my case a brilliant Negroni; a walk on the beach; and amazing sex. When someone is passionate about cooking, crafting a cocktail, making wine, or having great sex, that experience is thus elevated. It is this passion, when shared with others, that makes one's day a little brighter and much more fulfilled . . . simply.

"I created the Buck Naked to bring together the passion of

each; the craft of the winemaker and the creativity of the mixologist, inspired by the art of the porn star. This refreshing tipple doesn't pretend to be anything more than what it is: a stimulating aperitif before a festive meal, a quenching draft on a balmy afternoon, or a restorative bracer after some rousing sex—just a little pleasure, plain and simple. Cheers and happiness!"

—**TONY ABOU-GANIM** of TheModernMixologist.com has spent the past thirty years of his life behind bars, and has had a splendid time doing so. He is the author of the book *The Modern Mixologist—Contemporary Classic Cocktails*. He lives in Las Vegas, where he strives daily to achieve the perfect cocktail experience.

ELEVEN

The Most Delicious Women and Dessert Wines I've Ever Had Have One Thing in Common

One of the best assignments I've ever had as a booze writer was a piece I did on Savanna Samson. You may be familiar with part of Savanna's work—probably the part that has to do with her being one of the world's biggest porn stars. But in recent years she's begun to explore a different area of passion: winemaking. My assignment? Figure out if she's the real deal (as a winemaker, that is—her porn credentials are unassailable) and write about the experience. My research for this basically entailed drinking a lot of wine with a gorgeous and notoriously sexually voracious celebrity and talking fermented grape juice. I was a wee bit excited. Kind of like a kid in a candy store. If candy stores had giant, gorgeous tits in the window and a serious case of fuck-me eyes.

And if that weren't enough, she makes wine. Better yet, she makes *good* wine. When she first launched her wine project back in 2005, Savanna told me she fully expected to get bent over a barrel by skeptics. But before the purists and prudes could pounce, her debut release, Sogno Uno, received a ringing endorsement from none other than Robert Parker. Parker is the single most influential wine critic in the world, and while he declined to weigh in on her cinematic achievements, he felt that what she was putting in bottles was nothing short of astounding. He gave Sogno Uno a 91. And this man does not mess around when it comes to wine. Scoring above a 90 with him is considered a major achievement.

When I arrived at Savanna's spacious yet homey New York City apartment, I found her dressed not as a dominatrix and with nary any latex or ten-inch clear heels in sight, but rather barefoot in black sweats with a long-sleeved paisley T-shirt and her hair up in a ponytail. At that moment I realized how small a corner I had unconsciously painted her into. This was no tweaked-out freak of nature. In fact, she looked downright girl-next-door adorable. I felt more churlish than usual (which is saying something) when it dawned on me that this woman, who had been the featured player in so many of my own fantasies, was a real, flesh-and-blood person with a job, a life, an apartment. And a name. Natalie. Natalie is someone's sister and daughter and girlfriend. She has friends she's known since high school, most of whom work nine-to-five jobs. And apparently a kid, judging by the toys that were strewn about the place (and not the kind you'd find in her movies).

But just as I was getting used to her being a regular chick, in short order she proceeded to punch me in my mind again, when over a bottle of Krug Grande Cuvée she held forth on the physical logistics of both gangbangs and pop shots. I made a mental note to call my therapist.

Stretched out on an oversized love seat sucking down Champagne like ... well, like porn stars, if you must know, Savanna and I chatted about everything from her apparently perfectly normal childhood in upstate New York to her favorite sexual positions both on and off camera. (Note: This is the conversation where I finally, at long last, got confirmation that there *are* women—at least one anyway—who actually prefer anal.) Then, once the Krug was drained, she let her hair down (literally) and threw on a pair of jeans, and we made our way over to Les Halles, the cozy Park Avenue brasserie where celeb chef Anthony Bourdain worked before his books and TV shows turned him into the Sid Vicious of the culinary world. There, more expensive wine was consumed (on the company dime, of course—thanks, Hef!), and we really got down to the business at hand—discussing the ins and outs of pairing wine with sex.

This is when she started saying things like "When I'm working with a big guy, I like to have a glass of wine of equal stature on set." But when she followed up with specific details about her favored vintages, it became clear she'd put in a whole lot of time spitting in a bucket (the reader is encouraged to make up their own joke here, and then take a long look in the mirror and ask themselves how much their own jobs have in common with a porn shoot). Turns out a Ridge Monte Bello or Binomio from LaValentina pairs nicely with a well-endowed fellow. Solid choices.

About three vintages later, the talk, perhaps inevitably, turned to girl-on-girl sex. This is when Savanna revealed that sapphic action goes best with Moscato d'Asti, an Italian sparkling wine that's (appropriately) a kissing cousin of Asti Spumante. It's a dessert wine: light, feminine, bubbly, and delicately sweet. She told me her favorite bottle is Michele Chiarlo Nivole Moscato d'Asti, adding that "The most delicious women and dessert wines I've ever had have one thing in common: They taste like peaches." For some reason I was suddenly having trouble concentrating. But it was OK. My tape was running, and Savanna was essentially writing the article for me.

She proved no less knowledgeable when talk turned to cellaring. Apparently, the life cycle of a wine has much in common with the career of an adult-film star. "Young porn stars can be pretty volatile. They definitely need to be handled with care," she opined. "Sure, they're hot shit when they first arrive on the scene, but most aren't worth keeping around to see what they'll do a few years down the line. But if you know how to spot them, those rare few that age well end up doing spectacular things." To illustrate, she cited the career of Cara Lott, a fixture on the porn scene in the early eighties, who made a successful comeback in the aughts headlining MILF flicks. It seems that for porn stars, as with wine, "a little seasoning can be a very good thing."

My head was swimming. But Savanna was having the time of her life. This was no tragedy case right out of central casting, playing the real-life role of "troubled eighteen-year-old from Iowa with a bus ticket and a dream lands in L.A. and finds out the hard way about how the world works." Savanna was smart, funny, and in control, and one thing was for sure—this girl knew her wines.

At about this point I tuned in to the two middle-aged women at the table next to us. From their disapproving looks I gathered our conversational topics weren't quite their cup of rough sex. Savanna noticed too, and decided to have a little fun with them.

"When was the last time you had a big cock up your ass?" she asked loudly.

"Last week," I replied. "Total pain in the butt."

"Would you like to stick your cock in *my* ass?" Savanna asked gamely, causing one of the women to make frantic check-requesting motions at the bewildered, out-of-earshot waiter.

"Are you kidding me?" I replied. "I'm always looking for good stories I can tell my grandkids." I simultaneously wished Savanna wouldn't see how much I really would like to actually do this to her, and hoped that she was seriously considering letting me.

Thankfully for my blood pressure, the conversation cooled after the two biddies hustled out, shooting all manner of dirty looks at us as they did so. "Don't mind them," Savanna admonished. "They're just jealous. They can't handle fun. Or freedom. A good drink and a rousing fuck would sort them right out. They're living by somebody else's rules. And once you start doing that, you start dying." I could feel myself falling in love again. I wondered if Savanna had any interest in relocating to the West Coast.

As I walked her back to her apartment, she reminisced about one of the defining moments in her dual career. "I was once at a porn-industry event where a major director told me he thought I had the best on-screen presence he'd ever seen. Later that night, my then boyfriend tried my wine for the first time. He poured it down my chest while I sat on his face. We ruined a set of my really nice sheets. And it was worth every penny it cost to replace them. You only get to run around the world once; you gotta make it count."

I was inclined to believe her.

When the Savanna feature appeared in *Playboy*, it garnered more attention than anything I'd written for the magazine before or since. It got picked up by a number of media outlets and I was interviewed about it on several radio and television programs. I even ended up creating a tasting flight for a local

Santa Monica tasting room, Pourtal, that paired wine with *Playboy* Playmates. No one seemed to mind that I wasn't actually a capital-E expert on wine. Like Tall Paul taught me: If you can't be right, be funny. If you can't be funny, have tits. To be safe, I tried to be funny *and* have tits. Which is how I ended up comparing the Rocca Family Vineyards Bad Boy Red to Pamela Anderson, and the length of its finish to Tommy Lee's . . . well, you've seen their home video, right?

Long story short, I almost lost my *Playboy* column over that one. But the way I see it, the entire experience was an exercise in remembering that wine is supposed to be fun. Once you start learning about wine it's really easy to get lost in the solemnity and complexity. And the minute you do that, you lose (as does everybody who has to listen to you).

Truth is, wine appreciation is so airy and complicated, you can do a pairing with just about anything and people will buy it. Like porn. But as Savanna taught me, the similarities don't end there. Just watch . . .

Porn and Wine: An Evening of Daring Pairing

First up, we have a 1945 Mouton-Rothschild. We've paired it with *Deep Throat*, a 1972 vintage. Gerard Damiano's most famous film celebrates the life of a woman whose clitoris has migrated to her esophagus, and chronicles all the men (including the inimitable Harry Reems) who help accommodate her unconventional anatomy. The 1945 Mouton-Rothschild is likely to produce similarly orgasmic results in the back of one's throat. Alas, like women with hirsute nether-regions who can get off by giving head, this stunning, drinkable sixty-five-year-old vintage is a very rare bird (a swallow, perhaps?) indeed.

From there we move on to a 1992 Screaming Eagle, which we paired with the 1978 megahit *Debbie Does Dallas*. When the perky, pom-pom waving co-ed played by Bambi Woods made this film an instant classic, we all expected to see much more of her. But despite her immense popularity, the enigmatic Ms. Woods appeared in a grand total of four adult films. Similarly, the Screaming Eagle scored an unheard-of 99 from Robert Parker, yet only 225 cases of the esteemed Oakville cabernet were ever made. As a result, you won't find a bottle for less than five figures. (But at least you can buy some if you really want to. Ms. Woods is, unfortunately, off the market for good.)

In this portion of the program, we confront a monster, Guigal Côte-Rôtie 1978 la Landonne, Guigal's first vintage of this cru. We've paired this sinfully delicious bottle with *The Devil in Miss Jones*, in which the irrepressible Georgina Spelvin attempts to "earn" her way into hell by engaging that horny old dog Lucifer in all manner of deviant sexual behavior. The connection between these two legendary vices is tenuous, but it's a well-established fact that this far into any tasting, most people have stopped paying attention entirely, so one can really say anything one likes. Plus, when you've got vintage wine in the glass and golden-age porn on the telly, there's no sense sweating the details.

Our final combination pairs one of porn's most delicious vintages, 1972's *Behind the Green Door*, with an equally classic bottle of 1973 Chateau Montelena. In the film, the savvy/sleazy Mitchell Brothers (of San Francisco's O'Farrell Theatre fame) introduce a fresh face to the wank-happy masses. And we do mean fresh—as in 99 and 44/100% pure, just like the Chateau Montelena. Indeed, Marilyn Chambers (formerly Marilyn Ann Briggs) was the Ivory Soap cover girl before she decided to give pornography a whirl. Obviously, the folks at Procter & Gamble were none too pleased. But the ensuing brouhaha helped make Chambers and the film an international sensation, with

Green Door going on to gross more than $20 million. In the wine world, the Chateau Montelena created an equally massive and unexpected stir when it won the Judgment of Paris in 1976, helping establish California wine's bona fides and wresting winemaking hegemony from European producers.

Big Enough's Not Going to Cut It

A week or so after my article on porn/wine pairings hit newsstands, *Playboy* flew Savanna out to L.A. so that she and I could appear in a Playboy TV segment in which she got naked and flirty and I tried my best not to appear too flustered. After the taping we went back to her hotel, the Roosevelt on Hollywood Boulevard, and got pissed as farts in the hotel bar. Eventually we wound up in her room. And here's where I wish to all fucking hell that the story *really* got good. Only it doesn't. I'm normally not in the habit of choking on the finish line, but that's exactly what I did. Instead of making a move, instead of bringing any kind of game *whatsoever*, I just sat there like a lump on a chair, conducting the following agonizing dialogue in my mind as she stretched out seductively on the bed.

> *Just climb into bed with her and have a go right now.*
>
> *No, man, I need to keep things professional between the two of us. I'm a journalist, and she's my subject.*
>
> *Professional? You're both fucking wasted and she invited you up to her hotel room.*
>
> *Maybe she's just being nice.*
>
> *Nice? She's a porn star! Porn star! Hotel room! Hotel room! Porn star! Gah!*

What's that supposed to mean? You can't just automatically assume that if a porn star acts friendly toward a guy, she wants to screw him. I bet she gets that all the time.

She probably does, but in this case all the evidence points to serious carnal interest.

What evidence?

Dude, she took her jeans off as soon as you got in the room.

She put on shorts, though.

In front of you. And she put on hot pink, shorter-than-Marc Anthony shorts with the word "Juicy" across the ass. She may as well have slid on a pair of crotchless panties and handed you a condom.

What if I don't measure up? The guys she's used to fucking have anacondas between their legs.

Your penis is big enough, man.

Big enough's not going to cut it here.

Bullshit. You know how they say the camera adds ten pounds? Same thing applies to dicks. John Holmes? I bet that motherfucker was only packing eight inches, tops.

On second thought, maybe I could get her off with the thumb thing.

Yes, of course, the hitchhiker! That works every time. Now you're talking, man.

And there was that time she asked if I wanted to put my cock in her ass.

Exactly! She WANTS you.

Still, I dunno…

What now?

I just… I can't shake that look.

What look?

You remember. That girl. The actress from one of Randy's films. She was a first-timer, a scared little off-the-bus chick. She said the lines and moaned and pretended to like what was going on and everything, but there was this moment, just before the money shot, this scared little look toward the camera. Like it finally sank in that her dad or brother or priest might see this. Stripping for dumb hillbillies and frat boys at some out-of-the-way hole-in-the-wall is one thing, man, but getting reamed by a dude with a ten-foot pole on camera for the whole world to see… that's some serious shit. Porn's fine for the people who want to be there. But those who don't? Or aren't sure? That's some really fucked-up shit.

Jesus Christ, you're bumming me out, man.

I'm not saying I don't want to do it with Savanna. It's just that I need to focus and…

No, man, forget it, you self-cock-blocking asshole. Just forget it…

I looked over at Savanna. She was passed out hard. So I left without making a move. Since then we've become pretty good friends, but I still can't help but wonder where I went wrong.

Since no one knows more about porn stars than Randy, I figured who better to turn to for answers. So one bright L.A. morning a few weeks later, I swung by his Van Nuys production facility. I tend to drop in on Randy when I'm having trouble writing; seeing how he lives has a way of inspiring me, because I know that if my inkwell ever dries up, I'm going to end up being his gaffer. I've found that reminding myself what that would be like provides extremely effective motivation. Anyway, the place was littered with raunchy magazines, DVDs, a printout of an adult Web site directory, even an issue of *YM*. A familiar feeling of unease came over me. I could feel my sphincter tightening and my writer's block loosening. "Hey, Randy, you ever worry about getting too involved with, you know . . . with your work?" I asked.

"Whaddaya mean?" Randy replied without looking up from the *Hustler* he was flipping through.

"Like those undercover narcotics guys who wind up getting hooked on junk," I said.

Randy shot me a dismissive look. "You stay around this shit long enough, you become immune to it. Shit, I haven't jerked off to porn in five years."

I picked up the copy of *YM* and studied the fresh-faced cover model, outfitted in a diaphanous summer dress. "So what *do* you jerk off to, Randy? And please don't say this," I said, tossing the magazine onto the floor.

"You really want to know?" he asked.

"No. But now I have to know."

Randy cracked a sinister smile. He was enjoying this. "I wax my candle to infomercials."

"Come again?"

"Infomercials," he repeated. "Usually the ones about cleaning products on TV on Sunday morning. You know, with the women all done up like fifties TV."

Huh. One of the crucial elements to success in journalism is the capacity to accept that people of all walks of life are capable of practically anything. All the same, this development threw me.

"There's this one they do for the Fuzzy Wuzzy Microfiber Mitt.... Jesus, that babe is a first-class piece of ass. She wears this beige pantsuit from The Limited, sports Jaclyn Smith's hairdo circa 1977, and has the sexiest ice-blue eyes this side of Carol Alt. I'm telling you, the Fuzzy Wuzzy Microfiber Mitt lady could give a chubby to a Buddhist monk."

I really didn't want to think about Randy's unintended uses for infomercials, let alone his unintended uses for the Fuzzy Wuzzy Microfiber Mitt. But I wasn't going to begrudge him his good time. He wasn't hurting anyone, and in a way it was kind of adorable. And it just goes to show that people are freaks all over. Even professional freaks. The sad part is that when you do the math on how much porn is consumed in this country, versus how many people feel comfortable admitting to it, you're left with the inescapable conclusion that most people are hiding their freaky light under a bushel. Which is why I find certain parts of the porn industry refreshing. Too bad the other parts are so depressing and disturbing. But to the parts where they traffic in honesty and a healthy flowering of human weirdness, I say, right on, sisters. Plus, the nondamaged performers I've met are a hell of a lot of fun when you get them out on the town. So if you are lucky enough to find yourself out with a porn star and would like to avoid a tragedy on the scale of my unfortunate strikeout with Savanna Samson, do yourself a favor and remember the following rules.

How to Hang Out with Porn Chicks

1) Hold the anchovies.

It's common knowledge that porn chicks lose all self-control around pizza deliverymen. Ditto for pool boys, men in uniform, and guys with Tom Selleck mustaches. Should you encounter any of these types while out with a porn chick, you need to whisk her away immediately—or risk losing her for the next twenty-two minutes.

2) Adjust for inflation.

There are a number of factors that determine how quickly an individual will be affected by alcohol, body weight being first and foremost among them. For instance, it takes only two drinks for a 120-pound woman to be considered legally intoxicated, but a 200-pound man requires double that amount to breach a Breathalyzer's red zone. That's why whenever I'm drinking with a lady I always size her up to get an idea how much booze she can reasonably throw back without becoming a puddle. Puddles, by definition, being messy and hard to transport to the next bar—let alone my bed. I've gotten so good at guessing a woman's weight (and thus her tolerance), in fact, that my margin of error is around two pounds. But here's something else I've learned: Porn stars throw a bit of a wrench into the equation. That's because once you take into account such artificial additives as breast implants, collagen injections, tattoo ink, hair extensions, body piercings, and fuck-me pumps, the average porn chick's net body mass is at least fifteen to twenty pounds *less* than her gross weight. So keep that in mind, because the line between her blowing you and her blowing chunks can be a thin one, my friend.

3) Don't ask her about work.

If she wants to talk about it, she'll bring it up. And there's a good chance she doesn't want to talk about it. Because guess what everyone who meets her wants to know about? Don't be just another one of the predictable masses. If you want to know what her work is like, google it after you get home.

4) Choose carefully.

Believe it or not, not every porn star you meet is necessarily someone you're going to want to hang out with. Like in all professions, however, the people at the top of it are doing something noticeably different than the writhing faceless masses below them. For every poised, sophisticated Savanna Samson, there are seventeen thousand dim-witted, drug-addicted train wrecks. This latter group needs love and compassion, not a booze-fueled night on the town followed by an attempt to re-create the therapy breakthrough scene in *Deep Throat*.

5) Avoid Charlie Sheen at all costs.

Like a moth to a flame, that guy. But if you see him, run for the hills, because in all likelihood that deviant bastard's already fucked her, and who wants to go there? Plus, nothing kills the mood faster than Charlie Sheen.

All glibness aside, though, I had to wonder if this was really the time to start dating a porn star, given how insecure I've been lately about my relationships with women. Nothing against them, mind you. Hell, it's already been established that some folks in the adult-entertainment business rank among my most favorite people. It's just that dating porn stars is graduate-level relationship territory. You've got to be a seriously stable, confident dude to handle it well. And my internal conversation about putting the moves on Savanna was proof enough to me that, exciting though the idea might be, I probably couldn't handle it.

My shrink is happy with this course of action too, but for different reasons. She somehow has it in her head that dating someone who makes a living having sex on camera wouldn't constitute a "healthy relationship." For the record, I think she's prejudiced. I also think she's secretly jealous because she's hopelessly in love with me. I should also note that The Shrink is a stunner from Austria who grew up in the same town as Freud. And I'm sure she'd say my impression of her crush on me is a classic example of projection. It's also a classic example of what I like to call LLD (Ladies Love Dan). And pointing this out would add defensiveness and overcompensation to my tally sheet behind projection. Sometimes I wonder if therapy isn't just an elaborate mating ritual.

Speaking of which, I've been doing something of an elaborate one with Jen Topping of late. After we reconnected at Mood we started seeing a lot of each other. I don't know where it's headed, exactly, but it's been a long time since I've felt this at ease with a woman. I've even had inklings that she might have commitment potential. I also made the mistake of admitting this to Randy after I'd had a few beers at a Los Angeles Kings game.

"Jen and I happened to be at the King's Head the week before my birthday. Turns out it was karaoke night," I said. The King's Head is one of my favorite local watering holes in Santa Monica. "We just went for it."

"You fucked her in the bathroom?" Randy blurted excitedly. "That's freaking awesome!"

"We sang a duet, you douche."

"You did karaoke? This is getting disturbing," Randy said.

"I thought so too, at first, but I kind of think it turned out to be a transformative experience," I explained. "When we got up there and sang together, it was like we were the only people in the world. I was completely in the moment. I haven't felt that in a long time."

"You know, despite the sheer gayness of what you just told me, I also get how nice that would be."

"Thanks, man."

"So, what did you do?"

"Huh?"

"What song did you and your new soul mate perform?"

"That's the best part—we sang 'We're an American Band.' "

"Grand Funk Railroad?"

"Fuck yes."

"That's not a duet."

"I know—I did the verse, she sang the chorus."

"OK, you're absolved. Maybe you're not gay after all."

"Thanks. That means a lot."

I was sharing with Randy here, sure, but I still figured some things were better left unsaid. In particular, I hadn't been completely forthright with him in regard to my actual "knowing she could be the one even though I seriously doubted such a thing even existed" moment. While the karaoke duet certainly represented a major turning point in my music career as well as in my relationship with Jen, Cupid's arrow finally lodged itself in the general vicinity of my heart a week later, on my birthday. After dinner at one of my favorite L.A. eateries, Roscoe's Chicken & Waffles, we drove up the coast to Zuma Beach. It was ten p.m. by the time we arrived and the place was deserted. I had a case of Sogno Uno in the trunk (you're the best, Savanna), so we grabbed a bottle and a blanket and headed down to where we could hear the surf rolling in. I had an opener but no glasses so we passed a bottle that scored a 91 with Robert Parker back and forth, swigging it like it was Boone's Farm.

The weirdest part was, we weren't talking. Just staring out at the sea and stars. We were two thirds of our way through the bottle when I thought of something worthy of breaking the silence.

"It's the part of the movie they leave out," I said.

"What's that?"

"This is where they do the montage—running on the beach, toasting at dinner. Then maybe on the blanket looking up at the stars, sure, but for five seconds only, then it's on to unloading antiques from a vintage VW Beetle and one person drops their end and stubs their toe or some shit. But they never just leave the camera rolling, showing people looking up at the stars for thirty minutes. They leave out the long quiet part."

Jen didn't reply for a few minutes.

"I have a surprise for you," she said. "Close your eyes."

I did as instructed and heard Jen rustling around in her bag. I wondered what she was up to. Some birthday thing, I suppose. That's sweet. So, what, an iPod? Cologne? Was she taking off her clothes? Then I heard the flick of a cigarette lighter and soft cursing (it was windy). Fireworks, maybe? Were we about to get stoned?

"Open them," she said.

So I did. And there was no weed or Roman candles or Obsession by Calvin Klein, and Jen still had her clothes on. But by God, did she look beautiful. She started to sing "Happy Birthday," and with each note I felt myself hurtling faster and faster through the void toward a place I'd rarely visited before. And though I'd always feared this particular unknown in the same way professional athletes tremble at the idea of random drug tests, I wasn't afraid anymore. In fact, I was pretty sure I was ready.

"I hope you like chocolate," I heard her saying as, unbelievably, a tear rolled down my cheek. It reached my chin and dangled there for a while, like it wasn't familiar with the route, unsure where it was supposed to go next or how in the world to get there. Hanging on. Hanging on. Hanging on. And then it finally fell and plummeted through the air. It landed on the frosting of the tiny round cake Jen was holding and nearly extinguished the flame on the gold-flaked, D-shaped candle, the kind you get at kids' party stores. Hell, the candle was almost as big as the cake.

"Is that from an Easy-Bake Oven?" I asked, my voice cracking ever so slightly.

"Not just *any* Easy-Bake Oven," she said. "This was made in an original model Easy-Bake Oven from 1963. After you told me that story about your first love I knew I had to get you one."

"How'd you find it?" I asked.

"eBay. And don't ask what it cost, because you'll feel like you owe me, and I don't want you to feel like you owe me ... even though you *definitely* do owe me!"

"I know I do," I said, as I leaned in for a kiss. Then we both took our clothes off, and there were fireworks of a different sort, and it was really kind of amazing.... At least until we really got going and were rudely reminded that having sex on a beach sounds awesome, until the reality sets in that sand ranks up there with feces, Bengay, and Lady Gaga atop the list of stuff you don't want anywhere near your genitals, ever.

"Christ, it felt like you were giving me a Screaming Seagull back there," Jen said in the car, as I drove hastily toward my place so we could pick up where we left off.

This was a new one to me. She explained that it's a dubious sex maneuver that calls for a guy to pull his dick out while having sex on a beach, lay it in the sand, then resume fucking.

"There's really such a thing as that, eh? No shit?" I said.

"No shit at all, actually," she continued without missing a beat. "You want shit involved, you gotta go with the Dirty Sanchez or Cleveland Steamer."

"You ready to give that a try?" I kidded (at least I *think* I was kidding).

She flashed a mischievous smile but said nothing.

Which is about when I thought that, yeah, maybe finding The One is possible after all.

"Slip of the Tongue"

CREATED BY JOSH DURR

1 3/4 oz. Brugal Extra Viejo

1 oz. Dolin Vermouth de Chambery Blanc

3/4 oz. fresh-squeezed grapefruit juice

3/4 oz. fresh-squeezed orange juice

1–2 dashes Kübler absinthe (as a dash is subjective,
*   this should measure 1/8 oz.)*

Grapefruit zest, for garnish

Add all ingredients in a mixing glass with quality ice. Shake well with a Boston shaker, then double-strain into a coupe glass. Garnish with a large zest of grapefruit using a channel knife.

"When I started to think of a concoction that was going to capture the essence of this chapter, I knew I had to create something that was a breath of fresh air. Given the influence of the Dominican Republic and Brugal rum, of course we could start there. When I think of rum I immediately think of a perfectly made daiquiri and its simple allure. Yet when I think of refreshing, my mind drifts to the Corpse Reviver #2. So with both of these influences I created the Slip of the Tongue, a bright and refreshing cocktail that will brighten the mood of even the most royally screwed imbiber."

—**JOSH DURR** is a cocktail and spirits geek who directs and runs Molecularbartending.com and Hawthorn Beverage Group. When he is not traveling and doing educational and creative development for clients you will most likely find him drinking bourbon at his home-base bar, Tonic on Fourth, in Cincinnati, Ohio.

TWELVE

I Open Up to You and You Bust My Friggin' Balls?

||||||||||||||||||||||||||||||||||||||||||||||||||||||||||||||||||||||||||||||||||||||||||||||||||||||||||||||||||||||||||||||||||||

Dispatch from Puerto Plata, Dominican Republic:

||||||||||||||||||||||||||||||||||||||||||||||||||||||||||||||||||||||||||||||||||||||||||||||||||||||||||||||||||||||||||||||||||||

J'd like to impart a vital travel tip for visiting the Dominican Republic: While some sections are tourist-friendly, for the most part it's a desperately poor third-world country with roaming flocks of ultraviolent bandits who would much rather cut out your tongue than sell you a puka-shell necklace. Inadvertently stray too far from your cozy Punta Cana resort after sucking down a couple (twelve) mai tais and you could easily find yourself bound and gagged in the trunk of an '82 Celica praying someone back home gives enough of a shit about you to fork over ransom money.

Yet aside from the prospects of kidnapping, dismemberment by machete, and finding out your family is a bunch of dicks, the D.R. is a fabulous place to visit.

First off, about half the players of our national pastime hail from this diminutive Caribbean island. That alone is reason enough to make the journey. Get an autographed baseball from every athletic-looking kid you meet down here, because odds are there'll be a future Hall of Famer somewhere in the mix. We're talking mucho cash-money on eBay, my friends. Which reminds me—go get 'em, Pepe Ortega! I'm pulling for ya, kid.

Plus, there's legal prostitution everywhere, which is nothing to sneeze at. (Side note: If you *do* suddenly start sneezing after a roll with a Dominican hooker, see a doctor straightaway. Trust me on this one.) And while we're on the topic of cheap sex, I'd be remiss if I didn't mention the mystical Dominican concoction known as Mama Juana and its purported aphrodisiac powers. I felt news of this beverage warranted investigation. Unfortunately I had to conduct that investigation in a room full of pasty U.S. journalists, so needless to say, those powers were more wasted than I was.

But the best reason to visit the land of Sammy Sosa is its delicious rum. Or, as I've said to every bartender I've met, "You can't spell drunk without the D.R.!" They hate me here. The most-quaffed brand here is Brugal. Though most Americans have never heard of it, Brugal ranks third in sales worldwide (right behind Bacardi and Captain Morgan). And somehow, even though I love rum and am supposed to be a professional drinker, prior to being invited down here to sample the stuff by the fine folks at Shaw-Ross International Importers, I'd been oblivious to the joys of this 120-year-old brand, made with molasses from 100-percent Dominican-grown sugarcane.

Not anymore. Right now I'm pouring Brugal over my Corn Flakes as I lounge on the balcony of my suite overlooking the ocean at the posh Casa Colonial Resort and Spa in Puerto Plata. Thanks, Shaw-Ross International Importers! I'd say I owe you one, but that would be a clear violation of this thing they call journalistic ethics.

So where was I? Ah, right, objectively singing the praises of Brugal Rum ...

I've grown quite fond of the exceptionally smooth Extra Viejo ("extra old") variety. It's a blend of older reserves that commands attention with a dark crystallized amber appearance and a mouthwatering bouquet of raisins, toasted oak, and pipe tobacco notes. Its textured, seemingly weightless body delivers long-lasting flavors that include French roast coffee, warm toffee, hot cocoa, and hints of nutmeg and anise. It tastes timeless, classic, and elegant. Surely, my dearly departed rum-loving granddad would have shit himself if he'd tried this stuff. Actually, in his later years he would have shit himself pretty much no matter what. But definitely if he got hold of some Brugal.

And I'm not alone in loving this stuff. In his best-selling tome *Kindred Spirits,* leading U.S. spirits authority Paul Pacult refers to Brugal Extra Viejo as "stunning ... all the sensory delights promised in the color and nose are fulfilled in a balanced stately manner." And I agree wholeheartedly. Except I would have used "opulent" instead of "stately." I'm frisky that way.

And with that, friends, it's time for me to call it a luxury junket here in the Dominican Republic. I've got a car coming any minute now to take me to the airport. In fact, I believe it just pulled up now ... wait, an '82 Celica? That's odd.

I Hear You're a Columnist for *Playboy*

"I'm not sure how much longer I can handle the physical demands of this job," I told my editor at *Playboy* upon filing the

D.R. dispatch. In the interest of shielding him from any fallout, we'll call him Steve.

"I can only imagine," he replied. "Traveling the world, drinking and eating, having to type all those big words with your tender little fingers. I'm sure it's simply devastating." I think I detected some sarcasm there. Or was it derision?

"What? I open up to you and you bust my friggin' balls?"

"Um, no. You're busting *mine* with this whiny-ass bullshit. You have what 99.9 percent of the adult male population would classify as a sweet motherfucking gig. Says so right on your business cards. You are a nightlife columnist–slash–public menace for *Playboy* fucking magazine. And now you want to tell me you can't handle it? I suggest you man up. There are only about a hundred and thirty million people in line behind you."

"It's a grind, is all I'm saying," I whimpered. "Being on the road all the time, the booze, the jetlag. Deadline pressure. And the pay isn't what it used to be. It takes its toll."

"So does shoveling shit for a living, but I bet you wouldn't trade places with a shit shoveler, would you?" he said.

"But I *am* a shit shoveler, no? At least judging from your last round of edits?" I laughed.

"That's *right*," he replied. "You'll have to remind me to get you some new business cards."

Ah, the witty banter with Steve. I think it's what I'll miss most after I no longer have the job that tires me so, which Steve claims 99.9 percent of the adult male population covets. And make no mistake, that day is sure to come sooner rather than later. Hell, I'll be amazed if it hasn't happened by the time this book goes to print.

Steve's all right, though. And while he's a few years my junior, he's also clearly the adult in our relationship. It only makes sense, given that he's responsible for a wife, four kids, a house, and a mortgage, and juggles all that while managing a stable of needy, neurotic, complaining writers. I, on the other hand, have a dog. And the only reason I got her in the first place was that I thought she'd help me score dates. Steve is a grown-up by obligation. Me? Only when it suits my needs, like when I cite family emergencies to get out of doing things I don't want to do.

Steve is something of an oasis in the wasteland that passes for the magazine business these days—an editor who actually gives a shit about his writers, about the craft, about tradition. On several occasions he has had to talk me down off the metaphorical ledge . . . and once, off an actual one. Remember chapter 8? Tales of the Cocktail in New Orleans? Here's something I left out. One afternoon I was drinking with a lady friend at the Carousel Bar in the Hotel Monteleone. We were both about as sauced as a pot of gumbo. Not yet willing to abandon all pretense of being a working writer on assignment, I checked my BlackBerry. There was a message from somebody with a gender-neutral name. I'll call this person Terry.

Terry's e-mail was brief but to the point: "I hear you're a columnist for *Playboy*?"

My reply was similarly succinct: "That's correct."

"So you're a columnist for *Playboy*. I'd love to see some of your columns for *Playboy*," came the reply.

"Sure," I wrote back. "There are a bunch posted on Playboy .com. Check 'em out." I'd assumed Terry was among that odious breed of publicists who pitch story ideas to writers chosen randomly off some database and are too goddamn lazy to do their homework and find out who it is exactly that they're pitching.

"But you're representing yourself as a columnist for *Playboy*, correct?" Terry prodded. "Where can I find your column in the actual magazine?"

At this point I should clarify my exact position regarding *Playboy*. I am not, nor have I ever been, a *Playboy* employee. I am a regular contributor, a contract guy. I and my ilk supply the bulk of the magazine's content because, frankly, it's a hell of lot cheaper for these operations to pay freelancers than it is to maintain a staff of writers who might cling to such quaint notions as an actual workplace, health benefits, job security, and cute coworkers to flirt with at office parties.

Most of the time when my writing appears in the magazine it doesn't even have my name next to it. I do it for the money and to maintain a relationship with them, in the hope that it might lead to something bigger. A feature here and there, or a regular column. Which was the idea behind doing the "Imbiber" column for them. It was originally going to appear in both the print and online versions of *Playboy*—weekly online, monthly in the mag. However, due to a series of unfortunate events including a major recession and the continuing death spiral of the entire print magazine industry, some cutbacks were made to the magazine's page count, and somehow my majestic prose didn't make the cut. Since then, while I still contribute anonymous booze material to the mag, my actual named and bylined "Imbiber" column has appeared exclusively online. You get it, right?

"If you're telling people you write a column for *Playboy*, I'd like to know where in *Playboy* I can find your column." Terry clearly *didn't* get it.

Now, had I not been drinking so heavily, nor had the desire to chuck my BlackBerry and resume flirting with my lady friend been so strong—in other words, had I behaved like a working writer on assignment instead of like, say, myself—it probably would have occurred to me that sending the e-mail I was about to send Terry wasn't such a great idea. I mean, I *assumed* this was just some hack publicist with an attitude problem, but I didn't *know* that for sure. If you stop to think about it, he or she could be anybody, really. Of course, I didn't. Stop to think about it, that is. In my supreme wisdom I also didn't take the time to check the domain these e-mails were coming from.

"Who the fuck are you and why are you up my ass?" I replied.

"Look it up," came the reply, accompanied—at least in my mind—by one of those ominous musical cues that occur in movies when someone realizes a moment too late that they've done something really stupid and some seriously fucked-up shit is about to go down.

It turned out Terry really *could* be anybody. Say, for instance, a high-ranking *Playboy* executive based in Chicago that I'd never met, or so Google informed me when I did some belated research on my BlackBerry at the bar. It also turned out that Terry had a friend, a perfectly lovely woman I'd met at a dinner party the night before, and that she'd e-mailed Terry to tell him—yes, Terry was a him—she'd met one of his *Playboy* colleagues. Terry was understandably concerned that some drunken savage might be running amok in New Orleans passing himself off as one of Hef's hired hands for lord knows what devious purposes.

And now I was in a world of shit, having just drunk e-mailed something fairly offensive to someone who could very easily have me eighty-sixed from what little was left of my career at *Playboy*. On countless occasions, my drunken antics have led to positive results. Like a decision to give skydiving a try at the tail end of a twelve-hour bender that turned out to be one of the most exhilarating experiences of my life. (Note: The instructor was sober. I'm not a complete idiot.) Oh, and there was that naked dash through the lobby of a resort hotel in Borneo that culminated with an all-night romp with a Thai stewardess. Also ill-advised, also ended well.

This time, though, I'd dug a massive drunken hole and heaved my own ass into it. One lousy e-mail was going to cost me my column at *Playboy*, which suddenly did seem like the sweetest motherfucking gig of all time.

Now what am I going to do? was the first thought that ran through my head, followed almost immediately by *I wonder if that guy who owes me that favor is still over at* Maxim, leading to *Ah, fuck! Nobody reads* Maxim *anymore anyway.*

What disappointed me most, though, was that I'd broken one of my own cardinal rules about . . .

How to Not Ruin Your Life While Drinking

1) Never do drunk what you wouldn't do sober.

Unless it involves the following: striking up conversations with supermodels, running with bulls in Pamplona, flashing your boobs on Bourbon Street, shopping for lingerie and sex toys, hanging out with Gary Busey, filling out your census form, fielding calls from telemarketers, bowling, eating microwave burritos at two a.m., telling your asshole coworker to go fuck himself, flashing your boobs in Pamplona, sending lurid messages to your Facebook friends' hottest Facebook friends, shaving your head, naked skateboarding, telling your asshole roommate to go fuck herself, or writing a book. Note that I did not include anything about responding to e-mails from strangers who turn out to be your boss's boss.

2) Don't shit where you eat.

We went over this in chapter 10, when I talked about hooking up with the staff at your favorite bar. You may get laid a few times, sure. Maybe it will even turn into a nice little fling. But when, inevitably, things go south with the hottie who slings drinks at your own personal Cheers, she'll go back to work and tell you to go to hell—hell being anywhere but her bar. And then where are you going to watch Phillies games and eat pork chops drizzled in apple chutney and balsamic reduction, you fucking moron? WHERE?!!! Oh, God, this is too painful. Moving on . . .

3) When making decisions with women, apply the 70 percent rule.

This applies to all decisions more significant than what to eat or what movie you should see (for those, don't even waste your time; just let her have her way). For all subjects with graver consequences than this (Should we move in together? Keep the baby? Change our Facebook statuses to "It's complicated"?), you need to do some quick math in your head. Tally the ten most recent times you and this girl were together. Were you drinking heavily on seven or more of those occasions (i.e., 70 percent)? If so, the answer is no. Whatever it is she wants, if you need to get wasted around this person to find her tolerable, the answer is no. Unless she wants to break up, of course. If the tally is under 70 percent, you don't have to say no, but you should wait until you sober up to actually make a decision. As a side benefit, this makes you look like the responsible one.

4) Carry rubbers.

Like my dear old grandma always used to say before her liver finally gave out (my *other* grandma, that is; not the one who got hit by a bus), nothing takes the shine off a drunken roll in the hay faster than a baby. Or an STD. Or a baby with an STD. While researching this item I googled "drunk sex" and came across a video made by a cute recovering alcoholic in which she waxes nostalgic about the days when she used to get blotto and screw every guy in sight. Among other things, she claims she loved drunk sex because it's "sloppy and crazy and messy and no one cares and you're bleeding out of different orifices." Been there. Luckily you can avoid the vast majority of the problems associated with awesome drunk sex just by tossing a bag over Mister Happy at the right moment. But that isn't going to happen if you're not holding. So be holding.

5) Don't consume forty shots of vodka and take a nap.

In the trade, we call this "riding the John Bonham express." Next stop: Pulmonary Edema; everybody off the train. And I hear that town *sucks.*

6) Avoid cameras.

Hard to overstate the importance of this one. Thanks to this newfangled thing they call the Internet, there's a high probability that any remotely embarrassing thing you do in front of a camera will be available almost immediately for scrutiny by millions. Indeed, a Google search for "drunk photos you don't want to be in" turned up nearly 9 *million* results, including those great ones of Mr. Braveheart himself, Mel Gibson, in a bar with two blondes about a half hour before he called a female cop, and I quote, "sugar tits."

Remember, cops carry cameras too. Just ask Nick Nolte, whose mug shot following a 2002 arrest for DUI can best be described by one word—tragilarious.

Same goes for video. It might even be worse. You just know some smartass is going to remix it and it's going to go all viral and . . . oh, poor David Hasselhoff.

And while the Hoff was pathetically wasted when said video was taken, there's something that goes even beyond pathetically wasted. And that thing is called Brad Ferro, the now infamous Queens schoolteacher who claims to have been so befuggered at a North Jersey bar in the summer of 2009 that he has no memory of punching a girl in the face. Unfortunately for everyone—particularly Brad Ferro—his stupendous feat of fuckheadedness was caught on film and broadcast on a little reality-TV show you may have heard of called *Jersey Shore*.

And that guy wasn't even on a reality show; he was just in the proximity of one. Which brings me to a little-known corollary to rule number 6:

6a) If you are on a reality show, don't be The Drunk.

Oh, but wait, silly me. You're on a reality show. That means it's too late for you—you already ruined your life. As you were.

Now bear in mind that while my rules will keep you out of most of the major forms of booze-inflicted trouble, they are by no means an ironclad guarantee. Alcohol has strange and mysterious powers to create havoc in the most unexpected of circumstances. Which is, after all, why I love it so. But even the things you love can bite you sometimes. Just ask Siegfried and Roy.

It's like Steve said when I called from the Carousel Bar to tell him about the e-mail: The worse you are at thinking, the better you are at drinking. I was a mite agitated. Strike that— I was basically foaming at the mouth and hyperventilating. He quickly calmed me down, though, and promised to make things right with Terry. Not surprisingly, he did just that by convincing Terry that the volatility and scabrousness of soul that begat the offending e-mail is part of the formula that helps said soul connect on such a deep level with the many adult-beverage lovers out there who are bored to tears by my more urbane colleagues in the international drinking press corps. It's probably a load of bullshit, but Terry went along with it, which is, of course, different than buying it.

Still, it got me thinking again about the negative side of alcohol. They say that alcohol brings out the truth—*in vino veritas* and all that—but sometimes the truth is that even fine, well-adjusted people occasionally turn into assholes when they're blotto. We all understand this. But one of the most aggravating negative effects of alcohol is the way it's used by celebrity pricks and their damage-control teams to explain away all manner of truly despicable behavior. This upsetting trend we've seen over the past few years is a shameful bit of subterfuge that gives honest bad drunks a bad name.

Look, I've seen plenty of usually responsible drinkers overdo it on occasion and act like baboons hopped up on Adderall. Indeed, I've been the baboon more times than I care to remember (when I can remember it at all). But I don't care who you are or how much you've had to drink, the intoxicating qualities of alcohol cannot be blamed for the following:

- Being a raging racist

- Breaking into a bank with a loaded revolver (also, having a name like "Rip Torn")

- Shaving your head, attacking a photographer's car with an umbrella, and leaving your young children in the care of Kevin Federline while you check into rehab

- Marrying Billy Bob Thornton

- Pedophilia

- Recording a Heidi Montag CD

Now, at this juncture, professional writer that I am, I would be remiss not to point out the following etymological distinction: An excuse is not the same as an explanation. When Nicole Richie was arrested for driving the wrong direction on an

L.A. freeway a few years back, she admitted to police that she was higher than the prices in the gluten-free aisle at Whole Foods. Being hopped-up doesn't *excuse* horrendous driving, but it is a reasonable *explanation* for it. Similarly, if Richie tried to refute allegations that she's bulimic by claiming a particularly potent appletini made her forget to eat for eighteen months, well … you see my point. Booze isn't to blame for an eating disorder any more than it is for Mel Gibson's incoherent ranting against Jews or a disgraced congressman's predatory behavior toward young boys. You can go to as much rehab as you like; I'm still going to think you're an asshole.

That said, I'm well aware that excessive consumption of alcohol is to blame for all sorts of fucked-up stuff in this world, but to use it as a scapegoat for your personal and enduring demons is irresponsible, disingenuous, and dangerous. Unless I'm the one doing it, of course.

"Abstinence"

CREATED BY AISHA SHARPE

19.2 oz. Guinness

1 1/2 oz. shot of whiskey (Note: Your favorite spirit can be substituted for whiskey)

Preparation:

1. Select a clean, dry imperial pint glass. Hold the glass at 45 degrees under the spout.

2. Pull the handle slowly toward you and allow the beer to flow smoothly down the side of the glass (note: do not submerge the spout into the beer).

3. As the glass fills, straighten it up—fill glass until 3/4 full.

4. Stand the glass on the counter and allow the gas to surge through the beer.

5. To create the legendary head, push the handle backward slightly ("topping off"). The head should rise just proud of the rim.

6. Put shot aside.

7. Drink your nutrient-packed beverage, aka Guinness, while staring longingly at your shot.

"If you decide to give up the sauce for a predetermined period of time, there is always a little bit of wiggle room where a Guinness fits perfectly. If pregnant women can drink it, and they are told to give up booze, then we who are not pregnant should get the same free pass. The shot is ordered and not consumed, for those who still have a little guilt about the Guinness.

"This 'cocktail' is a twist on one of my favorites called a shot and a beer, which changes slightly seasonally."

—AISHA SHARPE'S mixology skills have been acclaimed by the *New York Times*, *New York* magazine, and top restaurant and club owners. She is the cofounder of Contemporary Cocktails, Inc., a global, full-service cocktails and spirits consulting firm.

THIRTEEN

It Looks Like You've Been Sleepwalking

I woke up naked on the dining-room floor.

Bad enough in any case. Doubly so when you don't know whose dining room you're naked in.

I tried to lift my head and winced. It was full of whiskey and regret. My eyes burned with a hot blue flame, and clearly Satan had taken a dump in my mouth at some point during the night. I was like the chorus to the most depressing Smiths song ever written (that would be the six-and-a-half-minute caterwaul of pure sadness that is "How Soon Is Now?" by the way).

The producer, I thought. *That must be whose house this is. Oh, good. I'm hungover and naked in the dining room of a high-powered TV producer. This is just how I wanted this to play out.* See, I'd been pitching him a pilot I'd written (about the hilarious and pathetic travails of a hard-living booze writer, naturally) and he'd seemed kind of interested. Wanted me to show him "how this whole thing worked." This "whole thing" being the boozy caricature that passes for my social life. He wanted to go drinking. What was I going to say, no? I remember meeting him at Formosa Cafe. I think we ate something. Then things got fuzzy. I recalled doing several Jäger Bombs at a place called Jones on Santa Monica Boulevard. Not a good sign. If I was doing Jäger Bombs, something had gone seriously wrong. I hate Jäger Bombs almost as much as I hate Hollywood.

This guy had gotten several big-time shows on the air. And he'd read my first book. *And* he thought my life could have juice as a scripted series. And now I was naked on his floor. Excellent.

Oh, dear God, what was that? Bolts of pain swept majestically across my skull. That was a noise. My eyes darted to the doorway into what I figured was the kitchen. There was someone in there. I painstakingly dragged myself a foot or so across the floor to get a better peek. A blond woman in a bathrobe was sitting at the kitchen table drinking coffee and reading the paper. Had to be the producer's wife.

A quick survey of the area told me that one of two things had happened: Either the producer's wife had entered the kitchen through the window over the sink, or she'd walked right by my naked ass sprawled out on her dining room floor. I wanted, in this order, three Advil, a glass of water, and a gun. All for use on my head.

As I had none of these things, I needed to figure out what to do next—a bit of a conundrum. Save for a sock lying nearby, my clothes were nowhere in sight. There were doors, all closed except the one into the kitchen, and a staircase. I figured it was entirely likely that there was a housekeeper, and possibly some children lurking around somewhere. And my bladder was telling me that I needed to get to a toilet or potted plant posthaste. Which one of those doors led to a bathroom?

Which is when I realized I had even bigger problems. Or rather, one problem that was bigger than it should have been. My penis, to be exact. I had a boner. And not your standard morning wood either. This was a pee boner. I could hear some nightmare exterminator in my head explaining (in a voice like Cliff Clavin from *Cheers*, for some reason) to a housewife who wanted to be rid of an infestation, "Naw, ma'am, your typical pee boner sticks around until the urine has entirely left the premises." This morning (or was it afternoon?) was going swimmingly.

Another noise from the kitchen. Shit. The wife was on the move. I realized I was lying on an Oriental rug. Maybe I can hide under it! Oh, mother of all divine fuckups, the rug's nailed to the floor. Stupid idea anyway. I scrambled to my feet, seeing no options but a run for the front door. And when your best option appears to be taking to the streets of Los Angeles without any clothes on, you are the living embodiment of totally fucked.

"So you're a sleepwalker," a male voice said.

"Huh?"

It was the producer, smiling matter-of-factly (did I detect a trace of pity?) as he handed me my clothes. This seemed a tad odd to me. Was this something that happened often? Helping a naked stranger who's trying to rip a rug off his dining room floor while his wife eats breakfast fifteen feet away?

"I said, it looks like you've been sleepwalking."

"It does look that way," I replied, "doesn't it?"

"Can you fuck off on your own," he drawled, "or do you need a hand?"

"Oh, don't worry—I've done this before."

It wasn't until he'd deposited me safely in a taxi that I had an epiphany. I should stop drinking. Not permanently, mind you. I'm not crazy. They say you've got to hit rock bottom before you quit for good, and frankly, as unfortunate as this incident was from a professional standpoint (let's just say you won't see that producer and me on the stage accepting an Emmy together anytime soon), in my world, waking up naked in some high-powered Hollywood player's mansion is still on the good side of the divide between rock star and rock bottom.

Still, my ego was sufficiently banged up from the experience that a temporary self-imposed booze ban seemed in order. Just to see what would happen. Actually, the thought of it energized me; I like challenges. Trouble was, my typical challenges involved trying to chug a beer faster than the guy next to me. Best to be realistic about this. I'd quit drinking for a full month. Long enough to count, but not so long I couldn't see the light at the end of the tunnel.

Driving home, once I'd retrieved my car from the Jones, where I'd evidently left it the night before, I looked in the rearview mirror and saw the eyes of a determined man, a man who'd been driven to extreme measures by extreme circumstances—like the Ving Rhames character in *Pulp Fiction* about to get medieval on the asses of Zed and the Gimp. Barely missing a parked BMW, I set the mirror back, focused on driving, and found myself humming Dick Dale's "Misirlou." Arriving home, I parked, hopped out of the car, and raced, with a newfound spring in my step, up the stairs and into my beachfront town house. I was a man with a renewed sense of purpose. This was going to be great. Just what the doctor ordered. And before he and the liver transplant team had even ordered it! I needed a break from the sauce anyway, just to take stock. This hiatus was going to be the best thing I ever did. It was going to be liberating. Cleansing, even.

Two days later I was staring down my home bar like a homeless dog looks at a steak dinner.

I realized that if I had any hope of making it through the next twenty-six days, three hours, and eighteen minutes (but who's counting?), I had some serious preparations to make. Like what? Glad you asked.

How to Prepare for a Month on the Wagon

1) Provide just cause.

Nothing helps kick-start a serious commitment to teetotalism like a blowout booze bender that leaves you feeling as though you've spent fourteen hours getting skull-fucked by a horse—a giant, horny horse that learned to screw from watching rabbits. The kind of bender that when you wake up next to the toilet you discover your tongue has been replaced by a giant furry cat, your eyes have been coated with gypsum plaster, and you've somehow acquired a second heartbeat inside your skull. You've vomited profusely all night long and are sure to vomit again just as soon as you try to ingest any food or fluids or hear a noise or breathe. On the off chance your wallet happens to still be in your possession, it will be light at least a credit card or two, left behind at wherever the hell you continued partying after you blacked out (you'll have no idea, of course). When you feel this bad, the thought of leading an alcohol-free life is the single most comforting thought you've ever had. If only wicked hangovers lasted forever, maintaining sobriety would be a breeze. They don't, however, which is why it's important that you . . .

2) Talk it through.

Separation anxiety can be a real bitch, so before going cold turkey you need to remind yourself that everything is going to be OK. You can make it through this. It's not permanent. You may also want to reassure your favorite booze that it's not over forever, like I did. Let Johnnie Walker know that it's you, not him. Tell him that in the long run, a little time away from each other could turn out to be the best thing that's ever happened in your relationship. If he continues to press you as to why you're doing this, you can cite the fact that you're currently engaged in an emotional conversation with a bottle of scotch. This is as sure a sign you need a break as anything I can think of. If he can't sympathize with that, well, he's not right for you anyway.

3) You've got to hide your love away. (Or not.)

To limit temptation, you may want to remove any and all alcohol from your home. Store it in a garage or some other storage space. This is easy enough for most folks. Unless said folks happen to be professional wine-and-spirits scribes who receive upwards of twenty alcohol-laden review samples per week. It took the better part of my first day of sobriety to move barely half of my liquor supply to its temporary digs in my neighbor's shed. Then UPS arrived with a whole new shipment of bottles. I realized that bailing water was futile, given the size of this leak. Plus, my back was killing me. And it dawned on me that hiding the booze that I planned to eventually come back to was akin to the dubious strategy AA folks have dubbed "pulling a geographic." That's when a drunk decides it's not him but rather his surroundings that are the cause of his drunkenness, and that all he needs to do in order to get straight is relocate to a new place, find a new job, and get some new friends. That never works. And, like I said, all that free booze I've got is really, really heavy.

4) Keep it to yourself.

Telling your friends you've decided to not drink for any extended period of time is a bad idea because no matter what their reaction, it's likely going to suck. For instance, if you tell a friend you've decided to lay off the sauce and he responds with something along the lines of "That is the smartest decision you've made in a long time," you probably won't feel very smart. Plus, you'll realize your friend thinks you're a raging alcoholic. If, on the other hand, your friend, faced with the prospect of losing a boozing buddy, responds badly and tells you that it's the dumbest idea he's ever heard, you can rest assured that for the duration of your self-imposed abstinence he will dangle drinking opportunities in front of you like they were bare titties and you were a stack of dollar bills. Another possible scenario is that your friend will decide to join you in your temperance experiment, which will eventually lead both of you to the inevitable conclusion that, devoid of the social lubricant that is alcohol, you really don't have very much in common.

5) Don't punt on first down.

One of the biggest—if not *the* biggest—challenges you'll face in going on the wagon is doing things for the first time that in the past have always involved alcohol consumption; things such as going on a date, watching a sporting event, taking a vacation, having sex, spending time with your kids, summoning the will to get out of bed in the morning, etc. That first time you go it alone is when it really hits you just how much you've come to rely on booze to feel whole, and how, in many ways, booze has become the dominant figure, the driving force if you will, in the relationship. It's a panicky feeling not at all unlike what I imagine poor Andrew Ridgeley must have experienced the day George Michael told him he was going solo. The thing is, no matter how uncertain, even terrified, you feel the first time you do *anything* without booze, you have to remind yourself of something: While it's unlikely he will ever again achieve the level of fame and fortune he did with Wham! during their "Wake Me Up Before You Go Go" heyday or, in all likelihood, even get recognized by anyone on the street (including George Michael), Andrew Ridgeley is still standing. He even managed to hook up with the hottest chick from Bananarama, who he's been with for twenty years, and as of this writing he's never been arrested for blowing a stranger in a public lavatory. And that's something. Isn't it? Please tell me that's something.

Three Lousy Days and You're Already Giving Up?

Day One was cake. I was a warrior. I could do this. No problem. I strutted around on a superiority high all day long. Day Two, however, was another story. Almost immediately upon waking up I was struck by how very different my town house felt. What was once my calming, comfortable sanctuary now seemed like a ... what? Tomb? Trap? Lie? Albeit a spacious, well-decorated tomb/trap/lie, replete with a well-thought-out color scheme, accent track lighting, and hard-to-clean deco detailing. And it wasn't even drinking time yet.

But I managed to crawl out of bed and up the expensive spiral staircase I'd had installed—all the while wondering whether one roll in the hay with that hot interior designer wannabe had really been worth all this. What are *post*-postmodern iron balusters anyway, and wouldn't the small fortune they cost me have been better spent on, say, helping the poor or, better yet, a long weekend in Vegas? Then again, I thought, she *did* give me a sweet deal on the brushed-steel kitchen countertops.

Back to bed, I thought. *Call it a sick day.* Once I was securely under the covers, though, sleep didn't seem to be in the cards. My mind was racing, alternately panicking and rallying. I could do this. It was February. Not only is it the shortest month on the calendar, but with the exception of the Super Bowl there is nary a special occasion in February that calls for alcohol consumption. March, on the other hand, has Fat Tuesday, the NCAA Tournament, St. Patrick's Day, and the vernal equinox. (I always get loaded on the vernal equinox, but only sleep with druid chicks. One has to have standards.) December has Christmas, Festivus, the annual end-of-the-season collapse of the Dallas Cowboys, and the awarding of Nobel Prizes. July contains the thirty-one-day bacchanal that is my birthday celebration. Had it been any of those months, I wouldn't have stood a chance. But February? I could totally do February. All I had to do was make it through the Saints-Colts championship game and I would be home free.

By my third day of sobriety I was seriously on edge. In my normal everyday life it's not completely unprecedented, nor does it seem so painfully difficult, for me to go three, four, even five days without touching a drop, but the fact that I'd made a conscious decision to abstain from drinking was gumming up the works something fierce. I'd *committed* myself to staying straight, and commitment is one thing I've never really been any good at. Round about dinnertime I received a text message from a model I'd been seeing off and on. She asked if I'd like to meet her out for a drink, which in the casual dating parlance of Los Angeles translates roughly to "Let's get drunk and screw." I typed, "Sure, where?" and was about to hit Send when I suddenly experienced a pang of something that felt an awful lot like guilt. And I couldn't have a drink to make it go away, either.

"Three lousy days and you're already giving up?" Guilt jeered.

"What's the point?" I shot back. "It's not like I'm quitting booze forever. And I could do it if I wanted. What's the difference if I resume drinking now or twenty-five days from now?"

"The difference is you promised yourself you'd stop for a while," that clever bastard retorted. "If you break that promise you're a fucking weakling."

"I'm not a weakling!" I protested.

"Yes, you are," Guilt insisted. "A weakling *and* a drunk."

"Oh, so now I'm a drunk, too. How do you figure?"

"Because if you weren't a drunk you could handle not drinking for one measly month."

"Listen, Guilt, I don't *have* to drink, I *want* to. . . . There's a difference, you know."

"Do tell," Guilt said.

"Look, Guilt. This model is really hot. She wants to meet for a drink and fuck. What red-blooded male in his right mind wouldn't want to do that?"

"But nobody's saying you can't go meet this model and fuck her. Go for it. Let her have a cocktail. You order a club soda."

"Yeah," I said, "but then she'll wonder why I'm not ordering a real drink, and I'll have to explain, and I don't feel like getting into all that with some fuck buddy. It's easier just to have the drink."

"Wait, get into all *what*?" Guilt asked.

I was growing irritated. "Get into anything, man! I dunno. Like, the reasons I decided not to drink for a while. Sheesh!"

"What are the reasons?"

"Oh, c'mon, give me a break."

"Is it because instead of going out and making a great impression on a powerful TV producer who literally could have changed your life, you got bombed and made a complete ass of yourself?"

"He got drunk that night too!" I countered.

"Whose floor did *he* wind up sleeping naked on?"

"You know what, man? Fuck you. You think I'm a weakling? I'll show you how weak I am."

I sent a text to the model: "Trying out a new prescription allergy medication ... Can't drink ... Come over here instead?"

"Be right over," she wrote back.

"See," I said to Guilt, perhaps too smugly. "No problem."

By the morning of Day Five I was feeling pretty good about myself. Things had gone swimmingly with the model on Day Three (read: we made crazy sober monkey love without any whiskey-dick issues). Then the following night I went bowling with friends and didn't touch a drop. Let me just repeat that so I know it happened: I went *bowling* and didn't drink. That's like skiing without snow. I bet Jesus couldn't even do that. And I had a great time. Turns out I'm a far better bowler sober than I am sauced. The pins are just so much easier to see without the booze goggles on. And there was no issue with the drive home afterward. Hell, it was all so damn easy, I began to wonder why I insisted on making things so hard on myself by drinking all the time.

As Day Five wore on, however, a feeling of trepidation came over me, no doubt because I was aware that the Super Bowl loomed ahead, on Day Six. Long before I decided to give up drinking, I'd accepted an invitation to a party that an actor friend of mine was throwing in the Hollywood Hills. There was sure to be an obscene amount of alcohol, drugs, gambling, and loose women there. Certainly it would prove to be an environment that no reasonable person who's trying to remain sober would willingly subject himself to. Thank goodness, then, that I am not a reasonable person. I'm more the daredevil thrill-seeker type. To me, this party represented the ultimate challenge—it was the Mount Everest of abstinence, and I would climb it, goddammit. Indeed, I was convinced that if I could emerge from this Super Bowl party unsauced, I would have proven to myself that, much like Sir Edmund himself, there is nothing I can't do once I've set my mind to it.

Still, I had a few lingering doubts, both about attending the Super Bowl party and about the quitting experiment in general. In the hope of clearing a few things up, I put a call in to the one guy I knew who was a bona fide expert on both drinking and not drinking. And someone I knew would shoot absolutely, perhaps painfully, straight with me: my dad. The guy who introduced me to P&J's all those years ago, and the guy who's been alcohol-free for going on twenty-five years now. Here's how the key parts of the conversation played out.

ME: Dad, what finally made you quit drinking?

DAD: It dawned on me that I was either going to quit drinking or I was going to die.

ME: Wow, that's pretty heavy.

DAD: It was heavy. And crazy. Literally. I'd learned some truly insane behavior because I was an alcoholic. I was a crazy person.

ME: What was the hardest part about quitting?

DAD: Why are you asking me this? Are you thinking about quitting?

ME: Yes, but only for a month.

DAD: ...

ME: What?

DAD: Why would you do that?

ME: Just to prove to myself that I can.

DAD: ...

ME: What?

DAD: Well, Dan, if you need to stop for a month, that's a good sign you probably need to stop permanently.

ME: Why do you say that?

DAD: Because why would anyone even consider it if it wasn't a problem?

ME: Because too much of anything can be a bad thing, right? So I'll take a break. Clean out the pipes, hit the Reset button and all that.

DAD: ...

ME: Dad, *what*?

DAD: I'm sorry, Dan, but if someone feels as though they need to stop drinking, or if people close to them are suggesting it, there is no doubt in my mind there's a problem.

ME: ...

DAD: What?

ME: This isn't how I imagined this conversation playing out.

DAD: Did you expect me to tell you it's perfectly normal for someone who claims to not have a problem with alcohol to suddenly decide they need to give up alcohol?

ME: Claims not to? So you think I have a drinking problem?

DAD: I don't know. Do you think you have a drinking problem?

ME: You sound like my freaking shrink. But no. I don't.

DAD: Then there you have it.

ME: Look, let's forget about why for now. What I want to know now is this—what advice would you give to someone who's trying to quit drinking yet has to go to a party where there's going to be booze and drugs and all sorts of other temptations?

DAD: Why would anyone who's trying to quit drinking go to a party like that?

ME: I don't know, Dad. Let's just say they do. What advice would you give them?

DAD: I'd tell them to quit fooling themselves.

ME: OK. Well, thanks, Dad. I appreciate the insight.

DAD: Dan?

ME: Yeah, Dad?

DAD: You sure you're OK?

ME: Yeah, Dad. I'm good.

As expected, the Super Bowl party was off the hook. Beer, booze, babes, and a game so exciting it would turn out to be the most-watched TV program of all time. Everyone was drinking and having a fabulous time. Everyone but me, that is. Oh, I was having fun all right, but I was determined to stick to my guns and stay sober. You see, while I believe my dad had made a legitimate point—why would someone who didn't suspect on some level they might have a drinking problem ever the feel the need to quit drinking?—I wasn't completely buying into it. I could see the shades of gray that my dad had overlooked.

In my opinion, a major failing of the 12-step treatment system is that it keeps harping on the concept of *denial* as being a key component of alcoholism. The way people like my dad see it, alcoholics have a pathological penchant for overestimating their ability to control their drinking, and feel that anyone who believes otherwise is full of shit. In other words, if you think you're not fooling yourself, you're fooling yourself. Which means the conscientious soul can't win. As soon as you deem it necessary to question whether you have an alcohol problem, you automatically have one. I'm no logician, but something seems off about this. And the more you argue this point, the drunker you look.

Look, I'm not denying that AA has done an immense amount of good in the world (see also: giving me my dad back; putting countless out-of-control drunks back on track to a meaningful life; completing the narrative arc of countless movies and memoirs). I'm simply arguing that it has the same sort of groupthink problem that exists in the military and in cults. There's no denying groupthink can be effective in certain situations (e.g., war, or full-blown alcoholism), but it's also famously intolerant of creativity and fantastically bad at handling shades of gray. I hesitate to knock AA too hard, though, because I believe my dad is 100 percent correct about one thing—had it not been for AA, he'd be six feet under.

That said, there's another school of thought espoused by what's known as the Moderation Management community (really, that's a thing). This progressive theory posits that there exists such a thing as "problem drinkers" (i.e., those who sometimes wake up naked and snockered in stranger's homes) who aren't necessarily "alcoholics." For me, this critical distinction goes back to what my friend and mentor Hunter S. Thompson once said about The Edge: that there is no honest way to explain it because the only people who really know where it is are the ones who have gone over.

For now, I am simply not able (or willing) to concede that my occasionally going overboard means I am powerless over alcohol. Occasional overindulgence doesn't make me or you or anyone else an alcoholic any more than occasionally eating junk food makes someone a glutton. Sure, I like to drink, and yes, sometimes I like to drink a little more than is probably good for me. But in the grand scheme of things I believe I'm doing just fine. I enjoy the hell out of my life. I dig my friends. I love the places we hang out. I've got a career predicated on alcohol consumption, and it's a pretty good fucking gig as far as things you do to pay the bills can go. And if thinking all that means I'm a delusional drunk, well, then, go ahead and elect me governor of the state of denial. Just don't expect me to show up for work on Monday.

Driving home from the Super Bowl party (and, hey, *there's* something I haven't been capable of doing in many years), my mind drifted to Hunter. It was February, after all. *Football Season Is Over.* Those were the four words Hunter scrawled in black marker at the top of a grim missive he penned to his wife before he shot himself in the head back in February 2005. He wrote, "67. That is 17 years past 50. 17 more than I needed or wanted."

I last spoke to Hunter two days before he turned out the lights forever. It was a Friday night and I'd called from Los Angeles to let him know I was headed to Aspen the following Thursday. We made dinner plans at Butch's, a lobster shack in Snowmass Village not far from Woody Creek, where Hunter lived. He asked me to bring along a bottle of tequila he liked that wasn't readily available in Colorado, El Tesoro. Sure, man. I'll bring it. See you soon.

In a brilliant eulogy he penned for *Rolling Stone*, Hunter's dear friend the historian Douglas Brinkley dubbed him the Patron Saint of Righteous Rage for the voiceless outcast.

"With a fierce vengeance, he lashed out, creating chaos from the mundane, psychedelic sparks out of the terminally placid," Brinkley wrote. "Most of us would never drive our Jeep through plate-glass windows or whiff rotten cocaine in a Huddle House parking lot . . . so Hunter did it for us. Mayhem was his calling."

Though I hesitate to compare myself to him as a writer, I have no problem comparing myself to Hunter as a man. Like him, I've always felt more comfortable—although there's often very little that's comfortable about it—operating beyond the fringes of polite society. Out where people are fucked-up and crazy in myriad ways. Where there are bars like P&J's scattered all over the place, filled with drunken rejects and outcasts wearing 5-CENT MUSTACHE RIDE T-shirts while chowing down on shit-covered pretzel mix and having sex behind Dumpsters. Where you meet the porn stars and the strippers you almost marry, and learn how to handle yourself in a street fight one bloody nose at a time. Where mayhem can come at you in the form of unsavory fight promoters who don't like you hitting on their hookers, or tatted-up religious crusaders wielding Fender Stratocasters instead of Bibles.

People drink out there beyond the fringes because, well, life's more fun that way, or more tolerable at least. Or because, in rare instances, they make a living writing about it. I didn't arrive at the decision to stop drinking for a month out of desperation or fear. I decided to do it for the same reason I tried skydiving or once ate an entire can of Spam—because I wanted to see if it would kill me.

It didn't. To risk using a cliché, these made me stronger (well, except for the Spam, which made me incontinent). Seriously. I felt like I was made of steel when I woke up on Day Seven of the sobriety experiment. I'd made it through Super Bowl Sunday without so much as a sip of alcohol, and in the process I'd proven to myself that, hell, maybe I wasn't as much of a hopeless lush as I'd thought! Plus, I felt as spry as I had in a long time. I could think clearly, and my muscles didn't ache. No shakes or bedspins, and fewer, if any, spontaneous nosebleeds. I think I may have even dropped a few pounds. Frank Sinatra's famous quote floated through my head, the one about how he felt sorry for people who didn't drink because when they woke up in the morning, that was as good as they were going to feel all day. Maybe Frank wasn't as spot-on as I'd previously thought. I mean, I love a great buzz as much as the next bipolar crooner, but the hangovers don't get any easier to handle the older you get. Just ask some of Frank's Rat Pack pals, like Peter Lawford.... On second thought, don't bother—Lawford died of liver failure in 1984.

Later that night I got another text from the model, asking if I'd like to meet her for a drink.

"Sure," I responded, and she suggested Copa d'Oro, my favorite Santa Monica cocktail bar. They make a mean gimlet at that place. The thought of it made my mouth water a little. I could handle it, though. I'd stick with vodka and soda, only I'd make sure the bartender knew that when I said vodka and soda I really meant just soda. Or maybe I'd go with the allergy-medication excuse again. Hey, last time I checked, the phrase "clean and sober" doesn't mention anything about honesty. It's a well-known fact that drunks who are trying to keep drinking lie all the time. I never realized that drunks trying to *stop* drinking lie more than politicians.

As I entered the bar I heard a familiar voice inside my head.

It was that pain in the ass Guilt again, but he was singing a different tune this time: "You know, man, it kind of sucks to waste a whole night with a beautiful lady in great cocktail bar only drinking club soda, doncha think?"

Figures. Guilt always was a two-faced motherfucker.

I didn't drink that night. But four days later I did. In retrospect, going bowling again was too much temptation for me to handle. Hey, I'd made it eleven days, seventeen shy of the twenty-eight I'd been going for. Not even halfway. But it was OK. The way I figured, I'd made it through the Super Bowl; that was victory enough. Besides, if I have this whole denial thing figured right, staying sober to the end of the month would indicate that I felt the *need* to do so, which would mean I really was an alcoholic, right? So I had a drink, just to prove I wasn't a drunk. I knew that logic class I took in college would come in handy one day.

"The Troubled Conscience"

CREATED BY PHILIP DUFF

> 2 shots of a conscience-tweakingly expensive
> fine tequila such as Excellia Reposado
>
> 1 shot Carpano Antica Formula sweet vermouth
> (That's vermouth, but business class.)
>
> 3 dashes orange bitters (I prefer The Bitter Truth.)
>
> A rinse of French or Swiss distilled absinthe,
> like Kübler
>
> Zest, sprayed and rimmed, of fresh, firm grapefruit

Stir the tequila, vermouth, and bitters with cold, hard ice and strain into a frozen, empty, absinthe-rinsed martini-coupe glass no larger than 4 oz. Garnish with the grapefruit zest by spraying the zest, peel side down, over the surface of the drink, rubbing it around the rim of the glass, and then throwing it away, because if you wanted fruit in your drink you'd order a damn mai tai.

"Like a decent Rolex, an expanding waistline, or a retreating hairline, a conscience is one of those things you acquire with age, and you can never be entirely certain whether it's a blessing or a curse. That moment of indecision before ingesting a pill stamped with the same kind of logo teenage girls routinely get tattooed on their bikini lines; the twinge a born-in-the-seventies gentleman experiences when he fails to call a lady the next day; the worrying thought, to channel P. J. O'Rourke, that teenage girls who play with your wing-wang while driving drunk may also be the ones who get pregnant the easiest. This, then, is conscience, and as with all mixed bags it must not be shied away from; nay, it must be embraced like a blowsy stripper after two bottles of Dom (you, not her). On the face of it a delicious tequila Manhattan, the intriguing absinthe rinse and the bitter grapefruit zest set off even the charming Mr. Dunn's radar, leaving him to wander aimlessly the rest of the day, wondering: Was that her sister—or her mother?"

—**PHILIP DUFF** is a jet-set bar guru, CEO of Liquid Solutions Ltd., founder of award-winning speakeasy door 74 (Amsterdam), trainer, drinks writer, presenter, womanizer, and Irishman. His most fraught decision every day is espresso or cappuccino?

FOURTEEN

You're Living the Dream, Buddy. Don't Forget It.

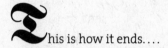his is how it ends....

I was at home one weekday, taking a break after finishing an-other brilliant column for Playboy.com ("How to Not Spike Egg-nog," if you must know; the "not" was added by their lawyers) and getting my ass handed to me in Xbox live FIFA soccer by a fifteen-year-old who goes by the handle Darth Timmy when I heard the doorbell ringing through the glorious sonority of Toots and the Maytals' "54–46 (That's My Number)" at high volume.

I sang my way over to the door: *"I'm not a fool to hurt my-self/ I was innocent of what they done to me/ They was wrong/ Listen to me, they were wrong...."*

I grabbed the knob, placed a foot in the "block forced entry" position (better safe than sorry, I say), opened it three or four inches, and peered out into the smiling face of Matt Denning. Matt's a friend from my early childhood in Philly who recently relocated to L.A. with his family. He's a corporate defense attorney and partner at one of the city's largest firms.

"What's happening, buddy?" Matt said, following me into the kitchen.

"Nada, counselor. Just getting a little work done," I replied, gesturing at the TV. "Scotch?"

"Uh, how about some coffee?"

I looked at him curiously. "You suddenly don't like scotch?"

"It's eleven o'clock in the morning," he said.

"You're right, it's early. Let's go with wine instead."

I opened a bottle of 2002 La Joie from Verité, a kick-ass (and prohibitively expensive if you don't get it sent to you as a sample) bottle from Sonoma County. *What the hell*, I figured. *I don't see Matt very often.* And it *was* almost lunchtime.

"What brings you to the dark side this fine day?"

"I had some free time, so thought I'd swing by to see what you're up to," Matt said, glancing around, looking alternately uncomfortable and fascinated. "So it's casual Friday every day here, huh?"

"Definitely," I replied. On the Internet, no one knows you're pantsless. "How are the wife and kids doing?"

"They're doing," he replied.

Matt was the first guy from my circle of childhood friends to get married. At twenty-two. Before he got hitched, Matt's nickname was Captain Nightlife, which he earned due to the fact that no fewer than three taverns near campus had cocktails named in his honor. But everything changed the moment Matt said "I do." Did he ever. The onetime namesake of the "Matt Finish" martini now had three kids, the eldest of which was about to graduate high school. And somehow I hadn't managed to put on pants that day.

"What's it been with you and Lisa—two decades now?" I asked.

"Something like that," Matt replied.

"That's amazing," I said, half meaning it.

"It's all right. Pain in the ass sometimes."

"But overall worth it, no?" I asked.

"Are you asking if I'm bummed I never got to sleep with a Playmate or something?" Matt asked. "Sure. I bet that would have been fun."

Since I'd briefly cohabitated with a former Miss February, I assured him that it would have been.

"But where is she now?" Matt asked.

"Who? The Playmate? Married with kids and living in Phoenix, I believe."

"Exactly. And where are you?"

"Wherever I wake up," I replied.

"No, I mean where *are* you?" Matt repeated. "In life."

"Sounds like a trick question," I quipped. "Do I get a hint?"

"I'm just saying, your Playmate has a family with some other dude. I bet most of the other five hundred or so women you've slept with over the years have families now too. So do all the guys you grew up with. Except for Randy, if you figure him for a grown-up," Matt said.

Well. Wasn't it a bit early to be this judgey? I mean, I hadn't even had my scotch yet.

"What's your point, Dr. Phil?" I countered.

"You're forty, never been married, never as far as I know even considered having kids," Matt said. "Do *you* have any regrets?"

"Well, there was the time I had unprotected sex with that junkie hooker in the Congo. That was regretful."

"I'm serious," Matt said, quite seriously.

"Oh, we're being serious now? In that case, I'd have to say"—

and here I did my best Frank Sinatra—"regrets, I've had a few, but then again, too few to mention. . . ."

"What a dickhead," he said and laughed. "No wonder nobody wants to marry you."

"Might also have something to do with me not popping the question to anyone."

"No doubt."

I briefly considered telling him about my burgeoning romance with Jen Topping, but quickly thought better of it. Best to maintain an image we were both more comfortable with. I also figured my proposal to Alison the stripper wasn't germane here either.

"OK, so gay banter aside, why are you really here?" I asked. Matt dropping by unannounced in the middle of a workday was severely atypical. "I know you're not just in the neighborhood killing time."

"Am I that obvious?" he asked.

"You bill at five hundred dollars an hour," I said. "With you, there's literally no such thing as free time."

"Indeed. Well, the reason I'm here is I'm hoping you might be able to help me line up a girl. You know, a pro."

"Am *I* that obvious?" I countered. "So much for conjugal bliss, huh?"

"What? Aw, Jesus, no. Lisa'd find out in a second. She'd know as soon as I walked in the house. Then she'd tie me up and chop my nuts off, then feed 'em to me and set me on fire and fuck the pool boy in front of me while I burned. The pro's for Matty Jr."

"You want me to line up a hooker for your kid?" I asked incredulously.

"Hey," Matt countered, "he busted his stones in high school and graduated with honors. He's going to Stanford, for chrissakes! I figure a hot piece of ass would be a fitting gift for all his hard work."

I laughed. "C'mon, man, Matty's a good-looking kid. He's probably bagging more hot pieces of ass than me!"

"But they're young girls," Matt said. "They don't know what they're doing."

"Have you seen some of the eighteen-year-olds who work for Randy? They screw like champs."

"I was thinking someone with some experience would provide him with something he'd always remember. You know some hot MILFs, right? Through your porn connections?"

"Well, yes, but something about this feels wrong," I said. "I was at Matty's first communion, for chrissakes."

"And I was at yours," Matt replied. "Then I found out you banged my sister at her junior prom!"

"*Senior* prom," I corrected. "And it was only a blow job."

He didn't punch me, but I think it was only because he still needed a favor.

"All right, all right, I'll see what I can do. Any special requests?"

"Like what?" he asked.

"Black, Asian, big tits, likes anal—"

"He likes blondes."

"OK. Anything else?"

"Uh, I dunno . . . the anal, maybe."

"OK, I'll make sure she brings a strap-on," I said, enjoying this a little too much.

"Wait, what?" Matt shot back.

"And if I put in a word with Randy, he might give you the unfit-parent discount," I rolled on. "It'll be cheaper than taking the kid to a Lakers game. A play-off game, but still cheaper. You thinking hotel room?"

"You think that's best?" he asked, bewildered.

"Actually, fuck it. Why don't we just send her over to Junior's tree house? She and Lisa can do a little MILF bonding while the boy hydrates between rounds."

"I don't think that's a—"

"You know I'm not actually going to help you get a hooker for your kid, don't you?"

"Oh. Right."

"Like, you know that's completely wacked? Jesus, how am I suddenly the responsible one? I've worked hard at being a fuckup. It's not an easy thing to get right. And I've made a lot of mistakes. Just don't ask me to start making them for other people."

"I just figured—"

"Assumed. You just assumed. Assumed I hadn't thought this shit through. Assumed I just do things by the seat of my pants. Having this much fun for this long takes a fuckload of planning, my friend. And along the way you get to see a lot of people have too much fun. Or the wrong kinds of fun. And you see those people not being able to handle the fun. I'm not going to be one of those people. So I have a code. And part of it pertains to this."

"What part?"

"I already told you, don't make other people's mistakes for them. If Matty wants to discover the for-pay side of sex on his own, more power to him, but he should do it the way the rest of us did. Nervous. Alone. Unsure. You're his dad; even if you're the biggest whoremonger in town, you should still let him make his own decisions, and this is a big one."

"Oh, fuck you. Spare me the lecture."

"Fine, spare me the assumptions. Have you told him to jack off?"

"Have I what?"

"Told him he should jack off? Every day?"

"I think he's probably got that one covered."

"Yeah, but does he feel weird about it? I felt weird about it for *decades*! You want to make him feel better about something? Give him a stack of *Playboy*s and a bottle of Astroglide and tell him it's time he started doing his own laundry."

"I thought you were going to help me."

"I *am* helping you. You got married back when you were just a kid, but Lisa keeps you on a short leash. Always has. What does she think about you jacking off?"

"I don't exactly advertise it."

"Again, problem! It's part of your life. It's part of who you are. I'm not saying she should watch you or whatever, but she should know you do it on the regular. Hell, she might even fuck you more."

At this point I should pause to say that I have lots of married friends who are in great relationships, couples who seem to accentuate each other's best qualities instead of limiting them. But at least 20 percent of my friends fall into a category I call "best-behavior marriages." By that I mean there's a thick dividing line between their life with their spouse and their life without her. They're fully yes-dear domesticated—until you get them out on the town. Then they're puking on your shoes and babbling incoherently at you about how much they want to fuck the waitress who is several light-years out of their league. Then they use their wives as an excuse for not even trying. Like she's the only thing holding them back. Which is a complete fucking cop-out.

I'm not saying they necessarily should go fuck the waitress. I couldn't care less. I'm just saying that *you* need to be the one who can kick your demons' asses. Demons are a lot of fun and all, but if you give them an inch they'll take over. If you let them drive the bus because you know your wife is going to take the wheel any minute, you're in even worse trouble because now those demons own your ass. Plus, it's unfair to your wife. Christ, they aren't even her demons! And the more you let the demons get the upper hand, the more you turn a blind eye to who's in charge, the more dependent on her you are. And the more you will grow to hate her. And the more she will grow to hate you. In that awful yes-dear best-behavior marriage sort of way. I've seen it happen time and time again, my friends.

Look, every guy wants to cheat. In fact, every guy wants to bone just about every piece of ass he passes on the street, even if he's literally on his way to getting laid. That's just a fact. If it bums your girlfriend or wife out, have her take it up with Darwin. But tell her. If you want to do a shitload of coke and ten shots of whiskey and fuck her like a rented mule, fine! Tell her! Want to know the best part? You can want to do all that without actually doing it! Sometimes the fantasy is better than the reality anyway. Our therapy-obsessed culture seems to celebrate sharing your feelings about intimacy and needs, but it too often leaves this kind of thing out. If you're spending most of your life with this person, she should know what a freak show you are. I may be unmarried at forty, but at least I'm honest about who I am and what I want out of life.

"Maybe you're right, man. I don't know," said Matt. "You really don't think I should get a hooker for Matty?"

"Absolutely not."

"Can you at least get me into the Playboy Mansion?" he asked in his best lawyerly attempt to slip one under the radar. "You said you'd try."

"I'll keep trying." The truth is I have a hard enough time getting in there myself, but I figured at this point, why burst his bubble?

"You're living the dream, buddy. Don't forget it," Matt said, handing me an empty wineglass and getting up to leave.

"I guess so. Not sure it's all it's cracked up to be."

With Matt gone I was left alone with a three-quarters full bottle of Verité at half past noon. And while I was cognizant that solo drinking at home in your boxers during so-called normal business hours isn't everyone's idea of time well spent, I could not in good conscience just sit there and let an opened two-hundred-dollar bottle of wine turn into vinegar. Some people would save it for dinner. Those people lack imagination.

Turns out Toots and the Maytals pairs beautifully with Verité, by the way: *"Funky Kingston, is what I've got for you/ oh yeah/ Funky Kingston, yeah is what I've got for you/ Funky Kingston/ oh yeah ..."*

The phone rang—my mother. Screen it. Hadn't heard from her in, what? Over a month now? Maybe two? Voicemail kicked on. Per usual, she left a long and rambling message that began deceptively sanely—something about a landscaper she'd hired who "overmulched" her garden. Then ...

"I think he's in cahoots with the people from the mayor's office who snuck in here and broke my leg when I was sleeping," she sort of yelled.

There it is. Still got it, Mom!

Then she suddenly switched gears and started to talk cheerfully about taking a trip to Rome to see the Vatican. Nothing unusual about that. She's been talking about taking a trip to Italy for as long as I can remember. Dollars to doughnuts she'll never do it.

"John and I want to make sure we get there before we get too old to enjoy it," she said, before falling silent for a good ten seconds. "OK. Call me." She left her phone number and hung up.

I shuddered involuntarily at the mention of John. That'd be my stepdad, John Taylor. The mention of him reminded me of a call I got from her back in August 2004. She had called to tell me she'd done something she hadn't done in nearly a decade—drink alcohol. A bottle of wine, to be specific. Unlike my dad, my mother doesn't have an alcohol problem. Rather, she has a sanity problem, and alcohol tends to exacerbate it (the problem, not the sanity). And to her credit, she doesn't tend to drink much at all because of it.

When I'd asked what special occasion had prompted her to lift her self-imposed ban, my mom told me there wasn't one. She said that she and John—her husband of twenty-three years at the time—had been sitting around the house on a warm summer's evening and more or less decided it was high time they tied one on. Just seemed like a good idea. So they opened a bottle of Frontera merlot, popped in a Creedence cassette, and grooved to the music like teenagers at the prom. It's a touching story under any circumstances: dancing cheek-to-cheek on the back porch with a long-overdue buzz. She said it was the most fun she'd had in years. I love that story. It reminds me why we call them "spirits" and how the simple pleasures of moderate drinking can truly add to the miracle of every day. Plus, she didn't wake up in the psych ward the next morning, which is a bonus.

My stepdad was a captain in the Philadelphia Fire Department. Two nights after the impromptu wine date with my mom he was on the job when a call came in for a fire in the basement of a row home in Port Richmond, a run-down section of the city. He answered the call. Put on the suit. Got into the truck. Drove to the house. Went down into the basement. But John didn't come out alive.

He died trying to save one of his men and was given a hero's funeral. Everybody from the mayor to seemingly every last firefighter John had ever worked with showed up to pay their respects. It was little consolation to my mother, though. She was off the deep end with it, and got worse afterward. One of the few plus sides to her increasing dementia is that she probably can't remember him, or how much she misses him, anymore. Now there's a happy thought to be getting on with!

I remember, though, even though I wasn't there. It's like a dream. I picture my mother dancing with him on the back porch, enveloped in an eldritch light. And John Fogerty serenades them as they sway: *"Put a candle in the window, 'cause I feel I've got to move."*

"Hello?" she sounded groggy. Must have already taken her meds.

"Hi, Mom."

"Hi, Dan."

"Got your message. You doing OK?"

"Well," she said, and groaned, "my leg hurts pretty bad. I told you they barged in here and broke my leg, right? Through the attic?"

"Yeah, Mom. You told me."

"Sonsofbitches," she spat. "Torturing me!"

She started into a rant about covert government operatives/landscapers conspiring against her, but I cut her off: "So you're thinking about taking that trip to Rome after all, eh?"

"Oh, yes. I tell John all the time we need to go there."

"You mean you *told* John that, right? Before," I said.

"Yeah, that's what I mean."

Silence. A long one. Am I an asshole? Moments like this I really can't tell. I just wish she'd say something.

"You coming home anytime soon?" she asked finally.

"I don't know," I said. "Maybe not for a while. Work's been crazy. And now that Summer is gone, I've got nobody to watch the dog if I want to travel."

"But it's winter."

"No, Mom, Summer. The girl I was living with?"

"What girl?"

"I'll tell you later."

More silence.

"You should get some sleep, Mom. You sound tired."

"I am," she murmured. "Yes, quite a bit tired. I should get some rest. Make sure I stay on my toes. Can't be too careful."

"You're right about that," I said.

"Danny?"

"Yeah, Mom?"

"When did you get a dog?"

After I got off the phone with my mom I opened another bottle of Verité. Fuck it. Turned out it was also the last bottle of Verité in my wine cellar, which is really just a refrigerator in the basement. (Sounds fancier when you call it a cellar.) It was 1:28 p.m. Buzzed en route to blotto, I began to muse on how unfair it is that solo drinking has gotten such a bad rap. While many people see it as a sure sign someone has hit rock bottom, I personally think getting shitty by yourself from time to time is a great restorative. Just you, your favorite elixir, and all the besozzled notions sloshing around your sauce-soaked psyche. It's transcendental, really. Best of all, you don't have to worry what anyone else thinks about what you're doing. Talk about jacking off! In many ways, this is the ultimate expression of self-love.

Halfway to the bottom of the second bottle of Verité, my iPod became a sudden source of fascination to me. Out of the shuffle came Michael Sembello's "Maniac," and suddenly I was on my feet, dancing like I'd never danced before. I tore off my boxers, spilled some wine down my chest, paused momentarily to think—do I *own* leg warmers? I was feeling footloose and fancy free. Wait, that's it—*Footloose!* Fuck Sembello; I needed me some Kenny Loggins. *Now I gotta cut looooooose....* By the time I'd polished off the Verité I'd gotten down to virtually every horrendous top-ten hit spawned from 1980s dance flicks. You could say I'd had the time of my life ... or you could sing it at the top of your lungs, like I did.

"Beat Street" ended and I was spent. I spilled myself onto the sofa. Naked. Drunk. Feeling warm and happy.

I thought, *You're living the dream, buddy. Don't forget it.* Then I wondered whether my mother could have even fathomed my life turning out anything like this on that day, those many years ago, when she consoled me after those little girls called me dumb for hawking homework help instead of lemonade.

"We'll see who's dumb," she said.

I believed her then. But now I think maybe we will and maybe we won't. At this point in my life I have seen dumb in most, if not all, of its manifestations. Hell, I've *been* dumb in most, if not all, of its manifestations. My saving grace is that most of the human race has too, so I get to grade myself on a curve. Let's face it: Human beings are all part of one big dumb fucking family. For proof just turn on the TV or log on to the Internet, or just walk down any street in the country. To be sure, rampant stupidity might be the best explanation of all for why so many of us drink—be it to get more stupider, or to quell the exquisite inner pain of coping with idiots.

Suddenly I was gripped by an urge to be industrious. I flipped open my laptop, intent on generating a list of great ideas for future "Imbiber" columns. All I could come up with, however, was something about how I'd reached—or at least was operating under the assumption that I'd reached—the exact midpoint of my life. That means I'm planning to live to be eighty years old. Too ambitious? Delusional? I don't think so. Eighty? Pfft, I can make eighty. Hell, Bukowski lived to be seventy-three. Bukowski!

So, yeah, eighty is attainable, but to get there I'm going to need a solid plan. We'll run this thing like an NBA Playoffs game and finally get down to some defense in the second half. Yes, a strategy . . . a set of guidelines for living that must be strictly adhered to from here on out. Well, what are we waiting for?

How to Live a Long and Loaded Life (Or, Mr. Beam, I'm Ready for My Third Act)

1) Don't fear the reaper.

Jim Fixx, author of the best-selling *The Complete Book of Running*, suffered a massive heart attack after a jog and died. He was fifty-two. Steve "The Crocodile Hunter" Irwin was killed by a stingray while filming a documentary about marine life. And Karl Wallenda, of the famous "Flying Wallendas," fell to his death while attempting to walk across a wire stretched between two buildings in Puerto Rico.

Yes, it's ironic. But the lesson here is this: Doing what you love could kill you, but you should do it anyway because you may wind up being referenced as a life lesson in a book someday. If their examples hold true, I'm probably going to die in some freak bottling accident while touring a distillery. On the plus side, the place will have a truly unique limited-edition offering on their hands. Who could pass up whiskey infused with real journalist spleen?

There are other lessons in here too: Avoid exercising too much, or swimming with dangerous sea creatures. And for chrissakes, stay off tightropes. You've been drinking.

2) Pity is a waste. Self-pity doubly so.

Because, you know, it doesn't fucking matter anyway. Not a lick. All the years I spent rolling my eyes at Randy's ridiculous recitations of Buddhist teachings? Turns out they're all true. Most of what happens in the world is beyond our control, so why waste precious time and energy feeling sorry for ourselves, or anyone else? Life is a bridge; therefore, build no house on it. Nothing is lost in the universe. Everything changes, and as soon as we think we are safe, we bump into our ex at the supermarket checkout and she got that boob job after all, and that surfer dude with her seems to get to the gym regularly. To cut off suffering, one must cut off greed and ignorance. Don't sweat the petty things and don't pet the sweaty things. The Dalai Lama said that, right?

3) Have a glass of wine, for chrissakes.

Wine has been shown to reduce the risk of heart disease and certain cancers and to slow the progression of neurological degenerative disorders like Alzheimer's and Parkinson's disease. Even the Bible commands us to drink it (I Timothy 5:23 ... hold that up at the next game, asshole). Wine has also been shown to taste fucking awesome and provide a killer buzz. So in other words, *not* drinking wine will not only kill you, you will die sober; and for my money, that's no way to go.

4) Know your limits.

Should the day ever arrive that you must choose between paying your rent and purchasing the vodka you need to make it through the day, it's time to hang up your drinking shoes. Thanks for playing.

5) Fuck your limits.

You have a friend's couch you can stay on for a while, right?

6) Fuck everyone.

Literally, I mean. A comprehensive study from the Harvard University Medical School revealed that middle-aged and elderly adults with healthy sex lives have an increased life expectancy. A related study showed that nobody needed a bunch of twits from Harvard to tell 'em to keep banging away for as long as they can. Men are chemically and neurologically wired to want to fuck every female they see. Don't fight it. The shame associated with it is probably the single biggest cause of misery in the world. Do you seriously think the Crusades would have happened if the Catholic Church let people masturbate? And don't get me started on the virgins that suicide bombers are promised in heaven. Don't they know that virgins have been categorically proven to be the worst lays in the world?

7) Find love.

Seriously. I'm not being sarcastic, for once. Provided, of course, that love doesn't interfere with rules 1 through 6 above. But, really, a wise man once said if you can't be with the one you love, love the one you're with. Then there's that other guy who told us all we need is love. And, of course, the brave soul who admitted he was, in fact, *addicted* to love. The common thread is love. Love, love, love ... it's easy. It's important.

8) Never overstay your welcome.

Now, well, this is awkward. As you've probably noticed, we're just a short way from the very, very end of this book. So I kind of have to go. And as you may have gathered by now, I'm not all that good at ending things. If I could wrap things up with this book by not calling it back, I'd be on familiar ground. But I'm told that won't work in this case.

I drink for a living. I wrote a book about it. It's pretty simple. So we'll close simply, with a story. A drinking story.

This guy is at home in bed with his wife and he hears a *rat-a-tat-tat* on the door. He looks at the clock on the nightstand—it's half past three in the morning—and he thinks, *I'm not getting out of bed at this hour* and rolls over. A minute later, he hears a louder knock.

"Aren't you going to answer that?" his wife asks groggily.

Pissed off and exhausted, he drags himself out of bed, throws on his bathrobe, and trudges downstairs. When he opens the door he sees a man standing on the other side. The guy is clearly drunk.

"Hi there," slurs the stranger. "Can you give me a pushhhhh?"

"Are you fucking kidding me, asshole? It's half past three. I was in bed. Now get lost before I call the cops!" He slams the door and heads upstairs.

When he tells his wife what happened she's shocked. "Greg, that wasn't very nice of you. Remember that night we broke down in the pouring rain on the way to pick the kids up from the babysitter and you had to knock on that man's door to get us started again? What would have happened if he'd told us to get lost?"

"But the guy is wasted," the husband protests.

"It doesn't matter," she says. "He needs our help, and the Christian thing to do is to help him." Chastened, the husband reluctantly climbs out of bed again, gets dressed, and heads downstairs.

He opens the front door, but he can't see the stranger anywhere. So he shouts, "Hey, man, do you still want a push?"

From somewhere in the distance he hears a voice cry out, "Yeah, please. That would be great."

Still unable to locate the stranger, he shouts, "Where are you?"

And the stranger replies, "I'm over here, on your swing."

I'd like to think that I'm basically that guy. Out in your yard, drunk, looking for kicks at three in the morning. Give me a push and I promise not to piss on your begonias.

The End

The Nightcap

"The Last Word, for Now"

CREATED BY SIMON FORD

3/4 oz. Jameson

3/4 oz. fresh lime juice

3/4 oz. Yellow Chartreuse

3/4 oz. maraschino liqueur

Shake with ice, strain, enjoy.
   (Festival shaker composed of 2 plastic beer cups held together ... add extra booze to compensate for spillage if this methodology needed).

"I was headed to the Coachella music festival near Palm Springs after an evening of partying with Dan Dunn in L.A., and I had a few things on my mind ... things like where I was going to stay, how I was going to blag myself a ticket, and what sort of cocktail to create as the final drink for this book. As I got closer to the festival site, it occured to me that, as it was for the end of the book, the drink ought to be a riff on the classic cocktail The Last Word. However, as it's for Dan's book it gets named The Last Word, for Now, since I know there's so much more to come from Dan in the future. The other thing that occured to me was that a music festival wasn't going to be the easiest place to obtain the fine ingredients that one would prefer to see in a classic cocktail, so it was necessary for my friend Dan Warner and I to load a few hip flasks with the good stuff and try our chances at getting it past security. Thankfully, security seemed not to care.

So next year I will be taking a few bottles of tequila in with me. The lime juice, incidentally, was obtained by buying 14 Coronas and fishing out the lime wedges from the bottles!

"The original Last Word is one of the great classic drinks to come out of the Prohibition Era and was allegedly invented at the Detroit Athletics Club (according to Ted Saucier's 1951 book, *Bottoms Up*). This cocktail is one of my personal favorites, and the thought of creating a twist on it and downing them during a performance by the Gorillaz in the blazing desert sun at Coachella seemed the perfect ending cocktail for a book about 'living loaded.'"

—Notorious ladies' man **SIMON FORD** is the director of trade outreach and brand education for Pernod Ricard USA and one of the author's favorite drinking buddies.

ACKNOWLEDGMENTS

Time to wrap up the proceedings with song dedications and toasts to the following exceptional human beings:

To Scott Alexander, my former editor at *Playboy*, who so often was the lone voice in the wilderness crying out in support of the "Imbiber" column, I dedicate "Higher" by Creed. I do so, Scott, not to insult your first-rate musical sensibilities, but because I know you'll never forget (and will hopefully find it quite funny) that of all the songs in the history of recorded music, I picked a godawful track by the ear-mauling sonic-shitfest that is Creed. The not-forgetting part is what's important here, you see. Oh, and having that chorus stuck in your head too. I really want that to happen. *Can you take me higher? To a place where blind men see…*

To Talia Krohn, my remarkable editor at Crown. First you turned the dream that was this book into a reality by giving me a deal, and then you took what I wrote and made it better.

For you, a little ditty called "Thank You" by Led Zeppelin. Here's to the future. May we continue to dream out loud at high volume.

To my agent, Scott Gould at RLR Associates in New York, who is—in the words of one Mr. 50 Cent—a muthafuckin' PIMP.

To my manager, Jeff Aghassi, and Josie Freedman at ICM in L.A.—"Don't Stop 'Til You Get Enough."

Sending out "White Rabbit" to my favorite hillbilly, the inveterate rabble-rouser Curtis Robinson. Knowing you all these years, my friend, has been a most intoxicating experience.

To all the brilliant bartenders (aka mixologists) who provided original recipes for this book, I dedicate "Standing in the Shower . . . Thinking" by Jane's Addiction, as I happened to be in the shower when the idea to hit y'all up for said recipes came to me.

It's got to be AC/DC's "Have a Drink on Me" for all the wonderful people in the wine and spirits biz, who make this feel more like a permanent vacation than a job.

To my friends, I dedicate "With a Little Help from My Friends" because . . . well, duh!

To my family, it's "We Are Family." (There's a pattern emerging here.)

To the Imbiber website's design and editorial team I dedicate Pink Floyd's "Money," 'cause Lord knows I haven't given them very much of my own.

The Clash's "Career Opportunities" goes out to the great magazine and newspaper editors I've had the privilege to work with over the years.

For Hugh Hefner, Jimmy Jellinek, Sam Jemielity, and everyone at *Playboy* and *The Playboy Radio Morning Show* I offer up Billy Idol's "Flesh for Fantasy."

And finally, I dedicate "South Central Rain" to Michelle . . . because I'm sorry.

INDEX